NEUTRALISM
and
NONALIGNMENT

THE NEW STATES IN WORLD AFFAIRS

Edited by

LAURENCE W. MARTIN

GREENWOOD PRESS, PUBLISHERS
WESTPORT, CONNECTICUT

Library of Congress Cataloging in Publication Data

Martin, Laurence W   ed.
    Neutralism and nonalignment.

    Reprint of the 1962 ed. published by Praeger,
New York.
    Includes bibliographical references.
    1. Underdeveloped areas--Foreign relations.
2. Neutrality. 3. States, New--Politics and govern-
ment. 4. World politics--1955-1965. I. Title.
[JX1395.M32 1976]   327'.09172'4   75-32460
ISBN 0-8371-8541-6

Originally published in 1962 by Frederick A. Praeger, Inc.,
Publisher, New York

Reprinted with the permission of Praeger Publishers, Inc.

Reprinted from a copy in the collections of the Brooklyn Public Library

Reprinted in 1976 by Greenwood Press, Inc.

Library of Congress Catalog Card Number 75-32460

ISBN 0-8371-8541-6

Printed in the United States of America

NEUTRALISM
and
NONALIGNMENT

Published for

THE WASHINGTON CENTER OF FOREIGN POLICY RESEARCH

at the

SCHOOL OF ADVANCED INTERNATIONAL STUDIES
THE JOHNS HOPKINS UNIVERSITY

ACKNOWLEDGMENTS

THE first debt the editor of such a book as this owes is to his fellow authors, who have all been considerate and helpful. I also owe thanks to the staff of the Washington Center and, in particular to Miss Gwendolyn Groomes, who has helped me in all my work on this volume and generously shared her extensive knowledge of the new states. Lastly, I must add yet another testimony to the debt that all his associates owe Arnold Wolfers for his friendship and wise advice.

L.W.M.

PREFATORY NOTE

I am very glad that my colleague Laurence W. Martin has under-taken this book on a topic of such importance for American foreign policy. The papers in the book have all been written by authors who are or have been associates of The Washington Center of Foreign Policy Research. Early versions of some of the papers appeared in the Center's earlier brochure, *Neutralism,* which was given a limited distribution.

These papers have grown out of the particular interests of the authors in various problems presented by the nonaligned states and consequently do not constitute a survey of the whole problem of neutralism. Nevertheless, they fall roughly into two groups, the earlier chapters being primarily focused on the nature of the new states and their behavior in foreign policy, whereas the later chapters deal more directly with the consequences of this behavior for American foreign policy.

The Washington Center of Foreign Policy Research is affiliated with the School of Advanced International Studies of The Johns Hopkins University. The purpose of the Center is to enable acade-micians and practitioners to conduct research, individually and as a group, on problems of international politics that are relevant to both the development of theoretical knowledge and the conduct of United States foreign policy.

ARNOLD WOLFERS, Director
The Washington Center of
Foreign Policy Research

Washington, D.C.
July, 1962

CONTENTS

INTRODUCTION: THE EMERGENCE OF THE NEW STATES

by LAURENCE W. MARTIN

THE appearance of several dozen new states on the world stage within the space of a few years would cause considerable revision of diplomatic thought under any circumstances. Given the actual recent influx, there have been sufficient similarities among the newcomers to give the appearance of collective as well as a set of individual challenges to the policies of older powers. Thus we have come to speak of the poor or underdeveloped countries in general, of the anticolonial or postcolonial states, and of the colored or Afro-Asian nations. Just what will be the influence of these states upon the interests of the West, and how it can best be handled, have been the subject of rising and frequently acrimonious debate.

Diplomatically, the most conspicuous characteristic of the new states has been a policy that has become known as neutralism— the determination of the majority of the new countries to resist entanglement in either of the great-power blocs in the Cold War. Neutralism seems to be something of an innovation. Like its name-sake, neutrality, neutralism implies abstention from an existing or potential conflict. But when a neutral of the past tried to maintain permanent neutrality—rather than merely to avoid a particular war—it did so by minding its own business and remaining aloof from the rough-and-tumble of world affairs. Such a policy was generally confined to smaller and weaker states, whose chief ambition was to be left alone.

Today's neutralists are very different. They are far from resigned to their fate. Even those new states that do not have territorial grievances or projects for wider groupings are made restless by their own internal economic needs and political instability. Modern neutralism is therefore not confined to nations content to remain as they are; it is also a course chosen by many states anxious to get on in the world. The new states have recognized this distinction by searching for some other term—positive neutrality, nonalignment, noncommitment, positive policy for peace— that will express both their ambitions and their feeling that there is something ignobly passive about mere abstention.

Neutralist policies seem to have a wide variety of purposes, both international and domestic. Internationally, they may be designed to preserve newly won independence, either by isolation or by an activist policy of playing one great power against another, attracting aid from both, and forestalling encroachment by either. Some neutralists may welcome the opportunity of playing a mediating role between the great powers, thereby reducing the danger of wars that might, at best, merely disrupt their own economic plans, or at worst, engulf the world in a conflict so total as to reduce to absurdity the traditional neutral hope of surviving unscathed. Domestically, neutralism and militant anticolonialism may serve as a distraction from internal problems, an excuse to avoid awkward disputes among political groups, and perhaps most fundamentally, a device to rally an ill-assorted people and inject purpose and coherence into an embryonic state.

But if the new states share many common experiences and problems that lead them to respond to the Cold War in similar ways, each also faces the world from a unique position. Each has its own variant form of the common slogans and emotions. It seems almost axiomatic that the promotion of neutralism serves very different purposes for a Nehru, with his philosophical bent and extensive territory; a Nasser, with his local and regional ambitions; and a Tito, with his European state and Communist ideology. Neutralist nations have some sense of solidarity and some congruity of interests; but they remain individuals who pay lip service to the tenets of nonalignment, but rarely allow them to impede opportunistic pursuit of their several goals. This gives a profoundly confused appearance to the neutralist camp as a whole. It is not easy, in fact, to be sure whether there is such a camp; nor is it easy to define what gives any lesser grouping of new states its coherence; nor can one even be sure, in any one instance, whether neutralism is a policy at all or merely an aimless and emotional reaction to day-to-day exigencies. The confusion is increased by the internal instability that frequently changes the outward character of a state overnight. In some cases, noncommitment merely signifies the absence of any authority capable of making commitments; in others, the alignment of the moment is illusory because authority is on the point of collapse.

It is not only to Western eyes that the picture is puzzling. The preparatory conference at Cairo in June, 1961, that established qualifications for attendance at the Belgrade conference of noncommitted nations, had considerable difficulty in agreeing on what the term "noncommitted" meant. It was finally decided that it demanded a policy of independence, "clear tendencies and efforts" to sustain such a policy, coexistence with states of different social systems, abstention from military blocs, and, for members of military alliances, evidence of being free from involvement in conflicts. Even this agreement did not prevent differences over who should be invited or serious disputes among those who attended.

According to one view, the chief purpose of the multitudinous conferences of new states is to call the roll and decide what the countries have in common. The latter task, difficult enough in itself, is made virtually impossible by the stream of new recruits hurrying to join the ranks at the last minute. In this respect, the continuous increase in membership that lends the neutralists much of their collective importance also deprives them of the coherence that is widely believed to be their most impressive weapon.

The Belgrade conference of September, 1961, and the earlier Afro-Asian conference held at Bandung in April, 1955, are probably the two most important landmarks in the series of meetings at which the new states have tried to define their relations with each other and with the world at large.

Unofficial attempts at cooperation among the peoples of colonial areas have a quite lengthy history, but meetings of sovereign Afro-Asian states are the product of postwar colonial emancipation. The outbreak of hostilities between Indonesian and Netherlands forces led to a meeting of fifteen Asian nations at New Delhi in January, 1949. At this meeting, the fifteen agreed on certain collective measures against the Netherlands and also decided to coordinate their actions at the United Nations. The following autumn, the Indian delegate, Sir Benegal Rau, convened the first *ad hoc* Afro-Asian caucus at the United Nations, and this group remained sporadically active, especially during the Korean War. It was in the course of efforts to bring about a settlement of the Korean conflict that Nehru seems to have first used the term "positive neutrality."

When the war was over, the Afro-Asian caucus continued and was established on a permanent basis after the Bandung conference.

The then Prime Minister of Indonesia, Ali Sastromidjojo, was one of the first heads of government to propose steps toward Afro-Asian cooperation when, in a speech to his Parliament in August, 1953, he outlined the purposes such cooperation might serve:

> Because we are convinced that close cooperation between the Asian-African countries will strengthen the efforts toward achieving permanent world peace, we therefore consider cooperation between those countries very important. Cooperation between the Asian and African countries conforms with the United Nations regulation concerning regional arrangements. Moreover, in general these countries have the same views with regard to some aspects in the field of international relations; they have thus a common ground for the establishment of a special group. Hence we will continue and strengthen cooperation between these countries.

In April, 1954, at a conference of the Prime Ministers of India, Pakistan, Ceylon, Burma, and Indonesia held in Colombo, Sastromidjojo suggested a further conference of Afro-Asian states. After some months of continued exhortation, the same five Prime Ministers met at Bogor, Indonesia, to determine which countries should be invited to the projected conference and to define its purposes: to promote cooperation among Afro-Asian nations, to discuss their problems, including racialism and colonialism, and to consider their part in the creation of world peace.

The Bandung Conference was a gathering not of uncommitted but of Afro-Asian states regionally defined and including Asian members of SEATO as well as the Communist states of China and North Vietnam. Although the meeting supposedly had no racial basis, racist undercurrents were plainly apparent. For many participants, the conference seems to have been attractive as an emotional herding together for mutual reassurance in a puzzling world. Many probably had relatively little expectation of real results and went along for the sake of appearances. So far as specific purposes emerged, three divergent groups could be discerned. For the Communist states, it meant an opportunity to identify their traditional slogan of anti-imperialism with the anticolonialism of new states that could no longer be ignored. Ceylon and other members of Western military alliances, some of whose governments were soon to fall, launched an attack on Communism and warned of the dangers of infiltration. Nehru and U Nu headed a third group that seemed to have ideas of wooing China away from the Soviet Union in an effort to insulate Asia from the Cold War. At least, they hoped to lay the basis for an improvement in the diplomatic atmosphere, and they persuaded the conference to reaffirm the principles of coexistence to which Nehru and Chou En-lai had subscribed the previous year.* But although these divisions were sharp, and although the Bandung conference may not have achieved much in practical terms, it symbolized the emergence of a force that could no longer be ignored, and much energy has since been devoted to attempts to appropriate its symbols and appear as the true heir of Bandung.

The Belgrade conference developed from the initiative of Marshal Tito, in the spring of 1961, after he had made extensive tours of Asia and Africa. Belgrade differed from Bandung in several important respects. As the principles of selection worked out at the preparatory conference indicate, Belgrade was based not on regionalism, but on noncommitment. This principle was held to exclude those African states still closely associated with France, although, in the interests of casting the net of noncommitment widely, it admitted invitations (which were declined) to Austria, Sweden, and Ireland, and also to several Latin-American states. One of these—Cuba—sent a fully accredited delegate, and three— Brazil, Bolivia, and Ecuador—sent observers. The criterion was thus more explicitly diplomatic, as befitted the increased experience of the new states with independence. Whereas Bandung looked for definitions, Belgrade tried to assume one—nonalignment— and concerned itself with what to do. Sukarno had set the tone for the Bandung conference when he announced, "This is the first intercontinental conference of colored peoples in the history of mankind! . . . Our nations and countries are colonies no more." Tito's welcome to Belgrade was the warning that "as the Cold War has assumed proportions liable to lead to the greatest tragedy . . . it is necessary for the representatives of nonaligned countries . . . to take coordinated actions, primarily through the United Nations, in order to find a way out of the present situation. . . ."

The sharper focus at Belgrade was not sharp enough, however, to eliminate divisions. Some tried to have the conference devote

* In a Sino-Indian agreement on Tibet, April 29, 1954. The principles were: (1) mutual respect for each other's territorial integrity and sovereignty; (2) mutual nonaggression; (3) mutual noninterference in internal affairs; (4) equality and mutual benefit; and (5) peaceful coexistence.

itself to the peacemaking function of the new states. U Nu summed up this desire to bring about a "cooling off" by acting as a "catalyst of some kind," though he was not clear about how this should be done. The most important overt breach at the conference occurred over this question of mediation between those who, with Nehru, argued that the tasks of mediation should take precedence over emotional denunciations of colonialism, and those supporting Sukarno and Nkrumah in their insistence on keeping anticolonialism at the top of the agenda.

A similar combination of cooperative and divisive tendencies has been apparent in the efforts of new states to work together on a narrower regional basis. Such efforts have probably occupied more serious attention than the grandiose but remote world-wide gatherings. In part, they reflect fear that if the new states of a region do not work together, they will become the divided tools of the great powers. To some extent, enthusiasm for regional movements has thus become a device by which neutralists can vie with each other in demonstrations of true independence.

As early as 1945, the Arab League, composed of Egypt, Iraq, Lebanon, Syria, Saudi Arabia, and Yemen,* began cooperation at the San Francisco conference and set up a permanent secretariat. An Arab League observer at the United Nations presides over joint meetings of the Arab delegation. But if the League has been one of the most elaborately organized groups, it has also been one of the most divided. Both before and after the revolutions in Egypt and Iraq, the divisive feuds characteristic of the old dynasties continued. Even the supposedly unifying issue of Israel has provided as many occasions for quarrel as for agreement. In these circumstances, Nasser's enthusiasm for a federal approach to Arab unity has met with understandable reluctance.

The Asian states have not displayed great organizational tendencies, perhaps because there are a number of large countries, each with a reasonable hope of playing its own substantial part in the world. It is Africa that has spawned the most bewildering array of nations and international groupings. In comparison to the Afro-Asian meetings, the gestures toward Pan-African unity seem to be taken more seriously by the African states; their weaknesses and problems enhance the appeal of greater integration, perhaps combined with withdrawal within their own continent.

An unofficial Pan-African Congress was held in 1919, but the

* Libya joined in 1953; Sudan, in 1956; and Tunisia and Morocco in 1958.

movement for cooperation among African states gained momentum only after Ghana achieved independence, in 1957. In April, 1958, the first conference of Independent African States was held in Accra, with eight states participating—Ethiopia, Ghana, Liberia, Libya, Morocco, Sudan, Tunisia, and the U.A.R. Since then, the African states have split into two groups: the so-called Brazzaville group,* composed of formerly French states, which receives massive aid from France and has adopted a "moderate" view of the Congo and Algerian questions; and the Casablanca group, composed of Ghana, Guinea, Mali, Morocco, and the U.A.R.† The second group supported the Lumumbist faction in the Congo and has taken a generally militant anticolonial line, attacking the Brazzaville states as dupes of the former colonial powers in their efforts to divide and thereby maintain control of Africa. In May, 1961, a still wider grouping began to appear, when the Brazzaville states met with seven other African countries in a meeting at Monrovia, at which Nigeria played a leading role. Efforts to induce the Casablanca group to attend this conference were unsuccessful, and a further meeting of the Monrovia powers at Lagos in January, 1962, was also boycotted by the Casablancans, ostensibly because of the exclusion of the Algerian Provisional Government.

For both America and Russia, the emergence of the new states and their espousal of neutralism has posed exacting tests. The West, recognizing that Africa and Asia can no longer be held as colonies, now faces the danger that the new nations will aid the Communist powers either by joining them or by independently undermining Western interests. In the immediate postwar years, American attention was focused chiefly on Europe, and there was preoccupation over the fall of China. The Truman Administration gave overriding priority to Europe. So far as Africa and South Asia were considered, Americans regarded decolonization with favorable emotions based on dubious analogies with their own history. This enthusiasm was tempered in practice by tenderness for various interests of America's colonialist allies and certainly did not prevent the United States from becoming a target for anticolonialist charges.

When Secretary of State John Foster Dulles first devoted the

---

* Named after a meeting in that city attended by all the former French states except Guinea, Mali, and Togo, in December, 1960.

† Named after a meeting in that city attended by these five states as well as Ceylon and the FLN, in January, 1961.

earnest attention of the American government to relations with the new states, he postulated a bipolar world in which those not actively assisting the West were regarded as hostile and in which the favored form of assistance was alliance. In a famous remark on June 9, 1956, Mr. Dulles denounced neutrality as the fallacy that "a nation can buy safety for itself by being indifferent to the fate of others." He added that this "has increasingly become an obsolete conception and, except under very exceptional circumstances, it is an immoral and short-sighted conception." The policy of bringing new states into alliance met, however, with limited success. Many refused to enter an alliance, and other governments that did align proved shortlived. As a result, there has been a marked contraction of official American ambitions. Within a few days of the Dulles pronouncement, Henry Cabot Lodge, the American delegate to the United Nations, had put forward the modification that the "so-called neutral who irritates you occasionally is certainly preferable to the enemy who arises to overcome you. . . . We must not view these countries with petulance or impatience." Dulles himself later acknowledged that few nations actually pursued policies as negative as the one he had condemned and conceded that loyal adherence to United Nations collective-security measures against aggression was all that could be reasonably demanded.

After the death of Secretary Dulles, a further softening of American tone set in, and the Kennedy Administration quite explicitly concluded that a policy of independence on the part of the new states would adequately serve American interests. The new Secretary of State, Dean Rusk, spoke of the new states in words that sound very much like an extension of Henry Cabot Lodge's earlier comment: "They will criticize us specifically on certain points, sometimes in the most vigorous terms. But the test is whether they are determined to be independent, whether they are trying to live out their lives in the way in which their own peoples would like to have them shape it." As this remark suggests, the latter-day modesty of demands made on new states arose, in part, from a belief that American policy had hitherto paid excessive attention to the outward alignment of the new states, to the neglect of their inner stability.* Indeed, the new American policy was as much

---

* The Alliance for Progress in Latin America, at least as initially enunciated, marked a switch from demanding a diplomatic *quid pro quo* for aid to requiring domestic policies believed to conduce the kind of society likely to have an interest in independence from Communism.

the result of disillusionment with allies among the new states as of enthusiasm for the virtues of independent neutralism.

The new nations have also presented the Soviet Union with difficult problems of adjustment in the past few years. For all the oft-quoted sagacity of Lenin concerning the political role of peasants and the future importance of Asia, at the end of World War II, Communists had no adequate doctrine to deal with the success of national movements in colonial areas. The Stalinist regime welcomed anticolonialism as an attack on the rear of the capitalist enemy and an opportunity for Communists to infiltrate the colonial areas. But it conceived no special role for the coming national regimes. Most Communist parties in the colonies were adjuncts of those in their respective metropolitan countries, and their task was to work directly toward taking power. The rapid rise of independent governments in former colonies, their active concern with Korea, and subsequent moves toward cooperation compelled Communists to review their approach to the new nations. There was an increasingly obvious danger that the banner of anti-imperialism might be taken over by a force independent of Communism and that the revolutionary enthusiasm of underdeveloped countries would be articulated around a purely nationalist movement. At Bandung, therefore, the Chinese sought to identify themselves with the new anticolonialism and to split the more militant nationalists from those who still paid residual allegiance to the West. Khrushchev and Bulganin made their flamboyant tour of Asia later in 1955, and in February, 1956, the Twentieth Congress of the Communist Party of the Soviet Union laid down the theoretical base for exploiting anticolonial nationalism.

The five principles of coexistence already agreed upon between Chou En-lai and Nehru were easily reconciled with Leninism, from which they partly derived and which the Supreme Soviet had endorsed in 1955. Khrushchev informed the Twentieth Congress that the socialist nations and the neutralist nations could constitute a "zone of peace" to destroy the capitalist system. Because their political interests were opposed to those of the West, nationalist movements could advance the cause of social revolution. Nevertheless, in the Soviet view as it has developed, the nationalist leaders are still regarded as only a temporary expedient. Communist states may aid the nationalist governments and local Communist parties may cooperate with them, but credit for revolutionary successes is attributed to pressure from the masses, rather than to the nationalist leaders, and ultimately a proletarian regime must take over. Any tendency toward effective consolidation among the new states on nationalist principles is therefore highly suspect. Nationalist governments are "democratic and progressive" so long as they pursue policies acceptable to the Soviet Union; when they cease to do so, they quickly become "national egoists and exclusivists." Thus, the theoretical basis permits a large degree of opportunistic collaboration against Western interests without in any way limiting ultimate Communist intention.*

This adjustment of Communist policy has not been achieved without considerable friction, and debate both within Russia and between the Soviet Union and China on the wisdom of cooperation with non-Communist regimes has become notorious. These sharp debates suggest that, as Communist dealings with the new states multiply, so will opportunities for the two great Communist powers to differ both as to strategy and as to who shall dominate the campaign in any particular area. The advantages Communists enjoy in competition for underdeveloped areas are often noted—their reputation for speedy economic progress, their totalitarian mobilization of resources, their supposed freedom from the taint of imperialism, their Marxist program as a non-Western road forward for anticolonialist intellectuals harboring resentments against the West and fascinated with modern material achievement.

Much more rarely mentioned are the handicaps under which Communists labor—the full extension of their resources, the difficulties they have encountered in maintaining Communist influence in nationalist regimes not contiguous to Communist territory, the greater inroads on independence ultimately made by their system as compared with that of the West, the difficulty of timing the takeover of any particular country so as not to alienate or frighten those still to be won.

Whether these and many other factors will tip the scales for East or West is only one of many complex puzzles posed by the appearance of these states. Do we perhaps overemphasize the importance of the new states and underestimate the resources of our own camp? Do we exaggerate the danger that the neutrals may go over to the other side? Have we come to regard as an immediate danger a possibility that would take years to materialize?

---

* It should be noted that Khrushchev no longer seems to rule out entirely the possibility that nationalist leaders could learn to accept Communist goals and sustain a continuous revolution.

Are we bemused by the ideological labels new states attach to what may be mere political opportunism? To what extent do we need neutrals to provide the flexibility and pluralism without which international organization may not function and without which the East-West confrontation may become even more rigid, direct, implacable, and explosive? Answers to these and myriad other questions will not come easily. By approaching the problem from many directions, the papers in this volume perhaps will serve to illustrate the complexity of the tangled forces at work as the new states enter world politics.

NEUTRALISM
and
NONALIGNMENT

I

STATE-BUILDING AS A DETERMINANT OF FOREIGN POLICY IN THE NEW STATES

by ROBERT C. GOOD

THE demands of state-building in former colonies overwhelm all others. Inevitably, they impinge on foreign policy. The foreign policy of a new state cannot be understood exclusively in the light of domestic necessities; but unless the omnipresent task of state-building is allowed to illumine the objectives and motives of foreign policy, it cannot be understood at all.

Consider for a moment the dimensions of the problem. Kwame Nkrumah once suggested that the West has set for the emergent peoples "the pattern of our hopes." That is exactly the case. Many of the new states are still, politically speaking, more a hope than an actuality. From the colonial epoch they have inherited the form of the state, but not necessarily its prerequisites. Theirs is a legacy of expectation, not realization; of aspiration, not capacity.

The modern state—"the pattern of our hopes"—has several attributes. These relate to the precision of its boundaries, the completeness of its jurisdiction within those boundaries, the cohesiveness of its population, and the capacity of its government not simply to maintain order but, acting through institutions designed to represent the will of the people, to formulate and execute policy vitally affecting the welfare of the national community. When we speak of the modern state, we mean, then, the territorial state. However imperfectly this complex model may be realized in the West, these are its hallmarks; they are accepted without question by the leaders of most of the new countries; they are guideposts by which a new state must measure its approach to modernity.

The obstacles, however, are manifold. A new state must organize itself within the geographic frame of the old colony, and often the

3

very shape of the frame adds to the complexity of the task. Administrative units under colonialism frequently bore little relationship to the distribution of ethnic or linguistic groupings, or even to the logic of geography. There may be no such thing as a "logical" boundary to demarcate a modern state in a heterogeneous, traditional society. But colonial boundaries were more capricious than most. Often, a new state is unwilling to accept the legitimacy of territorial boundaries inherited from a colonial dispensation; many new states are still in search of their proper frontiers.

Every new state is engaged in a desperate struggle to become a nation. The familiar sequence of political development has been foreshortened—even reversed, in a sense. First comes nationalism, an emotional-intellectual ferment among a small elite. Then comes independence, precipitously and, for many new states, without a national struggle of any significance. Only last comes that which should have been concurrent with the first two stages, the long and difficult task of building something like a national society to go with the newly won juridic status of nationhood. The problem is highlighted in a line taken from the introduction of Congolese Prime Minister Cyrille Adoula to a mass meeting in Stanleyville: "Adoula is a great nationalist and he will explain nationalism to you."

A new state faces the task of effective and responsible government. Resources are slender and apprenticeship scanty. With the removal of the tight mold of colonial rule, long suppressed divisions and tensions emerge to threaten a fledgling state with "grave fissiparous tendencies," in Nehru's phrase. The requirements of effective polity are not necessarily those of responsible or accountable government. Democracy is based upon restraints on the exercise of power. But the problem in many new states is not one of restraining power, but one of accumulating sufficient power to make the government's writ effective across the land. Democracy demands a sense of the commonweal so compelling that the ruling elite and those who compete for leadership see themselves and each other as trustees of some larger interest than that of class or section. But the "opposition," such as it is, tends in many new states to express not national but tribal or sectional loyalties. The line between opposition and sedition is thus tenuous indeed.

The pattern of hopes of the new state includes progress and social equity. Again, the gap between aspiration and capacity, and the problems created thereby for the new country, are enormous. A subsistence economy lacking both infrastructure and investment capabilities; a dearth of technical, managerial and entrepreneurial personnel; an excessive dependence on the former metropole or on alternate sources of external aid to maintain even minimal governmental services and civil order—these are among the formidable obstacles.

The problem, however, is deeper than these instrumental difficulties. The search for progress and social equity adds to a colonial revolution an incipient civil war—a struggle against the institutions of feudalism and traditionalism. Society must be emancipated from the straitjacket of immemorial custom. The established order comes under attack—the landowner, the tribal chief, the feudal lord. Every aspect of life is affected. Change beckons; it also threatens. Men are torn between old habits and new methods, between ancient loyalties and strange new allegiances. A new state is cast adrift not only from its imperial moorings, but from its traditional ones, too. "The terrible experience through which our people are going," Nasser once wrote, "is that we are having both revolutions at the same time." These are the stubborn realities that must be made to conform to "the pattern of our hopes."

New states achieve juridical recognition of statehood far in advance of their capacities to perform as states. This is the salient fact to hold in mind when analyzing the foreign policy of a new nation. For, frequently, foreign policy is recruited to the state-building task—or is intimately affected by the immensity of that task.

Foreign Policy as a Continuation of the Revolution Against Colonial Rule

The leader of a new state is an impassioned and often verbose anticolonialist. One important reason is that anticolonialism is a cement that holds together otherwise incompatible domestic factions. The cohesive function of the "common enemy" must be perpetuated even when the foreign "enemy" is no longer a real threat, for the invocation of the putative threat is useful in maintaining unity at home. This, perhaps, is the reason why opposition to colonialism frequently grows more intense *after* independence.

Anticolonialism is a mood, a state of mind. It permeates countless speeches, declarations, and resolutions. However, the object of the anticolonial animus is often sharply focused. Sometimes the focus is territorial. Morocco demands the return of "national" territory still under French and Spanish occupation. The Arab states promise vengeance on Israel, which is variously described as an instrument of Western imperialism and as an imperial threat in its own right. Sukarno breathes life into the fading image of Dutch imperialism by warning of the dangers of Netherlands New Guinea. The radical states of Africa inveigh against the intrigues of a foe now pursuing "neocolonialism" and using as its base of operations the puppet governments of its former colonies. Ghana, Guinea, and Mali frankly admit that the revolution against foreign rule must continue until the beachheads of genuine independence have been expanded into an integrated Pan-African state.

The anticolonial animus may also focus on remnants of a colonial relationship that persist *within* a new state. Foreign policy is affected because relations with its former metropole are clearly involved. Most new states insist that the influence of the foreign community must be reduced; in extreme cases, the expatriates must be driven out—out of civil service, out of critical sectors of the economy, out of the educational system, out of military bases. If citizens of the former metropole no longer offer a worth-while target, others can be found—presently, the Chinese of Southwest Asia; soon, perhaps, the Lebanese of West Africa, or the Indians of East Africa.

Divisions within a new state are frequently and conveniently attributed to colonial machinations. Occasionally, these charges are justified. But, generally, the sweeping accusations are out of all proportion to the actual role of the former colonial power. A high official of an important Moroccan party took pains to explain to me that a competing party, one which attempted to give a certain political complexion to the grievances of the mountain and country areas, was a creature of the French Embassy, financed by French funds, and aimed at continuing traditional French divide-and-rule policies. A newspaper editor and leader of still another Moroccan party insisted that, in Morocco, there were no serious political differences. "There is only one struggle," he said, "that between the popular forces of the country and colonialists." Obviously, every "force" in Moroccan life not "popular" was held to be the instrument of France.

Similarly, colonialism is charged with fomenting divisions within the postcolonial world and preventing the achievement of solidarity among the new states. A highly placed official in Guinea expressed certainty that there are no tensions in Africa not accounted for by "the presence of continuing British and French influence." Cairo insists that unsatisfactory relations with Tunisia are the result of the increasing subservience of that country to "Western imperial designs." A spokesman for radical Pan-Arabism told the U.N. that the most significant manifestation of continuing colonialism in the Middle East is "the policy of the colonial powers . . . to perpetuate the division of the Arab nation into a multiplicity of states, territories, and spheres of influence." In Accra, it is argued that the European Common Market, which has extended its tariff-free zone to include the former colonies of France and Belgium, is "a new design for reimposing Europe's domination and exploitation in Africa." Similar examples could be cited endlessly.

The new states were nurtured on promises; but the present is filled with problems, and the future with uncertainty. There is almost no audience for sophisticated doctrines about underdevelopment in the political, social, administrative and economic realms, and about the painful process by which competence in these areas is achieved. It is no wonder that every problem of a new state is blamed on the legacies of the colonial era and on new forms of imperialism that are said systematically to thwart the new government in redeeming the heady promises of independence.

Foreign Policy as an Effort to Establish the Identity and Integrity of New States

Viewed from within, a new nation seems evanescent. It is riven with divisions; it lacks a tradition of common institutions and an awareness of the commonweal; indeed, its "public" constitutes a bare fraction of the population, for most of its citizens are oblivious to their membership in a national community.

However, in its external relations, the reality of a new nation—its integrity and its uniqueness—finds expression. Membership in the United Nations, recognition by foreign governments, and attendance at international gatherings confirm its existence. Differences with other nations in the international arena, particularly disputes with the former metropole, underscore even more emphatically the substance and the cohesion of the new state. Morocco asserts its Morocco-ness by opposing itself to France, by asserting against France its right to Mauritania, and by displaying indignation at French atomic tests at Regane and French intransigence in Algeria.

In short, the state's legitimacy is more easily asserted through its foreign than through its domestic policies, and it is more apparent when performing on the international than on the national stage.

Domestic issues divide the nation and disclose how little developed is its consciousness of itself; foreign issues unite the nation and mark it as a going concern.

Insofar as foreign policy serves to further the establishment of national identity, nonalignment presents attractive possibilities. Before independence, a colony was related to the external world only through the foreign office of its metropole. It participated in the international community only by proxy. Once independent, it wants to pick up its own franchise, speak with its own voice, and demonstrate its own capacities. Alignment with a bloc means a renewed loss of voice and identity. Nonalignment means an uninhibited voice, an independent role, and a sense of uniqueness—particularly in relation to the former metropole. As Prime Minister Nehru asked at Bandung:

> Has it come to this, that the leaders of thought who have given religions and all kinds of things to the world have to tag on to this kind of group or that, and be hangers-on of this party or the other, carrying out their wishes and occasionally giving an idea? . . . It is an intolerable thought to me that the great countries of Asia and Africa shall have come out of bondage into freedom only to degrade themselves in this way. . . . I will not tie myself to this degradation . . . and become a camp-follower of others.

Nehru's statement suggests that the issue is more profound than its political manifestation, for the mind and spirit are intimately involved. It is in the nature of colonialism to produce feelings of impotence and dependence. It is thus in the nature of the emancipated man to seek to assert power and independence. What is at stake, as Thomas Hodgkin has observed, is the restoration of the confidence of the colonial elites—confidence "in their capacity for political action; in their power, if they so choose, to affect the course of history." At home, the opportunities to demonstrate this capacity are severely limited. The new states and the new statesmen turn, therefore, to the international arena to validate their capacity to act—if not "to alter the course of history," then at least to declaim against those who do. The leader of the new state condemns the Cold War, the arms race, and nuclear tests; he advocates summit negotiations and disarmament conferences; his attitude is often one of impatience with, and even moral superiority to, the great powers. One does not necessarily question the genuineness of the leader of the new state in suggesting that these positions, quite apart from their merits, are responses to a deeply felt need to demonstrate an identity long concealed and a capacity long denied.

Foreign Policy as a Means of Keeping an In-Group in Power

This is the practical and political aspect of the proposition just discussed. There is nothing unusual about it. Leader X appears before the United Nations. His speech is later featured at home as the occasion when X set the world aright, advising his fellow statesmen of the course that must be pursued to avoid ruin and achieve justice. For a leader of a new state, all the world—the U.N., regional conferences, or state visits—is a stage on which to play a heroic role, partly for its impact on an audience back home.

It is much easier to demonstrate wisdom and political potency by "resolving" the problems of the world than by tackling the obdurate issues of domestic policy. Besides, if leader X poses as a mediator of global conflicts (for which he has no responsibility), he may avoid focusing attention on the insoluble problems at home (for which he is all too responsible).

For a leader anxious to speak his lines from the world stage, the posture of nonalignment again is expedient, perhaps even essential, because it is free from responsibilities. Curtailed by obligations to an alliance, the role of a Garcia or an Ayub Khan can never be as free-wheeling as that of a Nehru, a Nasser, or an Nkrumah.

Although foreign policy serves the efforts of "ins" to remain in, it also provides opportunities for heading off domestic opposition to a regime. Sometimes opposition takes the form of an organized political movement. More frequently it is an "opposition" operating within the regime—a radical sector of the ruling party, or younger members of the elite who are dissatisfied with the older, established leaders.

The radicals generally seek greater regimentation, discipline, and planning at home, and a sharp reduction of the influence of the former metropole. They seek to accelerate the "nativization" of the civil service, curtail the number of students studying in the former mother country, limit the activities of foreign entrepreneurs, and eliminate foreign bases. Their attitude towards the West is frequently one of considerable suspicion, if not one of outright hostility. Generally, they advocate expanded relations with the Communist bloc, from which they would have their country seek foreign technicians, trade agreements, development financing, scholarships, and, perhaps, military hardware.

The presence of this radical sector forces many new regimes into a position more vigorous, both in its anti-Westernism and in its support of the East, than the leaders themselves would care to take. But this is a cheap and relatively harmless way of containing the opposition—much safer than opposing them in domestic affairs, where the risk of their upsetting present leadership is a constant danger. Thus King Saud declares he will not renew the lease for the U.S. base at Dhahran—a gesture of independence from foreign influence aimed at capturing nationalist support. Haile Selassie entertains conferences of African nationalists in Addis Ababa and thereby identifies with restless Ethiopian radicals—but he does so on foreign issues that do not directly affect the domestic issues surrounding his personal rule. In Morocco, conservative Hassan II is more radical in his foreign policy than was his left-wing predecessor, Abdullah Ibrahim. This is a paradox until it is understood that the problem of containing the radical opposition is much more difficult for a conservative than for a left-wing government. Thus, a regime that resists reform at home moves toward the Soviets abroad—even to the point of accepting Soviet military aid, a step that the Ibrahim Government never pursued.

Foreign Policy as a Means of Reducing Foreign Influence at Home

All new states are more dependent on the outside world than they want to be; many are more dependent on the former metropole than they believe desirable. Particularly for the latter, there is an assumption that independence cannot be complete as long as the metropole remains enmeshed in the life of its former colony—acting as its major trading partner; the main source of its imported technicians, civil servants, and teachers; the dispenser of higher education for its students; the principal supplier of investment capital and even, in some cases, outright subsidies for government operations. "There is a difference between having and exercising independence," a spokesman for the ministry of foreign affairs of a new African state said to me. Togo's President Sylvanus Olympio once compared colonial independence to his own situation upon release from a Vichy French prison during World War II. "The jailer told me, 'You are free.' But what kind of freedom was it when the jail was in the desert, hundreds of miles from my home, and there was no gasoline for the truck we were to travel in?"

Paradoxically, the drive for development aimed at greater self-sufficiency means that, at least for a transitional period, the new state must expand its reliance on external aid—more technical assistants, more loans, more students studying abroad. For psychological and political reasons, attention frequently is directed toward diversifying the sources of aid. Interest in aid from the Communist bloc is increasing sharply. This is not simply because it offers attractive terms or because the new state believes that advances toward the bloc will induce more attractive offers from the West. These motives, of course, are not absent; in fact, the possibility of "blackmail" is built into the very structure of Cold War competition. But from the point of view of the excessively dependent, relatively impotent new state, this is not blackmail. It is the equally ancient but more honorable art of maintaining political equilibrium through the diversification of dependence, the balancing of weakness—in short, the creation of an "alternative" lest the influence of one side or the other become too imposing.

The attraction of Communist aid is enhanced for radical governments whose wariness of the intentions of the former metropole extends to the "capitalist-imperialist West" in general. Yet, as noted earlier, conservative governments—Morocco and Ethiopia, for example—are receptive to Communist aid. They want it partly to placate their radical oppositions and to hasten development, but also, one suspects, to pursue the first requirement of operational independence—the creation of a rough equilibrium among foreign influences in the life of the country. Conversely, radical governments that have developed extensive relations with the Communist bloc may seek the re-establishment of compensatory links with the West, as in the case of Guinea and the U.A.R.

The point, once again, is that foreign policy for a new state is mainly (though not exclusively) a response to domestic conditions, not to external problems. Rather than attempt to manipulate the external environment in ways suitable to the nation's interests, the foreign policy of a new state seeks to affect its internal environment in ways favorable to the building of the state and to the maintenance of the regime in power. To summarize: Foreign policy perpetuates the cohesive role of the revolution against colonialism; underscores the existence and integrity of the postcolonial state detached from the identity of its former metropole; enhances the prestige of the national leader at home while reducing the effectiveness of his opposition; and provides opportunities for diversifying the new state's reliance on external assistance, thereby diluting the potency of foreign influence in its domestic life.

At every point, then, the requirements of state-building impinge upon foreign affairs. For a new state, foreign policy is domestic policy pursued by other means; it is domestic policy carried beyond the boundaries of the state. Only recently freed from colonial domination and acutely aware of its impotence, a new state frequently suspects even the idea of "interdependence," which is thought to present the danger of renewed control by the strong over the weak.

This fear, after all, is not surprising. The notion of an international society can hardly be vital for a state still preoccupied with the creation of a national society. And the concept of a compatible world order can have little significance for a nation still trying to complete its emancipation from the colonial order, while spending itself upon the problem of establishing a viable order at home. For a new state, the wider issues of international politics may be important, but usually only insofar as they provide an opportunity to respond to the problems that really matter—and these, in large measure, are domestic.

II

ON UNDERSTANDING THE UNALIGNED

by CHARLES BURTON MARSHALL

ANY American having lived, as I have, for a considerable time in a distant but relatively accessible non-Western country is likely to have recollections of at least one homeland friend who stopped off on tour, saw the museums and landmarks, shopped in the bazaars, conversed with some cabinet ministers at tea, met a few bureaucrats and professors of the locality, chatted with students, and, after a week, went on his way aglow and atwitter with a sense of new understanding of the land and its people—leaving his host to muse upon the contrast between his guest's quick, confident conclusions and his own wariness about claiming to understand the environment. Apparent points of identity induced a sympathetic response in the guest, and this made him sure of having gained insights, whereas the more skeptical host would ponder on the subtleties of cultural diversity, the elusiveness of real insight, the ephemeral and misleading nature of sympathy without insight as a base, and the ambiguity of understanding.

That last word is one likely to recur frequently in discourse on foreign policy, whether at sentimental levels of discussion or in exacting forums of decision. Hardly a speaker nowadays omits urging international understanding. Rare is the report or resolution that fails to invoke it. Obviously, the quality and the function represented by this word deserve reason's endorsement. It is difficult to imagine anyone openly advocating its opposite, "misunderstanding." The synonymity of the word for "stranger" and that for "enemy" in most primitive languages suggests at least a tendency of comprehension to abate hostility and promote friendship in human affairs. The idea of creating understanding underlies a great many current undertakings in international relations. Its truth and utility, however, should be seen as relative rather than absolute.

13

Either must be weighed against warnings of dangers in intimacy uttered by such wise men as Aesop, Publilius Syrus, and Shakespeare.* Professor John Stoessinger has aptly pointed out limits to the idea of a necessary linkage between better understanding and closer mutuality.[1] A recent book by Stuart Cloete reflects the possibilities of increasing one's awareness of estrangement through greater knowledge of exotic cultures.[2] My own advocacy of understanding in world affairs—now recorded to fulfill the formalities—is conditioned only by a *caveat* against assumptions equating it invariably with affinity.

Here, however, the purpose is not so much to take a stand in favor of understanding as to examine what it entails, especially in the sectors of policy comprising the precepts and endeavors by which a government undertakes to relate itself to the portions of the world lying beyond the span of its jurisdiction. For relevant purposes, Charles Beard's definition of foreign policy serves: "A broad program of action to be followed by the Government in conducting relations with other powers and their nationals," consisting of "maxims, axioms, or principles to be accepted as official and applied in practice to concrete cases as they arise from day to day or circumstance to circumstance," and, "taken collectively . . . supposed to form a consistent whole, logical in its parts, devoid of mutually destructive contradictions." Foreign policy, to continue quoting Beard, "rests upon an image of the world. However disconcerting the thought may be, it is also an interpretation of all history, out of which all nations, provinces, and empires have emerged, in which they now have their being."[3]

Two of the several meanings of the ambiguous term "understanding" are relevant. It seems like a good idea to distinguish between them and then to relate them to each other. They are almost alike but not quite, and the difference is important. First is understanding in a sense of gaining a full mental grasp of the nature, significance, or explanation of something. Second is understanding in a sense including all such comprehension and, besides all that, developing a sympathetic attitude regarding the object of comprehension. Objective appreciation is common to both meanings, but the second has in addition a quality of favorable subjective response. The first involves taking measure of something, while the second involves that plus accord. The first embraces comprehension of qualities, but the second includes also some degree of community of

---

* According to each of the three, familiarity breeds contempt.

qualities. Even adversaries may understand each other in the first sense of the term—and indeed, as Professor Stoessinger has made amply clear, it is highly important for them to seek to do so.[4] Allies and friends understand each other in the second sense—at least to the extent of their understanding in this sense, nations may be described as being in accord.

The first sense of the term applies to consideration of phenomena in a detached, scientific fashion unencumbered by preferences and invoking no frame of values. The approach is akin to that ascribed to an anthropologist by Ruth Benedict:

> To the anthropologist, our customs and those of a New Guinea tribe are two possible social schemes for dealing with a common problem, and in so far as he remains an anthropologist he is bound to avoid any weighting of one in favor of the other. He is interested in human behavior, not as it is shaped by one tradition, our own, but as it has been shaped by any tradition whatsoever.[5]

Though intent to comprehend the values of any social group, one taking this approach does not himself invoke any scheme of values. He wants to enhance understanding solely as comprehension—not as a concept entailing sympathy, accord, or identity. He notes likeness and diversity as qualities of relationship between or among entities from which he stands intellectually aloof, but not as qualities of relationship between himself and others.

Far from being, like an anthropologist, concerned merely with comprehending other societies while remaining indifferent to points of community or diversity between his own society and any other, a policy-maker is enormously concerned about them. Points in common, insofar as they obtain or can be developed, are essential to the dialogue of policy and diplomacy. To find none whatever—to be in a world devoid of points of response—would amount to being alienated and isolated in the world of policy. The proponents of policy must seek points of community between the home base and the world environment. Recurring allusions in our discourse to the preservation and nourishment of diversity as an aim of our foreign policy tend to obscure this idea. The elements of diversity in the world are likely to suffice without being given attentive care. Policy must seek to bridge diversity—not merely to recognize it or to preserve it. This is not an absolute statement. Only a foreign policy dogmatic and totalitarian to the utmost degree conceivable would aim to wipe out all diversity or even to maintain animus against all diversity. Nevertheless, the concept of a need to bridge diversity is essential to the understanding of understanding in foreign policy.

Moreover, policy is concerned not only with understanding circumstances but also with affecting them. Policy involves the exercise of preferences; choice is its very essence. An important thing to focus on in Beard's definition is the basic relationship between concept and action. The "image of the world" and the "interpretation of all history" underlying foreign policy, according to Beard, are not simply passive intellectual appreciations of the external environment and of the nature of human affairs. They constitute major premises, articulated or unarticulated, by which to exercise choice, to make decisions, and to bring will to bear. Political decisions—like all decisions—involve opting for one course and renouncing alternatives, favoring one possibility to the disadvantage of another, committing influence and resources to a particular course in preference to something else. The business of states and governments, insofar as it is political, involves choosing sides and thus entails weighing values, not with uninvolved objectivity, but with an aim to invoking them as guides to action.

It would misstate the case to imply mutual exclusion between the two kinds of understanding, associating one solely with political endeavor and the other with scientific approaches. The two are neither inextricably linked nor altogether separate. The description given for an anthropologist's outlook surely serves in the field of policy. It applies to the approach of a political scientist as distinct from a policy-maker. Yet, walks of life other than political, even the most coldly detached and scientific, have aspects requiring understanding in the sense entailing accord or sympathy. For example, however objective and indifferent to questions of community of values in surveying the workings of society as an object of scientific interest, an anthropologist is involved, in a different sense, and must operate with a different kind of understanding in dealing with, say, colleagues and superiors. For then society is the element he swims in, rather than that which he scans and measures as it flows past. The point of distinction is which kind of understanding is instrumental and which is purposive. In the field of anthropology—to labor the example—a scientist may employ the second kind of understanding of the working of society to ensure an opportunity to pursue the first kind of understanding. In the field of policy, understanding in the first sense is instrumental to understanding in the second. Thus, while the anthropologist seeks to keep his preferences walled off from the phenomena he studies, the proponent of policy must surely find understanding in the sense of objective knowledge of use only as he brings it to bear in clarifying, refining, and helping to realize a set of preferences.

The policy-maker works at understanding the world from a base consisting of the essences of his own society's character, possibilities, and requirements, as he understands them. From this base, he sorts out what is relevant or irrelevant, important or unimportant, favorable or unfavorable, alarming or reassuring, and feasible or unfeasible in the environment. In doing so, he focuses on the frames of understanding, so far as he can understand them, dominant in other governments and other societies. He embraces in this quest an understanding of their understanding of his own government's understanding of them, and assumes that the process is reciprocated. He looks for points of response and assumes that potential respondents are doing likewise in return, in a complex and continuous interaction. The basic concepts from which the process of understanding begins can be subtly affected by the process—and here, again, the effects are assumed to be reciprocal. The continuously interacting essays in understanding elude measurement and definition. Approximations and generalizations must do—the "images" referred to by Beard. To gain even an approximate understanding of the understanding thus operative within another government's frame of policy is to understand it in the first sense of the term used here. To be able to concur substantially in another government's frame of understanding as thus understood and to sense a reciprocal concurrence is to approach understanding in the second sense of the term.

Anyone in a foreign government undertaking to understand the American understanding of the world—intent upon examining the "image of the world" and the "interpretation of all history," in Beard's words, affecting American approaches in the past or the present—would surely be well advised to take into account the body of premises and conclusions engrossed in the Declaration of Independence. The document was, in its time, primarily an undertaking in propaganda and psychological warfare. It was designed to explain the sundering of a bond of authority; it was not intended and could not have served as an instrument for governing. Its assumptions were in some degree subsequently modified and superseded by the Constitution. Notwithstanding these considerations—and despite the far greater numbers, scope, and ethnic diversity that now distinguish the nation from what it was at its advent in independence—the Declaration remains basic in the American appreciation of history and of the rights and reasons of nationhood. Its propositions—even though not memorized by all or even a great many Americans or invoked by them each time they appraise an event or an issue on the world horizon—nevertheless enter deeply into American assumptions and perspectives.

The doctrine in the Declaration is that of a people "born free"—an effective phrase used, in Professor Louis Hartz's *The Liberal Tradition in America,*[6] as an echo of Alexis de Tocqueville, who in turn echoed it from St. Paul. In Hartz's context, it describes the condition of being unencumbered by an overlay of relationships and restrictions left over from feudal order or a tribal system, the condition of being able to make a conscious collective choice about the character and limits of governing authority, to act as a society in ordaining an apparatus of government and bridling it, and to make such basic decisions as a society antecedent to the governing authority rather than being in essential respects a creature of it. Such are the conditions assumed in John Locke's theories of the state. The Americans fulfilled them on coming into independence. They regarded themselves as vindicating rights assumed inherited from ancestors who, in Thomas Jefferson's words, "before their emigration to America, were the free inhabitants of the British dominions of Europe and possessed a right, which nature has given to all men, of departing from the country in which chance, not choice, has placed them, of going in quest of new habitations, and of there establishing new societies, under such laws and regulations as to them shall seem most likely to promote public happiness."[7] These ancestors had been colonial in a classic sense of bearing elements of a metropolitan culture to distant lands and there applying them as the basis of new communities pervasive of the new locations. The situation was distinguishable from that of being colonial in the sense applicable to a people and a land subject to a superimposed alien authority. The American venture into independence arose from differences of constitutional interpretation and preference between political groups, however estranged by time and distance, still sharing common ancestry and language and drawing largely upon a common fund of history—namely, those groups dominant in the life of the British colonies in America, on the one hand, and those dominant in the political life of the homeland, on the other. Autonomy and self-government were asserted not as goals to be pursued but as realities to be preserved. Separation from a kindred people in an erstwhile homeland was proclaimed on the premise of its necessity to the preservation of conditions of government to which the Americans asserting independence not only felt entitled, but also were accustomed.

These points, however obvious, are often overlooked in facile attempts to overdraw the parallels between the American experience in venturing into juridic independence and the quest of independence among colonial peoples of the contemporary world. Those in colonial status today are characteristically peoples whose ancestors were once placed in colonial status through conquest by forces intruding from abroad. No simple formula for this can be presented. The presence of descendants of the Dutch in South Africa and of Portuguese-descended persons in the Portuguese enclaves of Africa, for example, is inveighed against as imperialistic even though, presumably, their ancestors got there ahead of the now subordinated Negro populations. Moreover, the equities, case by case, may become enormously complex. Often the rights asserted against imperial rule are those of peoples whose own ancestors, in their own time, arrived as conquerors.* The contemporary case against imperial rule seems largely to be based on impugning the last conquest and overlooking what conquests preceded it. In the main, the ones last coming from afar, or descendants of theirs, are the ones from whom, rather than by whom, independence is asserted. The American thrust for independence and the contemporary instances do have in common a repugnance for being ruled from afar, and the parallel between the American case and the present typical case would be more apt if the American quest of independence had been the work of Mohawks, Shawnees, Cherokees, and the like, rather than being, as it was, an effort raised by groups preponderantly of British antecedents on behalf of reasons appealing to them in part from British backgrounds inherited from British ancestry.

In asserting independence, the Americans might conceivably have stated their case solely on pragmatic grounds having particular application to their situation. They might thus have asserted

* An item in the *Washington Post* for February 1, 1962, relates charges of Arab dominance in the Sudan made by refugee Negro political leaders in Brazzaville. The gist is that Arab groups ruling since the withdrawal of British control are descendants of conquerors from the outside, with no more right to be in the country than the British had. Presumably, investigation might show even the complainers in this instance to be descendants of tribesmen who, in a distant past, captured land from earlier occupants. The notion of retroactivity correcting the results of every conquest obviously soon reaches absurdity.

that rule from abroad was not the sort of thing they were accustomed to and that they were simply not going to put up with it. This attitude, they could have added, made such rule unworkable, since it was scarcely feasible for the Crown to generate support enough to make it effective, and force sufficient to make up for the lack of support was proving excessively difficult and expensive to maintain. They could have pointed out that authority so far removed from the scene of its effects could not make practicable decisions and was bound to blunder. They could have asserted their own superior comprehension of their own problems. They could have concluded by saying that was the way they wanted things to be—and that King and Parliament had better take a practical view, recognize their reluctance for what it was, and yield to realities.

Besides marshaling particular reasons for a particular desired effect, the Americans had also, and more importantly, to use other and more abstract grounds. In that age, the dominant intellectual forces were strongly inclined toward universal concepts. The Americans had to find grounds convincing to themselves as partakers in the intellectual style of the times, and to those abroad whose support they needed, including sympathizers within the onetime mother country. They placed high store on the efficacy, as a factor swaying the policy of governments, of the group opinion of private men as distinguished from regimes—"a decent respect to the opinions of mankind." Arguments merely of practicability and self-interest would not have sufficed. Accordingly, the exponents of independence raised universal postulates, invoked principles declared to have validity everywhere, premised certain attributes as inherent in all men, argued for corollary restraining principles as incumbent upon all governments, asserted the obligation of obedience to be contingent upon fulfillment of these principles by governments, cited Divine authority, invoked natural law as a premise for their case, and asserted that governments fit to command allegiance must be lawful in that sense of law, and that in order to fulfill this requirement they must be based on the consent of the governed.

This argument was set down lucidly and dramatically. It was an argument designed for history, expressed with the apparent intention of producing a deep impression over a wide scope. The argument thus fashioned along a high line may be found circular if carried to a certain length. That is beside the point, for circular logic inheres in perhaps all deeply held political creeds. At some point, any proponent of such is likely to find himself having to rely on the fact of belief as his justification for believing. The aspect in focus here is a different one, of a sort latent in any instance of asserting eternal, universal reasons on behalf of a particular purpose. The question is whether the proponents were citing such huge reasons for restricted results or really hoped to see their purposes reverberate through a scope as wide as their argument. Were the Americans announcing independence concerned only with explaining themselves to the world and explaining the world to themselves, or did they intend to shape the world as well?

An answer at one extreme is the notion of a chosen people—to use Professor Hartz's apt way of characterizing it.[8] It involves in no degree the weakening of the assertion of universal principles. Rather, it combines it with a claim of their peculiar applicability. It argues that the application of the inherently valid principles must be deserved by those who would invoke them. The qualifications are a special grace and set of insights, accessible only to the elect. From this viewpoint, the precepts underlying American independence are regarded as giving the nation a special role in history, one setting the nation apart from others, rather than serving to relate it to others. The attributes making up the national character are therefore to be guarded rather than shared. Being governed rightly derives from talents in the people. Whether others in due course see the same light and thus are led to qualify is their concern, not that of the assertedly elect, and the validity of the insights by which the elect guide their affairs is not to be verified or discounted by the degree of their appeal and success among the rest of mankind.

At a contrasting extreme is the concept of a people with a universalizing mission—not the role of a chosen people, but one in accord with the injunction, "Go ye therefore, and teach all nations. . . ."[9] In keeping with it, the principles redeeming the political life of a nation are not to be hoarded, but rather exemplified, advocated, and promoted wherever feasible. This may come naturally enough to men who, besides believing themselves possessors of a great truth regarding the best of all possible ways to govern, hold some notion of a community or brotherhood of all. The precepts of governing, according to this view, rightly cannot be fulfilled if a nation is governed without its consent. Government by popular consent is obviously incompatible with government imposed from afar; therefore, it follows that every nation should have opportunity to determine its own government as a condition precedent to being governed rightly. It is, then, seen as a national mission to promote political self-determination everywhere and, beyond that, to coax, educate, abet, and press other nations to use independence rightly to develop political constitutions and practices consistent with the right way of governing.

As abstractions, either of those approaches can be made to appear either plausible or unsound. A nation disposed to regard itself as a chosen people leading a life in history all its own can be thought of as either modest or self-centered. The elitist idea implicit may be judged unbecoming in an age inclined to emphasize community and equality, but the busybody implication of the contrasting extreme may be equally subject to criticism. It is not reprehensible for a nation to do the best it can with its own opportunities without engaging in the dangerous folly of trying to determine history for everyone else as well. The notion of a universal political mission is likely to entangle a nation endlessly and vainly in other people's problems through the assumption of a general warrant to intervene. On the other hand, there are the clichés about no nation's being an island sufficient to itself. It is pretentious for an informed people to pose as uninterested in what may happen beyond its domain. It is fallacious to suppose that good may be the result of sparing other nations from critical judgment of their acts and standards. If the judgment of outsiders is to count, why should not our own be included? To assign ourselves no role beyond that of approving or remaining indifferent to whatever others may do is to make of us a nation with nothing to communicate, no standard to advocate in history.

How plausible either side of the argument may be made to sound was impressed upon me by an incident in Buenos Aires still recalled vividly from 1948. At an American Club luncheon, a visiting United States Senator, guest of honor of the occasion, spoke. Juan Peron was then in sway, and the United States' relations with the Peron regime was the speaker's theme. The drift of his argument was: Out in the world at large, Americans must see in proportion the principles which they value in their own institutions. Americans are for representative government, accountable authority, and free elections, and they are against dictatorship and totalitarianism. These abstractions are good, but it is pointless and mischievous to intrude on other nations with them. Whatever government suits the Argentines deserves American approval and cooperation. They owe that much to their neighbors. The important thing is to do business and to put aside any concern over the inconsequential question of how another nation is governed. A good rule is to run your own affairs and let other people run theirs.

The Senator spoke well and conclusively—or at least so it seemed for a moment, until someone offered a spontaneous rebuttal from the floor. The challenger introduced himself as an American in business in Argentina. This is what he said, as I caught it in notes at the time: "On arriving here a few years ago, calling myself a hardheaded, realistic business operator, I would have agreed with what the Senator had just said. I know better now. Tyranny is not an abstraction. The fears and indignities of life under an oppressive, vengeful, self-centered, unaccountable rule are realities. The notions of a free order and constitutional government are practical, sensible propositions. If how men govern is not important, then what is? The founders of our nation thought it so. Nothing has disproved them. We cannot impose their ideas on Argentina, but that is not the issue. The question is whether we still stand for them. Nothing compels us to yield our sense of truth. That we cannot order the situation to our liking is no reason for saying we like it. If we cannot give effect to our standards, we can at least avoid the futile relativism of declaring that whatever is, is good. I cannot think of business as separate from the human condition. We owe something to those Argentines aware and ashamed of the regime's true character. We owe them a recognition of their ordeal and a sign that we too hope for something better for their land."

The dialogue between these two propositions started at the beginning of the American experience in independence, as Professor Hartz has pointed out,[10] and continues into our own time. Its effect on the set of understandings composing United States policy toward the exterior world has been determined not solely, or perhaps even primarily, by intrinsic merits of the argument, but more importantly by the external situation and the prevailing estimates of opportunity and the factors of national power in relation to it.

It is relevant to recall the broad circumstances of the early decades of independence as background to the approach reflected in United States policy in those times. The state system, far from being universal, was centered in Europe and largely confined there. The metropolitan societies participating in it shared, at least as states, large elements of common culture. Diplomacy, as a set of equalitarian usages for relating different political societies to each other, operated within the limits of the state system. Relationships among entities of highly diverse cultures far removed from each other were carried on, if at all, through inequalitarian practices of an imperial-colonial order, distinct from the usages of diplomacy. In winning a place in independence, the Americans, in effect, succeeded in transferring their relationships with other areas from the nexus of the imperial-colonial order to the system of diplomacy. It was a highly contingent success. In Professor Thomas A. Bailey's phrase, the United States was then the "world's ugly duckling." For the time being, the newcomers to independence were having an extremely difficult time putting into practice the independence and self-government they had asserted. "Most Europeans," Professor Bailey recounts, "did not bother their heads about the new infant in the family of nations; or, if they did, their opinions were obscured by ignorance." Their indifference, however, he adds, "was not shared by the monarchs of Europe. . . . The ruling classes of the Old World were anxious, therefore, that the American experiment should fail. This attitude continued to be a basic factor in the relations between the United States and Europe far into the nineteenth century."[11]

In these circumstances, merely to hold onto national existence was enough exemplification of the precept of independence to the world. Of necessity, the role of a chosen people prevailed in policy, whatever was the temptation to indulge the notion of a universalizing mission in sentiment and rhetoric. The prevailing concept provided a dignified rationalization for a people still engrossed in realizing its asserted nationhood, preoccupied with filling out its land position, still striving to establish itself. The attendant habit of mind—in an oversimplifying correlation—underlay the United States' historic isolation and the accompanying attitude called isolationism, and its marks still linger and are important.* Conversely, the idea of a people with a universalizing mission tended to become reflected in United States policy in connection with an increasing role in world affairs—a development corresponding with what, for want of a better term, may be called the enhancement of

---

* My colleague Ralph McCabe points out that in internal undertakings the Americans who got the nation under way in independence adhered to the concept that self-government was not something to be bestowed without restraint, but rather an attribute to be earned through rigorous qualification. Self-government, he points out, was not spontaneously extended to territories of the United States. To the contrary, participation in the nexus of self-government through admission to statehood was made contingent upon qualifying for it through meeting standards laid down by the Congress to require appropriate willingness and capacity on the part of the population. This practice has continued into our own time. In this respect, internal practice implicitly has been consistent with the concept of a chosen people.

United States power. This, in turn, has related closely to successive changes in the dominant position of the imperial-colonial system centered in Europe.

The first relevant change was an erosion of that system with the assertion of independence by a cluster of Latin-American countries during a temporary breakdown of the European state system marking the Napoleonic period. Whether or not the North American colonies' earlier success in cutting transatlantic strings was a necessary condition for the emergence of Latin Americans into independence, the development gave Americans opportunity to claim authorship of a historic precedent, and the hope of having established an archetype for new nations. Henry Clay's prediction that "they will establish free governments" typified this hope. He saw the United States as "their great example." "They adopt our principles, copy our institutions . . . and employ the very language and sentiments of our revolutionary papers," Clay said. In answer to those doubtful of the Latin Americans' capacity to follow the American example, he assailed "the doctrine of thrones that man is too ignorant to govern himself" and asserted self-government to be "the natural government of man."[12] Doubt was typified by John Quincy Adams: "I have seen and yet see no prospect that they will establish free or liberal institutions of government," he said of the same claimants to nationhood. "They have not the first element of good government. Arbitrary power, military and ecclesiastical, is stamped upon their education, upon their habits and upon all their institutions. Nor is there any appearance of a disposition to take any political lessons from us."[13]

The differences in estimate did not produce differences in policy. Both views united on propositions of sponsoring the independence of the emerging states by early diplomatic recognition, and of asserting the exemption of the American continents from extension or renewal of European dominion. Both actions were consistent with the attitude of isolationism in respect to Europe yet tended also toward assumption of ranging responsibilities pertaining to the Western hemisphere. Yet, for more than half of the intervening experience of roughly 140 years, the relationship was mainly one of mutual indifference. In the next phase, which lasted about 30 years, the United States set a high mark for activity but an indifferent record for success in the role of exemplar and mentor of the forms and standards of the political life of its neighbors. For roughly the last three decades, effort has been guided toward combined enterprise in ensuring the political standards of the hemi-sphere.[14]

Much of this broad range of experience has borne out the dour predictions of Adams. Yet the notion of governments republican in form with accountable institutions and free elections, and with authority the reward for excelling in a free competition for politi-cal support, has come to prevail as a norm, if not as a per-vasive fact, in the American hemisphere. Failures to fulfill the pattern have customarily and conveniently been accounted for as tutelary phases and aberrations. That some of the participants have met the standards only intermittently, and others scarcely at all, has not disposed of the tradition. The notion of all American re-publics as destined some day to succeed in prosperity and demo-cratic institutions is still honored in discourse, along with the idea of "this hemisphere" as having a life apart—a new world "in-sulated from the follies and wickedness of the old."[15] The vaunted archetype has not been fulfilled; it has been challenged, but it has not been discarded. The goal remains easier to eulogize than to realize.

In considering the interplay in American attitudes and policy be-tween the concept of a chosen people, withdrawn, and living its history alone, and that of a people with a universalizing mission, one is tempted to dwell upon the Wilsonian period, concomitant with the making of war and peace in the second great breakdown of the European state system. With respect not only to Latin America in particular, but also to a larger frame, American discourse in Woodrow Wilson's time set a high point in projection of the as-sumed American archetype and the concept of self-determination. Here it would be easy to confuse the implicit universality of rhetoric of policy with actualities. In Professor Rupert Emerson's description, however,

> The ringing phrases . . . had all the sound of universality, but for practical purposes . . . were regarded as matters for application in Europe. The rest of the world barely entered in. . . . It is symbolic of the times that the man who set out to make the world safe for democracy went no further than to suggest that the interests—not the national desires—of the colonial peoples should be lifted to an equality with the claims of their alien rulers.[16]

All the great discourse on self-determination, self-government, and rights of representation undoubtedly entered into the world's general store of ideas and thus may have served as a factor in producing long-term results, unintended at the moment of utterance, in the great movements for independence and the proliferation of new states that developed a quarter-century later out of circumstances following the third great breakdown of the European state system in World War II.

If so, it could have been only a minor and marginal factor in phenomena whose causes and consequences reach into multifarious aspects of recent history and contemporary events. These phenomena are, of course, first, the wide and rapid progressive decline and disappearance of imperial-colonial relationships, inequalitarian in character, formerly serving as a basis for order between peoples of highly diverse cultures and levels of economic development living in widely separated places; and second, the concomitant emergence into juridic independence of increasing numbers of political entities with unformed political character.

Characteristically, though the degree of difficulty varies widely from one instance to another, these newcomers are having a hard time finding their place in the conditions of the middle of the twentieth century, striking a practical balance between ambition and capability and finding adequate standards for public life in independence. These trials are not unique to them, for even long-established political societies have to strive in order to cope with the demands of the times. Obviously some states are distinctly better off than others for having developed a sense of their place in history, a pattern of identity and allegiance, and institutions adequate to the requirement of making and carrying out decisions. Not all states of long standing have achieved these attributes in a satisfactory degree. Not all of the states newly arrived in independence are beset by a critical lack of them. Yet, broadly speaking, necessitousness in this respect does characterize the new states —along with what President de Gaulle of France has aptly described as "a passion for self-determination, for the right to make their own decisions" and "a growing desire to see their own living standards rise."[17] Characteristically, they are conscious of having a long way to cover before becoming going concerns, and they are not sure of how to close the gap.

Among these newcomers to independence, one finds prevalent the tendency called neutralism and nonalignment—an attitude showing some appeal among Latin-Americans as well. Each of the abstractions requires a referent. Neutralist and nonaligned in what respect? To name three illustrative examples, Indonesia is certainly aligned with respect to West New Guinea, as India is with respect to Kashmir, or Afghanistan with respect to a dream of access to the Arabian Sea, and all of them have in common the emotions of self-determination. Actually, a considerable tangle of alignments on one issue or another obtains among them. A disposition to describe them as neutralist and nonaligned reflects a recognition that what counts in their appraisals is not merely different but, indeed, notably different from what prevails in our own policy. There are gaps in understanding between them and ourselves— gaps important enough not to be obscured by customary sentiments regarding international understanding.

Neutralism—meaning merely a tendency toward vehement profession of expediential nonalignment—appeals to some of them as a way of bridging a gap between neediness and ambition for significance. It reflects at once a desire to avoid commitment—an understandable attitude for any people of meager resources—and a wish to be among those who count in world affairs. It is a way not of withdrawing, but of playing a role in global politics, of getting into the game, but staying out of the scrimmages. The character of contemporary international organization puts a premium on this approach. Being among those who are counted almost necessarily entails being among those who count. A state truly desirous of avoiding some role in world affairs would virtually have to exclude itself from the state system and avoid the United Nations membership, which now seems to follow almost *ipso facto* on the attainment of juridic independence, and, as the Western Samoans have done, renounce "the status symbols of world politics."[18] This is a course likely to appeal only in marginal instances. The motives guiding some underdeveloped new states to wish to frequent the machine shop and, at the same time, keep out of the machinery should present no puzzle to us. Even in the form of trying especially hard to placate the presumably less placable of the great antagonists in the contemporary world, the motives are readily understandable, in the first sense of understanding given above, however perplexing it may be to our own view of the realities and, therefore, less understandable to us in the second sense of the term.

A far deeper and more enduring significance implicit in the phenomenon of neutralism is a disjunction of ideas between ourselves and a great part of the emerging world. This gap in communication is due not to failure to say enough back and forth, not to a failure as yet to hit upon a right combination of words, not simply to a lack of common knowledge and terms, and not to an insufficiency of exchanges of visitors and students. It is, however, ascribable to some basic disagreements as to what counts, what is feasible, what the nature of authority is, and what the nature of history is in which nations have their being. If the lack were simply quantitative—a failure of parties to meet each other halfway —it could be readily met by doing more, giving more time, spending more on the effort to communicate. In fact, however, unprecedented volumes of words go into international communication, cultural exchange operates at a high level, and official good-will visits and the like have become commonplace. The problem seems to be not quantitative but qualitative; the question is not whether to meet each other halfway, but how to approach each other on intersecting tangents.

Professor Saul Padover, an astute observer, has stressed the point that, "although a measure of misunderstanding among nations is unavoidable, that which exists between the United States and a large part of the world is monumental and unprecedented. . . . Unless corrected, at least to the extent that it is possible to do so under the circumstances, the gap . . . may become unbridgeable. . . ."[19]

"Can a people 'born free' ever understand peoples elsewhere that have to become so?" The question is raised at the conclusion of *The Liberal Tradition*.[20] The phrase "born free" has been dwelt upon. The word "understand," in this context, presumably embraces both senses of the term discussed above, and especially, in relation to policy, the sense of mutually recognized common views. The "peoples elsewhere that have to become so" are a significant portion of the world exterior to the United States. The phrase "have to become" is indicative, moreover, of something unfulfilled, but not of historic necessity. No law of being compels peoples to achieve the state of being free. The process of becoming so is by no means necessarily to be equated with the achievement of juridical independence. If it were, in actuality, equivalent, then the progressive disappearance of the imperial-colonial order could be taken to signal the universalization of freedom in the domestic character of the societies concerned, as well as the riddance of rule from afar —an unwarrantedly optimistic conclusion.

Professor Hartz leaves his question unanswered, but the implication of his text is scarcely more affirmative than Professor Padover's account of "a measure of misunderstanding . . . which . . . is monumental and unprecedented." That question of understanding was obviated as a consideration of policy so long as the United States, in a marginal and highly insecure position in the early sequel to gaining independence, adhered in practice to the concept of being a chosen people. In later times, with widened scope, Americans have had to think of themselves as a people with a mission, although without a clear formula for performing it. Simple projection of the American image, as it appealed to Clay and Wilson, for example, seems scarcely adequate to cope with exigencies in the present. To a people whose independence was based on generalizations as wide as ours and whose founders declared "a new order of the ages," this is disconcerting. It is a concern not only of sentiment and pride, for it has a central bearing on the character of what new order, if any, will replace the disintegrated imperial-colonial system.

It is perhaps relevant to refer to some of the common expedients offered for getting around the difficulties. One of these is to cleave to old assurances of a world destined to follow the American example into independence and, thereafter, the American pattern of national success and affluence with freedom. This is coupled with assertions of American authorship and inspiration for recent and current surges into independence, and interprets the emerging world in the pattern of an American prototype. One notes, for example, an address by one of the State Department's hierarchs postulating the relevance and utility of the United States' early history as the key to understanding the future of the nascent states of Africa. He likened one-party authoritarian rulerships currently prevailing among them to the overwhelming American consensus behind George Washington as first President, discerning therefore a prospect among them of early polarization of politics along lines of a two-party competitive system as here. This, he said, equated their disposition for neutralism to the tenor of Washington's Farewell Address.[21] In a similar vein, an official of the United States Information Agency has asserted that the inspiration of African independence is American—citing as proof his having met some rioters knowledgeable of Jefferson.[22]

Another expedient is to view independence itself as a final good, ignoring all consideration of what to do with it. This attitude maintains that whatever practice may be indigenous is suitable, and whatever is suitable, is good. It judges the quality of government solely on the basis of the territorial location of authority, and is relativistic with respect to other qualities. It is reflected in an often-heard proposition that the all-important challenge for the emerging peoples is to find institutional patterns of their own suitable to native genius. That states only a fraction of the requirement. Government must be not only native but also effective; and if the society concerned proposes to act as and to be regarded as a going concern in a modern, respectable sense, the effectiveness must be judged by the relevant standards. An analog to Edmund Burke's warning of the folly of regarding freedom as a final good, irrespective of what was to be done with it, must surely apply to independence.[23]

A third approach is to pin hope on economic development as the key to the character of states and nations—a premise often encountered among the more enthusiastic rationalizations of foreign aid. The line of reasoning is simple and, within its limits, plausible enough: to be free and successful, societies must be able to make choices; to make choices, they must have alternatives; having alternatives requires margins; margins require increments of productivity; this will materialize in ratio to outside assistance supplied. Mr. Robert L. Garner, former Vice President of the International Bank for Reconstruction and Development, has cogently pointed out the questions begged by these propositions. Good use of foreign aid requires antecedent characteristics in a society and its government. It is Mr. Garner's "conclusion that economic development or lack of it is primarily due to difference in people and in their attitudes, customs, traditions and the consequent differences in their political, social and religious institutions." He declares it "no service to truth and realism to avoid the fact that much effort and sacrifice of the accustomed ways are the inevitable price of advancement."[24]

A fourth escape defines a solution in a negative term: anti-Communism. It attempts to describe a course by indicating a pitfall, to define a goal in terms of what it should not be. To a query of how to set up a going concern, it gives an answer of how not to do it. It supposes that things will end well if the emerging societies avoid the Communist formula, and that no guidance beyond that is required. This is roughly equivalent to a line in an old song: "O Lord, if you can't help me, then please don't help that bear!" This is far short of what is needed by a society in the predicament of being partly in modernity and partly still in the grip of a traditional past.

Much of the bias against the forces and ideas summed up in the term "the West" are consequences of a sense of that predicament, one suspects. Generally, the societies concerned were brought into such a predicament through contact with the West. What they label as imperialism are the experiences and influences that put before them concepts they feel able neither to achieve nor to renounce. So they tend to associate their frustrations with Western societies and cultures, with a consequent bias that sometimes affects their views on great issues.*

Our end of the dialogue with them is perhaps excessively affected by our sensitivity to this bias. Our interest can be served better by comprehending the bias for what it is and understanding how it arises, than by humoring it with uncalled-for sympathy. There is indeed a morbidity—not too strong a word, I think—in the preoccupation with the West and its values and precepts, and in the related dissents and grievances found among the peoples of the emergent countries.

On a recent occasion, I heard a minister of education from one of the more underdeveloped and militant of the new African countries expound plans to eliminate Western influences and restore indigenous values in the educational undertakings of his government. It was an eloquent exposition on inculcation of national morale, enrichment of public life, and development of a sense of a place in history. At the luncheon afterward, a wise Nigerian observed: "He said those basic ideas in French, and he could not possibly have said them in the tongue of his tribe. Such is the dilemma. To express his aspiration he must embrace that which he would scorn." This reminded me of thoughts I had once addressed to an Asian and African group, and I repeat them now in closing:

> At Bandung . . . a recurring theme was the necessity for the new states of Asia and Africa to develop political institutions and traditions distinguishable from those of the West. Those bespeaking this theme did so almost invariably in English—and not merely as a matter of convenience in communication, for in the general case it would not have been possible to express in native tongue the political abstractions being spoken of. I have heard the same idea over and over again from Asians and sometimes also from Africans, and one can understand the impulses behind it without being persuaded

* This sense of frustration related to the West and imperialism can indeed be carried to inordinate lengths. For example, a scholar from India recently told me: "Our grievance is not only because of what was taken from us but also for what we were prevented from doing. Electricity, atomic energy, the internal combustion engine—all those would have been within our capabilities. We should have had them first if it had not been for the burden and blight of imperialism."

of the merits. It is folly to take a position for abandoning ideas merely because they and the West have had something to do with each other, and one should not abandon a source before making sure that he has an alternative at least as good. It is folly—understandable folly, perhaps, but still folly—to speak of finding one's political traditions in the background of one's own country when that country manifestly has no traditions adequate for the problems of a political going concern under the conditions of the mid-twentieth century.

There is nothing wrong, moreover, with such ideas as accountability of ministers, with the right to be judged under law on the basis of evidence and with opportunity to put up a defense, or with the notion that bureaucrats should make their decisions on the basis of some pattern of public policy arrived at by discussion and established by processes free of coercion. These are hard things to achieve. They are not practiced perfectly anywhere. To maintain them is an onerous, Sisyphean task. The West, in its best sense, represents the achievement of such ideas and in its worst sense the failure of them; but for better or worse, they are identified with the West in some degree. To feel free to cut loose from them merely because they are in some way of the West is a course of egregious folly. The important thing is not that they are Western but that they represent the better impulses of men in the life of the state. The struggle between the better and the worse impulses as they affect political life is a general struggle. It knows no points of the compass. Anyway, the abandonment of something of value in the politics of any part of the world hurts all of it.[25]

III

THE CONGO CRISIS:
A STUDY OF POSTCOLONIAL POLITICS*

by ROBERT C. GOOD

THE first thing to decide about the Congo crisis is what kind of problem it represents. The crisis is not really constitutional; that is only symptomatic. Neither is it truly a colonial problem, for to call it such is to miss the significant distinction between the issues involved in the revolt of the colonies and the issues arising from the success of that revolt. Nor is the Congo crisis a function of the Cold War, even though that Midas-like conflict seems to transform all it touches. Nor is it best understood as a case of international aggression—surely not in the conventional sense. Since early September, 1960, Belgium has had no army deployed on Congolese soil. "Aggressor" she may have been, and for some states the case is beyond dispute. But if so, it was an "aggression" that can be understood only with reference to quite unique circumstances that demand examination, for they hold the key to the real nature of the Congo crisis.

The circumstances are disarmingly simple: Imperial power withdrew from the Congo. The power that replaced it had few of its attributes and almost none of its capacities of governmental authority, and a decline into chaos ensued. This led to competition among those, both within and outside the Congo, who tried to organize the chaos according to their own political and ideological patterns.

The Congo crisis, then, may be called a "postcolonial" problem. It is a tragic incident rather close to the final curtain of this his-

* This paper was completed in the spring of 1961, and Mr. Good's subsequent appointment as Director of African Research for the State Department has prevented his making substantial changes or additions.

34

toric drama that has seen the dissolution of a vast imperial structure, and has given rise to the grave complexities of reordering the political life and international relationships of the proliferating new states of the postcolonial era. The term "postcolonial" is used advisedly, for it suggests a set of data and a framework of analysis of critical importance to the theorist of contemporary international relations.

The Postcolonial Era

To speak of the postcolonial era is to point out the obvious; a key determinant of international politics in our time is the collapse of a vast imperial system. The metropoles of the system were Western (or, in the case of Japan, Westernized). It established itself in two great waves of expansion, that of the sixteenth to the eighteenth centuries, and that of the latter part of the nineteenth and early twentieth centuries. As the scope of this imperial system was unprecedented, so too has been the crisis occasioned by its collapse. Both have been world-wide.*

To the immensity of the change signaled by the collapse of the Western colonial system must be added the startling speed with which it has been accomplished and the remarkable shift in ethos that has accompanied it. There is no more vivid symbol of these changes than General de Gaulle's eloquent plea to the French army to support his Algerian policy. On December 10, 1960, at Blida, Algeria, he said:

> The Algerian question presents itself to France in conditions completely different from those of other times. . . . Because of the Moslem insurrection the population of Algeria, which is in the great majority Moslem, has assumed an awareness of itself that it did not have. Nothing will prevent that. There is also the fact that that insurrection and everything connected with it takes place in a new world, in a world that no longer resembles at all the world that I knew when I was young. There is . . . that context of liberation

---

* Historians will record the establishment of the Soviet and Red Chinese empires as the third wave in a historical sequence in which the center of imperium moved steadily eastward from the Iberian Peninsula to Western Europe and, most recently, to Moscow and Peking. For the analysis of contemporary international politics, however, the development of the Communist imperia must be viewed not as part of a historical continuum, but as a historical disjunction, for the rise of the Soviet and Chinese empires at the very moment of the collapse of the Western imperial system is one of the basic causes of imbalance between West and East today.

which sweeps from one end of the world to the other. . . . It is vain to pretend that Algeria constitutes a province like our own Lorraine or Provence. It is so vain that it is not worth saying because it is not true. It is something else. It is an Algerian Algeria.

The significance of this statement is apparent when it is measured against the intervention of a French diplomat at the United Nations just five years before: "Since 1830, that is for more than one hundred and twenty years, Algeria has been an integral part of French territory. . . . Algeria has been united to France . . . on an equal footing with the Ile-de-France, Brittany, or Auvergne, such that any Algerian, whether Moslem or Christian, is a French citizen."

The term "postcolonial," then, points first to the fact that Western colonial rule as a means of organizing the economic life and maintaining the political order of vast parts of the non-Communist world is now nearly defunct, and that the imperial ethos, according to which men did not seriously question the propriety of alien rule, is in thorough disrepute.

Secondly, it suggests that the new age is not totally new, but remains organically related to the old. The many legacies of the colonial past press upon and help shape the present and the future. Thus, the colonial era helped to determine both the form and the viability of the new postcolonial states. It conjured up numerous problems that now affect the relations of these states to one another and to international society. The colonial heritage helps also to condition the relations of the former metropole to its former colonies. It gives to the "anti-imperial" Soviet Union ideological access to the postcolonial states. It even importantly affects the American mind, as this country seeks to define its unaccustomed, and in a sense unprecedented, role as a hegemonic power in a passionately anti-imperial age.

The term "postcolonial," in the third place, suggests a mode of analysis appropriate to the theorist on international relations. The new states of Africa and Asia present a range of problems presently under intensive examination by scholars in several associated disciplines. Political economists seek ways to stimulate the growth of stagnant and primitive economies. Cultural anthropologists focus on the mechanics of social change, which, they point out, must be understood and manipulated to permit traditional cultures to be modernized with a minimum of social dislocation and tension. Political scientists are concerned with the difficulties of

creating viable political societies with a sense of community sufficient to produce national cohesion and a capacity for public service adequate to the demands of reasonably responsible government.

Each perspective, in its own way, is basic. But the theorist in international relations is oriented in another direction—the development of the new states, and intrastate dynamics as these project
themselves into the arena of interstate politics and help to create
the dynamics of international society to which foreign policy must
respond. For the student of international relations, the emergence
of the new states suggests certain structural changes in international politics. These changes involve the collapse of colonialism
as a form of international order, and the integration into international society of an unprecedented number of new sovereignties,
each reflecting the legacies of the colonial past, and each burdened
by the problems of adjusting to the postcolonial present. As "underdevelopment" defines the problem for the economist, as "tradition
versus modernization" orients the inquiry of the cultural anthropologist, as the "politicization of society" fixes the approach of
the political scientist, so the notion of the "postcolonial era" may
give the scholar of international relations an important set of
guidelines for examining the impact upon international politics of
these "transitional" or "emergent" or "quasi" states—to use labels
that are now in vogue. How may the internal instabilities of these
weak and untested nations affect international stability? The question is crucial, but it does not exhaust the subject, for the problems attending the end of an old order and the advent of a new
era are as various as they are complex.

Relationships long maintained within the colonial nexus must
now be conducted by diplomatic intercourse between juridically
sovereign entities. Economically interdependent societies whose relations were once handled by the exactions of the strong from the
weak now must relate themselves, not simply by the authority of
superior force, but by mutual efforts to accommodate interests.
Lines of authority that formerly ran from relatively few centers
of power to a vast array of subject communities are now in dis-
array, and the number of repositories of independent authority in
international society has vastly increased. So, too, have the sources
of international tension increased as the newly sovereign states
entered the arena of world politics, suddenly to encounter, in case
after case, conflicts of interest or ambition with neighbors now
equally sovereign. Disputes between former colonies and former
metropoles that, not very long ago, were "domestic" in character

now emerge as international issues no longer protected from international review by the reservations of the U.N. Charter. Accordingly, the agenda of political issues confronting the United Nations is seriously overtaxed, and growing more so all the time. If the advent of the postcolonial era has altered the very character of the United Nations, which indeed it has, this is no more than a reflection of the changes it has wrought in the international political arena at large.

These changes are the more pronounced because the postcolonial era coincides with the era of Cold War. The two are closely related. Exploiting the stands of the great powers and the desire of each side to gain their favor, the new states achieve a maneuverability and a leverage in international politics wholly incommensurate with their real power. A curious inversion has taken place. Never before has the gap been wider between the great powers and the miniscule powers. Many of the latter are dependent for their very existence on the assistance afforded by the powerful. Yet, the great powers are strangely inhibited in pursuing their interests among the miniscule states. Often, the great power is obliged to act exclusively by proxy, seeking its ends among the new states through native agents responsive to its direction, or perhaps through the United Nations. Not infrequently, the suggestions of the great power are peremptorily vetoed by the miniscule power, which can turn "elsewhere" for support.

The problems preoccupying the super powers in their contest with one another are generally peripheral to the interests of the new states, most of whom refuse to measure the issues of international politics with Cold War calipers. The meaningful choices are not between the "free world" and the "Communist world," nor between democracy and authoritarianism, nor between the economic systems of East or West. Insofar as these options are incorporated into the issues inviting choice between one or the other of the two opposing blocs, most of the postcolonial states are neutral. And if the Cold War is conceived as the development of spheres of influence by East and West, all the new states want is to "keep the Cold War out" of the postcolonial world.

The struggle that has meaning is the one that derives from colonial experience and postcolonial aspiration. It is the fight to end all imperialism. It is the attempt to nourish those roots of individual or cultural uniqueness that have continued to live in the subsoil of "Negritude" or "Africanism" or "Arabism," despite the working of the topsoil by a foreign culture. It is the effort to gain greater access to the economic levers of power—skills, productivity and capital—so that the new state will, more and more, be in charge of its own destiny. It is the search for the proper relationship of the new states to their former metropoles, to the great powers, and to one another, and the creation of a new order in those vast regions recently vacated by the imperial powers.

In greater or lesser degree, the advent of each new nation has brought to light these and related postcolonial problems. The Congo, however, brings the postcolonial situation into sharp focus. All new states must solve the problem of transferring the order-producing authority of imperial power to native hands. In the Congo, the problem of achieving order seems continuous and monumental. Many new states have found it necessary to staff government bureaus, educational institutions and technical services with expatriates. The Congo is totally dependent on foreign skills, grasping the twentieth century, as one journalist put it, with Belgian hands. Almost all the new states must create in fact what juridic independence concedes only in theory—a sense of nationhood. The Congo is not a nation; it is probably not even in prospect of becoming one if, by a nation, one means a community conterminous with the boundaries of the state and commanding the loyalty of a majority of its inhabitants. Many postcolonial states are dependent on their former metropole, yet fearful and resentful of that dependence; their attitude toward their former mother countries is ambivalent. In the Congo, ambivalence becomes schizophrenia; Belgians have been simultaneously condemned as "aggressors," and relied upon as advisors.

Here, then, is the lens through which the Congo crisis ought to be examined. It is a case study of postcolonial international politics, for it is beset with all the problems arising from the annulment of imperial authority, the rupture of the colonial relationship, and the struggle to create a new center of governmental authority and a new system of international order to replace the metropole.

The term "struggle" is used with forethought. For the postcolonial states are anything but of one mind. In the center of the arena, one finds the new states contesting, not with just the outside world —that is to say, the former metropoles and the great powers—but with one another. Throughout the first year of the Congo crisis, the competition of postcolonial leaders was in full view. The decision of the United States to act only through the United Nations, and the successful deflection of Soviet attempts to intervene unilaterally, gave competing Congolese leaders considerable freedom to maneuver, and afforded the new states a remarkable degree of access to the Congo, whether through the various agencies of the United Nations or through direct intervention. Thus, an analysis of the first year of the Congo crisis vividly illumines the positions of the new states and the divisions among them as they confronted the issues of postcolonial politics. What follows is an identification of these issues as they emerged in the particular context of the Congo debacle.

The Postcolonial Issues in the Congo Crisis

THE IDENTIFICATION OF THE "ENEMY"

The real issues in the Congo were not immediately apparent. They emerged slowly and in sequence during July, 1960. These developments are worth careful review. At the end of the first week of independence, units of the Congolese Public Force began to mutiny. Panic-stricken Belgians fled the country. Almost simultaneously, Belgian paratroopers arrived from Brussels. From these developments, the first issue arose: the proper identification of the "enemy." Was he the mutinous Congolese soldier, or was he the Belgian paratrooper? That is, was the problem one of internal disorder—a threat to the non-Congolese population and, ultimately, to the very existence of organized society in the Congo? Or, was the problem one of external aggression—a threat to the sovereignty of a newly independent nation?

The ambiguity of this situation was apparent. On July 10, the day on which Premier Lumumba first protested Belgian intervention, President Kasavubu pleaded with the Europeans not to leave, and Foreign Minister Bomboko made it known that his superiors had given him permission to call on the Belgian troops, if necessary.

On July 12, however, Kasavubu and Lumumba jointly signed an appeal to the U.N. for military aid against a Belgian "act of aggression." On July 13, Reuters reported that the Congolese Government had avowed the existence of a state of war with Belgium. The subsequent resolutions of the Security Council, however, did not mention Belgian aggression, although, with increasing insistence, they demanded the withdrawal of Belgian troops. The resolution of July 14 clearly implied that the problem was one of assisting the Congolese Government in the maintenance of order, while the resolution of July 22 referred explicitly to the "restoration of law and order." (These words were later repeated in the

General Assembly resolution of September 20.) Secretary-General Hammarskjold endorsed this interpretation in his first intervention in the Security Council debate: "The difficulties which have developed in the Congo . . . are connected with the maintenance of order in the country and the protection of life."

The new states of Africa and Asia were represented on the Security Council by Ceylon and Tunisia. Both acknowledged that the problem of restoring order was genuine. Ceylon's Sir Claude Corea noted that the treaty of friendship between Belgium and the Congo stipulated that Belgian troops could be called out only at the request of the Congolese Government; but, he said, the treaty "had to be overridden in view of the emergency." Tunisia's Mongi Slim found the Belgian attitude "understandable" in the light of the "deplorable acts that were committed against foreigners in the Congo." But neither Ceylon nor Tunisia was ready to acquit Belgium. On July 21, Sir Claude found that one of the chief causes of continued tension was "the presence of Belgian troops in the independent territory." And when, on August 8, Foreign Minister Wigny of Belgium pointed out that the Security Council had consistently refused to accept Soviet resolutions condemning Belgian "aggressions," Mongi Slim made it quite clear that this was to avoid "aggravating the feelings of the Belgians" and that the U.N.'s intervention indeed was "to prevent a continuation of what is considered to be a violation of [the Congo's] sovereignty and independence."

According to this view, the problem of disorder was real; but it was a problem exaggerated and perpetuated by the Belgian presence. Order would return to the Congo, Lumumba said, time and again, "five minutes after Belgium's withdrawal." For perhaps all the new states of Africa and Asia, the "enemy" during the early days of the Congo crisis was clearly Belgium, though the accusation in the Security Council was made without passion. Indeed, the issue seemed almost academic. Belgium, after all, avowed trust in the U.N., hoped the arrival of U.N. troops could be hastened, and expressed willingness to withdraw her men "without any delay" as soon as the safety of her expatriates could be assured. In the Security Council, Ceylon called attention to this concurrence of objectives: "What is required is to devise ways and means . . . of doing something which the people of the Congo and the Government of Belgium both desire. . . ." Soon, however, the proper identification of the enemy was to become more critical as the differing objectives of the new states became apparent, and as the schisms within the Congo grew more serious.

THE DEFINITION OF THE CONGOLESE STATE

By July 11, 1960, President Moise Tshombe had announced the secession of Katanga Province. The Belgian Cabinet met the next day and stated emphatically that their policy "has been and still is a policy based on the Congo's unity." Tshombe was said to have had second thoughts about secession, and the July 14 resolution of the Security Council did not even mention the phrase "territorial integrity."

But while the Council debated in New York, Tshombe was evidently having third thoughts in Elizabethville. "Let us face the truth," he said. "Democracy does not exist here. We have a tribal structure. The last election showed everybody voted according to his tribe." Under the circumstances, he concluded, the only solution was a federation with each province governing its own affairs. On the same day, Ghana, through its High Commissioner's Office in London, avowed that " . . . Katanga is an integral part of the Congo and . . . any attempt to detach it would amount to a flagrant violation of the Congo's territorial integrity."

Here then was the second fundamental issue in the crisis: the proper definition of the Congolese state. Was it the centralized organism maintained by Belgian imperial power, bequeathed to the legatees of Belgian rule in the Brussels Round Table Resolutions and the *loi fondamentale,* and established in legal practice by the elections of June, 1960, the convening of Parliament, and the creation of the Kasavubu Presidency and the Lumumba Government? Or was there a deeper reality based upon the essential disunity and artificiality of this thing called the Congo, and evidenced in the inability of a central regime without the aid of imperial power to maintain the cohesion of the whole? It was partly the question of central *versus* dispersed authority. But it was also the question of legal principle *versus* political fact. Was the Congo a legal entity established in inviolable law, or was it a legal fiction demanding to be re-established in accord with political fact?

For the Lumumba Government, as for the nationalists in general, there was never more than one objective—the imposition of effective control over the whole of the Congo. The Premier's mercurial attitude toward the U.N. and his erratic invitations to a variety of states to intervene on his behalf were prompted by this single, constant aim. At the outset of the crisis, the new states may have been critical of Lumumba's methods, but not of his notion of a unified Congo. Sir Claude Corea was emphatic: "When we speak of the Congo, we mean the Congo as the Republic of the Congo—the whole unit and all its provinces—that is the only basis on which the Security Council can proceed." From this view, there was no dissent.

Still, the problem of properly defining the Congo had been posed by Tshombe's secession. Soon it was to be sharpened by other secessionist movements and by the Lumumba-Kasavubu struggle, which was partly a dispute between centralism and federalism. On this issue, too, the new states eventually divided sharply.

THE ROLE OF THE UNITED NATIONS

As the first two issues dealt with objectives—the identification of the "enemy" and the nature of the Congo—the remaining two concerned implementation. They were: defining the proper role of the United Nations and settling the problem of unilateral aid—or unilateral intervention, depending on one's point of view.

The same ambiguity that made it difficult to identify the real enemy also affected the U.N. operation in the Congo. The Congolese Government had asked for U.N. assistance for the single purpose of coping with Belgian "aggression." But, as we have seen, the Security Council resolutions of July 14 and 22, 1960, identified, not one, but two objectives: the withdrawal of Belgian troops *and* the restoration and maintenance of law and order. Not just the issue of Belgian troops, but the problem of mutinous Congolese soldiers, came within the mandate of the United Nations Mission to the Congo—although it was a mission to be executed "in consultation with the government of the Republic of the Congo," while making available to that government "such military assistance as may be necessary." In a bitter speech read in the presence of Dag Hammarskjold during his visit to Leopoldville, Vice Premier Gizenga put the issue pointedly: "We do not understand why we, victims of aggression who are at home here, are being systematically disarmed [by the United Nations Force] while the aggressors, the Belgians, who are the conquerors here, are permitted to keep their weapons and their means of inflicting death."

Another aspect of the problem involved the limitations imposed on the U.N. troops. During the first sitting of the Security Council on the Congo question, Hammarskjold outlined the principles by which he would establish the force—principles deriving from the U.N. Emergency Force in the Middle East. The troops "would not be authorized to action beyond self-defense"; and "they may not take any action which would make them a party to internal conflicts in the country."

These limitations could have been made compatible with an effective U.N. action if there had existed a single, reasonable, effective governmental authority in the Congo to which the U.N. could have related its assistance, and if the several factions in the country had been willing to compete with one another without resort to armed violence. But as things developed, neither of these provisos obtained. So the limited and neutral character of the U.N. operation—utterly consistent with precedents deriving from the U.N.'s role in Palestine, Kashmir, Suez, and Lebanon, but now applied to an unprecedented situation—became the occasion for harsh debate. This was particularly true as the secessionist crisis of August, 1960, and the governmental crisis of September, 1960, hardened divisions within the Congo and created schisms among the new states.

Even at the very outset, however, intimations of the coming crisis were not difficult to find. On July 20, Lumumba told a press conference: "If no action is taken by the United Nations, we will understand that the United Nations is a tool of imperialism, a plot by capitalists to grab the Congo."

Lumumba's assessment was theatrical. The real issue was this: Was the U.N. to serve as an adjunct to the Central Government, contributing its force and authority to the realization of that government's objectives? This could be inferred from the language of the resolution of July 14, 1960: "To provide the government with such military (and technical) assistance as may be necessary." Or was the U.N. Mission to remain independent of Congolese authority and aloof from all internal political issues, answerable only to the Security Council? This was Hammarskjold's position; the U.N. Force, he said, "will not be under the orders of the [Congolese] Government"; further, the troops "cannot be used to enforce any specific political solution of pending problems or to influence the political balance decisive to such a solution." Or, to state the issue differently, how much initiative ought the U.N. to assume? It was charged with the restoration of law and order; it had endorsed the territorial integrity of the Congo. How far should it intervene to create the conditions in which these mandates might be fulfilled? Or, under the limitations of self-defense and abstention from internal conflicts, was the U.N. reduced to the passive role of neutralizing all Congolese initiatives that might endanger order while, whenever possible, it attempted to conciliate competing factions?

THE PROBLEM OF UNILATERAL AID—OR INTERVENTION

From the outset, Lumumba had made it clear that he would turn elsewhere if the U.N. failed to act. "We need the fastest and most efficacious help," he once said. "We are willing to accept anybody . . . the United States or Russia or anybody." Here, then, was the final issue: the problem of unilateral aid. It arose early. On July 12, Vice Premier Gizenga requested direct U.S. military assistance, which the American Government quickly refused. When this appeal became known in Accra, President Nkrumah contacted Lumumba urging him to act through the U.N. Lumumba's agreement was qualified, as evidenced by his repeated threats to turn elsewhere. In the cable requesting U.N. aid, he said he would call on the "Bandung powers" if the U.N. failed to act. On the same day, he requested troops from Ghana. On the day following, he, with Kasavubu, cabled Nikita Khrushchev indicating that the Congo might have "to ask for the Soviet Union's intervention should the Western camp continue its aggression. . . ." On July 17, Lumumba announced that a telegram requesting Soviet troops had already been composed; he would send it if the U.N. had not cleared out the Belgian troops within seventy-two hours.

As might be expected, the Soviets strongly endorsed the right of interested states to give direct aid to the Leopoldville government. In the Security Council, Kuznetsov pressed for a resolution demanding the withdrawal of Belgian troops within three days; after that, the Congo would be free to invite unilateral aid. The idea was resisted. Tunisia's Mongi Slim spoke of "the necessity of allowing the United Nations to give all the assistance demanded in the present situation in the Congo." Only in this way could the Congo crisis be insulated from great-power rivalry. An overwhelming majority of the new states shared this position that, in a sense, became the *raison d'être* for the U.N.'s intervention in the Congo, despite Soviet resistance.

Neither Lumumba nor Tshombe, however, endorsed the idea of prohibiting unilateral aid. Lumumba refrained because he sought assistance from anyone willing to help him force the Belgians out, and Tshombe, because he insisted that the Belgians must remain. "Belgian troops must stay in Katanga," he said, shortly after he had asked these troops to quell the rebellion of the Congo Public

Force in Elizabethville. "Otherwise we will have the anarchy and chaos which is happening in the Congo Republic."

Once again, a basic issue had been posed. Should all aid be channeled through the world organization in an effort to seal off the Congo power vacuum, which otherwise might be filled by rival external powers, possibly on the model of the Spanish Civil War? Or, in view of the U.N.'s limited technical services, was not such a prohibition meaningless and perhaps even a violation of Congolese sovereignty?

The month of July, 1960, disclosed the fundamental issues underlying the Congo crisis; succeeding months would demonstrate how intractable they really were. Divisions within the Congo grew with time, and finally settled into three camps. The radical nationalists were led by Premier Patrice Lumumba, and his successor, Antoine Gizenga, head of the rump government in Stanleyville. They wanted a unified Congo brought under the firm control of a central government by the instrumentality of a single mass party and, if necessary, by force. Belgium and other "neocolonial" powers were considered the principal obstacles standing in the way of this goal. The U.N. had to commit its full resources to the achievement of unity, or lose its legitimacy; moreover, help from any source was solicited. Lumumba and Gizenga, without scruple, accepted from the Soviet bloc military aid that the West, except through the U.N., consistently denied.

The second camp was that of the secessionists, led by Moise Tshombe, President of Katanga Province, and to a lesser degree, by Albert Kalonji who, following Tshombe's example, declared on August 9, 1960, the secession of the southern fifth of Kasai Province, which he called the "Mining State." The secessionists viewed the Congo as an artifact of colonialism and urged that the only legitimate basis of political order is essentially tribal in character. The enemy was not Belgium, with whom these conservative leaders shared important interests, but the radical nationalists and the states supporting them. The role of the U.N. had to be minimal —the maintenance of law and order in those areas of the Congo unable to assure security by their own means. But in no sense was the U.N. to hold governmental prerogatives or to inhibit the several parts of the former Belgian Congo from the organization of their own affairs, including the hiring of foreign personnel and the soliciting of foreign aid.

Those in the third camp, whom I will call moderate nationalists, cannot be defined as sharply. Despite the differences among them, this group included President Kasavubu, the Mobutu regime, the Ileo government, and the moderates in the Adoula coalition. The moderate nationalists were committed to a unified Congo without espousing either the absolute centralism or the thoroughly uninhibited tactics of the radical nationalists. They participated in denunciations of Belgium, but at the same time, were willing, occasionally even anxious, to accept Belgian assistance. They were generally, though not always consistently, chary of the motives and the influence of other states, both East and West, radical and conservative. This has disposed them, more regularly than either the radical nationalists or the secessionists, to accept U.N. assistance and the legitimacy of the U.N.'s role in the Congo. At the same time, relations between the moderates and the U.N. were punctuated with unpleasant incidents arising from the sensitivities of a sovereign state patently unable to discharge its responsibilities.

Significantly, the three camps formed in the Congo also emerged among the new states as the crisis hardened and as the nature of the issues became clear.* The "radicals" have included Ghana, Guinea, Mali, Morocco, Egypt, and an Asian country, Indonesia. The "conservatives" have consisted of the former sub-Saharan French states excluding Guinea, Mali, and Togo. The "moderates" have encompassed Ethiopia, Liberia, Libya, Nigeria, Somalia, Sudan, Togo, and Tunisia, with Ceylon, India, and Malaya representing Asia.

It is the interaction between actors within the Congo and supporters outside that provides one of the fascinations of this drama for the student of international relations. It is regrettable that the story is too complex to be told here.[1] What does concern me are the fully matured positions of the new nations concerning the issues at stake in the Congo.

The New States and the Postcolonial Issues in the Congo Crisis

The premier of a new state once advised the General Assembly to listen carefully to the lesser powers because, in assessing international issues, they were more detached, more impartial than

---

* By "new states," I mean the nations of Africa and Asia that have achieved independence during the past decade and a half, and those more venerable states (Liberia, Ethiopia, and Egypt) that have assumed an active role in international politics only in recent years. The following review concentrates on the views of African states without, however, ignoring the positions of the four Asian states most actively engaged in U.N. debates and actions: Ceylon, India, Indonesia, and Malaya.

the great powers. "In a sense," he added, "the small and uncommitted nations can be said to represent the unbiased conscience of
mankind."

If that is true, mankind's conscience has been well-represented
in the Congo—but it has not always spoken with one voice. The
new states are building their tower heavenward. But as the goal of
total national independence is approached, the children of the postcolonial era find themselves speaking in different tongues. Great-
power designs and rivalries continue to affect the new states, but
they are by no means the only channels through which the babel
of confusion is introduced to the postcolonial world. The Congolese representative in the Security Council once complained that
Western capitalism had provoked Katanga's secession, while Communism fomented the secession of Orientale. "It is not the Congolese that are divided, it is the world that is divided. Therefore,
leave the Congo alone. . . ." There is enough truth in this plea
to make it poignant. But it is a half-truth. The other half relates
to the perfectly obvious dissensions among the principal actors in
the Congo, and among the new states themselves.

There is, of course, a relationship between the great-power conflicts and emergent conflicts among the new states. For the rival
interests of the great powers roughly concur with the rival positions
held by the new states, or for that matter, held by the rival leaders
within the Congo. When these concurrent interests between external sympathizers and internal actors are implemented—when, that
is, a great power directly intervenes to assist the faction sympathetic
to its interests—the mischief occurs. What began as a dispute
among postcolonial actors may overnight be transformed into a
Cold War conflict. Actually, the surprising fact about the Congo,
remembering that it represents an almost complete power vacuum,
is not how much, but how little direct and overt intervention there
has been by the great powers.* This is why the Congo crisis permits

* Surely, this is the case if one compares present behavior with the performance of the great powers in similar instances during the imperial era.
Though U.S. influence has hardly been absent, the American government
has minimized, while the Soviets, for the most part, have been deterred
from, direct intervention. The case of Belgium has been more difficult to
analyze. But if individual Belgians who have exercised influence in the Congo
were under orders from Brussels, it is hard to understand how those in
Leopoldville could have pressed for policies contrary to the policies advocated by the Belgians in Elizabethville. Leopoldville's Belgians and Tshombe's
Belgians hardly have seen eye to eye. The influence of Belgian business interests and the white settler population in Katanga is another matter, though

a relatively undistorted examination of the competing positions of the new statesmen on some of the basic issues of postcolonial politics.

One or two warning flags must be posted immediately. The following summary represents broad positions. Differences within each camp, admittedly important, are not adequately explored. Each position represents an orientation that obviously affects, but does not preclude, tactical maneuver. Moreover, we are examining "declaratory policies" that are often exaggerated for impact. Still, within these limitations, the following survey does illustrate broad differences among the new states in their analyses of the Congo crisis. These differences reflect some of the forces that will help shape political developments on the African continent in the opening years of the postcolonial era.

THE RADICALS

If one wishes to understand the position of the postcolonial radicals concerning the Congo, and concerning African developments in general, one must first understand the word "neocolonialism," for a complete world view attaches to it. We will "open a dossier which will be a historic one in the annals of the United Nations," as Guinea's Caba Sory said in the General Assembly during a debate on the Congo. "How do we label this dossier? Neocolonialism." In the radical ideology concerning neocolonialism, there are three tenets that especially concern us. The first is the notion of "pseudo independence," or what Ghana's President Kwame Nkrumah has called "clientele sovereignty." This, he explained, is "the practice of granting a sort of independence by the metropolitan power, with the concealed intention of making the liberated country a client-state and controlling it effectively by means other than political ones."

The second tenet is capsuled in the term "Balkanization." This is the basic strategy of the neocolonialists for maintaining pseudo-independent regimes. The colonial power divides an area—the Congo, for example—into a number of small states. None is viable,

---

it is of critical importance to distinguish between covert imperial control on the one hand and, on the other, a concurrence of interests between Belgian business groups and certain Congolese leaders. Tshombe has enjoyed too much political support from his own South Katangese population and has had too much leverage on Belgian business in Katanga to be labeled a puppet; however, from the point of view of many African states, he is scarcely an authentic "nationalist."

so all must remain "clients" of the former mother country. Balkanization is practiced not only on a country basis, but regionally and even continentally to divide the new states from one another. "We know the objectives of the West," Lumumba once said. "Yesterday it divided us at the level of tribes, clans and chiefs. Today—because Africa is freeing itself—it wishes to divide us on the level of states. It wishes to create antagonistic blocs and satellites and from that state of cold war accentuate the divisions with a view to maintaining its eternal trusteeship." If the African bloc has been fractured, it is the result, not of genuine, internal divisions, but of "sabotage" carried on by the colonial powers in order to wreck African "solidarity."

The saboteurs have accomplices recruited from the colonized population. These are the "stooges" of the imperialist powers. A third tenet of the radical world view deals with this "enemy within." Often, he is an unwitting puppet, the victim of a colonially corrupted mind, unable to distinguish between national and colonial interests. After a bitter exchange in the Security Council, the delegate from Guinea said to his opposite number from the former French Congo: "It is with great sadness that I have listened to the man that I . . . call my brother—sadness to see to what point colonization can change the very nature of the colonized. . . ." But whether knowingly or unwittingly, the stooge or the puppet is the instrument of the neocolonialists; he is the enemy within the gate—Bao Dai in Vietnam, Baccouche in Tunisia, El-Glaoui in Morocco, and now Tshombe, or Mobutu, or perhaps even Kasavubu, in the Congo.

Neocolonialism is the "enemy"; from this notion, the radical's position on the other issues follows logically. Thus, the proper definition of the Congo: It is an embryonic state threatened with extinction by the Belgians and their neocolonialist allies who have "set Congolese to fighting Congolese." But, advised the Indonesian delegate, get rid of outside interference and "the Congolese people as a whole will be able to express themselves freely through their elected Parliament." There is a whimsical and legalistic note in this remark which equates form with fact. The real Congo—unified and at peace—is the presumed reality. Evil and extraneous forces prevent this reality from expressing itself.

Other analyses by the radical states must have been more hardheaded. The Congo, whatever may be present realities, must be unified and consolidated at all costs. This is the "feel" underlying the views of Guinea, Mali and Ghana. Experience at home dictates appropriate action in the Congo. "Let me assure you that Tshombes do not exist in Mali," the delegate from that country told the Security Council. "And it is in the very name of justice and the security of our peoples that we have firmly decided to take traitors and conspirators out of circulation. Our state organization will be strengthened despite the desire of those who wish to see many parties in the country." The "traitors" and "conspirators," of course, are principally the agents of foreign governments. "At the time of our independence," the Guinean delegate declared, "the only problem confronting us was that we had to unite to end foreign domination."

The end of foreign control demands rapid consolidation against the dangers of Balkanization. It demands the decisive reduction of reliance on the former metropole, for a foreign-controlled economy means domination that is every bit as effective as outright political control. Finally, it demands the unity of the postcolonial states (Pan-Africanism), not only because there resides in unity the strength that is the only ultimate answer to imperialist designs, but also because a setback anywhere along the nationalists' front line may cause a breakthrough of neocolonialist forces that would utterly overwhelm the fragile new states. This is why the neocolonialist assault on the Congo must be defeated conclusively, for if it succeeds, said the delegate from Mali, it will encourage "the aggressive aims of the colonialists on other territories in Africa."* This notion of an interrelated pattern of peril has been articulated even more forcefully by Guinea: "We are convinced that if the policy of territorial division were to succeed in the Congo the entire world would undoubtedly be a spectator to the destruction and breaking up of Africa to the satisfaction of the colonial powers. . . . As far as we are concerned, Guinea could well be the Congo, and the Congo, Africa. . . ."

For the radicals, the legitimacy of a postcolonial regime relates in part to its legal mandate (the "legality" of the Lumumba Government, and later that of Gizenga, has been invoked constantly by the radicals); but even more, one supposes, legitimacy relates to the regime's credentials as a representative of genuine nationalism fighting against the intrigues of neocolonialism. This is why Lumumba was so extolled as the "best son of Africa," the "Lin-

* He referred specifically to the dangers deriving from French bases on the territory of Mali, from the enormous French armies in Algeria, and from the French presence in neighboring Mauritania and the Sahara. Morocco's view is conditioned by similar factors.

coln of the Congo," the "Black Messiah," whose struggle was made noble by his unswerving demand for centralism against all forms of Balkanization, and was rendered heroic by his unyielding resistance to the forces of neocolonialism that finally killed his body, but not his spirit.

According to the radical view, there is only one enemy in the Congo—neocolonialism; there is only one legitimate authority in the Congo—that representing genuine nationalism. What about the role of the United Nations? Clearly, if it is to have any meaning at all, the world organization must place its resources at the disposal of the legitimate regime. The doctrine has been stated most clearly by Guinea: "The United Nations must acquiesce in all requests of the [Lumumbist] Central Government since it, the Central Government, is the only body properly able to judge the appropriateness of measures that will lead to the re-establishment of order and security throughout the entire territory of the Republic of the Congo." If the United Nations fails to do this because it has come under the domination of neocolonial forces, it will lose its legitimacy and become an added cause of the crisis, rather than the cure. Under these circumstances, the U.N. must withdraw from the Congo.

This leads to the final aspect of the radical's view, that aspect dealing with unilateral aid or direct intervention in the affairs of another nation. If the U.N. fails to act effectively to thwart neocolonialist ambitions, action must be taken outside the world organization. "We cannot be passive spectators," said the Moroccan Ambassador to the United Nations, "[watching] the rebirth of colonialism and its return to the Congo. . . ."

The radicals have been accused of "intervention." But intervention, which is an illicit involvement of one sovereign state in the affairs of another, is a meaningful category only in the context of true international relations—that is, relations between sovereign and equal members of international society. Indeed, intervention is a violation of the norms on which international society is based. It is central to the radical view of African politics that no such international society now exists in Africa, nor could one exist until the plots of the neocolonialists have been exposed and defeated. Rather, Africa is seen as composed of a few beachheads of genuine independence struggling to consolidate against an implacable foe. Surrounding these enclaves are vast areas, nominally independent, to be sure, but still controlled in varying degrees by neocolonialist forces. These are what Ismael Touré, Minister of Public Works of Guinea, has called "regimes of surveillance," as opposed to "regimes of pure liberty."

Under Lumumba, the Congo had a fighting chance to frustrate the plots of imperialism. But the imperialists overwhelmed Lumumba. The Congo, except for Gizenga, came under the control of neocolonialist forces. A state controlled by neocolonialism is not a sovereign member of the international community at all. This being the case, one cannot speak of "intervention" in the Congo. Rather, one must speak of the continuation of the struggle of nationalism versus colonialism on a new front. Pseudo independence may change the form of the problem, but not the reality. On the same day (February 21, 1961) that the Security Council passed a resolution calling for "the solution of the problem of the Congo . . . without any interference from the outside"—a resolution cosponsored by the U.A.R.—President Nasser announced that he was giving unilateral aid to the Gizenga Government in Stanleyville! This is a contradiction only to those who do not share the radical view of African politics.

The questions raised by these several views are intriguing, the more so because they appear to apply to relations between the radicals and the many conservative states of the former French empire. When does the postcolonial era really begin? When do the rules of the game change? Obviously, the rules that obtain during the struggle for independence are one thing; the rules that govern relations between sovereign and equal members of international society are another. There is a tendency on the part of the radicals to assume that the rules will not change until Africa has established a position of strength independent of the former colonial powers, has thus voided the plots of the neocolonialists, and has created a true Pan-African state. Until that consummation has been reached, tactics that less radical minds might condemn as intervention, or subversion, remain perfectly fair game.

THE CONSERVATIVES

We may call these states "conservative" because, unlike the radicals, who want to upset the *status quo* in emerging Africa, the former French sub-Saharan territories (barring Guinea, Mali, and Togo) want to preserve it. Rather than disrupt the ties with the former metropole, they wish to maintain them. Rather than develop Africa as an autonomous continent, beholden to no external force, they want their states to develop, at least for the present, in close cooperation with Europe. Instead of advocating a Pan-African super state encompassing the entire continent, they prefer to seek modest accords of cooperation, first within the family of French-speaking states. Instead of the radicals' notion that the state system inherited from the colonial era is a form of Balkanization that does not provide an adequate, or even a legitimate, basis for relations among true African nationalists, the conservatives insist on the legitimacy of present boundaries—again, for the present.

These conservative states have achieved independence in amity with France. For the most part, they do not question the propriety of maintaining civil order and technical services with extensive French help. One supposes, therefore, that a radical's animus toward the former metropole is difficult for them to comprehend.

As the conservatives' approach to the problems of organizing the postcolonial world differs markedly from that of the radicals, so, too, does the entire problem of the Congo have a different structure for the conservatives. Belgium may be an "enemy," but not the only enemy, or even the major one. Mr. Thiam, of Senegal, found Belgium's failure to prepare her colony for independence "a grave and heavy error" that history will judge severely. "But," he continued, "I believe very sincerely that the threats now hanging over Congolese unity are due to objective situations deriving from the nature of the country, its size and diversity."[*]

For the conservative extremists—Cameroun and Congo (Brazzaville) are the clearest examples—the real "enemy" in the Congo situation is not Western imperialism, but Communism, the fountainhead of a new imperialism. Frequently, these states simply take over the categories of the radicals but fill them with opposite content. It is Gizenga who is scored as a "colonialist puppet," with Soviet imperialists handling the strings. It is the radical state that suffers "independence on parole," having sold itself to the "rapacious" Communist master. "You are not independent, Mr. Telli," said the delegate of the Congo (Brazzaville) to Guinea's Diallo Telli. "What naïve persons would believe you were?"

Whereas the radicals speak of conservatives as "imperialist stooges," the conservatives refer to the radicals as "Soviet satellites," Russia's "African colonies," and "crypto-Communists."

---

[*] Other "conservatives," namely those of Upper Volta and the Central African Republic, have been more vigorous in their attacks on Belgium. With the single exception of the attacks from Upper Volta, however, none of them has been as impassioned as those of the radicals.

Thus does the Cold War infiltrate postcolonial disputes, despite the best intentions of the new states to keep it out.

In reply to the radical's doctrinaire assertion that the Congo is, or must be made, one nation indivisible, the conservatives tend to stress its diversity. Instead of the "inviolable principle" of unity, they have emphasized "reality." After recording the enormous diversity that underlies the "myth" of the Congo, Mr. Thiam noted how complex were the problems of achieving unity, even among countries long exposed to modern life, like those of Europe. How much more difficult, then, in Africa! "We accused France of having Balkanized Africa. But who knows if we would not have found ourselves in a Congo-like situation if independence had been granted to us, not on the basis of each territory being one State, but the basis of a united territory." Added to the Senegalese sense of "reality" is French equatorial "realism." The Congo's near-neighbors in former French Africa are hardly enthusiastic about the emergence of a unitarian Congolese state, susceptible to control by a "radical" government.*

During the governmental crisis in the Congo, the conservatives, while emphasizing a "hands-off" attitude, have supported Kasavubu and Ileo as the carriers of the nationalist tradition, rather than Lumumba, a "newcomer." When Lumumba was assassinated, the conservatives politely participated in the denunciations of "political violence." Some noted, however, that Lumumba's death created even a greater sensation outside the Congo than within. "When a member of the family dies," said the Central African Republic delegate, "wakes are organized during which people weep. It is improper [however] for neighbors and friends to weep more loudly than the deceased person's own relatives."

If the radicals scored the U.N. Mission to the Congo because it would not intervene enough, the conservatives criticized the world organization because it intervened too much. While acknowledging the usefulness of the U.N. in preventing foreign intervention in the Congo, the conservative states have stressed that the United Nations must not practice "proconsulship" (Senegal), that it "should keep its hands clean in respect of the problems of African internal politics, which are a family matter" (Central African Republic),

* In general, the conservative states welcomed the Tananarive confederal formula for the Congo, for it was compatible with the conception, developed at the Brazzaville conference, of a loose association of French-speaking African states.

that it "can take no stand in the institutional crisis" (Ivory Coast), and that it must take no action tantamount to disarming the troops of a sovereign member of the United Nations as "this would be a grave precedent indeed" (Congo [Brazzaville]).

Most conservative states would probably agree with an observation made to Marguerite Higgins by a Cameroun official drawing a parallel between divisions in the Congo and the radical-supported Bamileke rebellion in his own country:

> We are lucky. Think of the terrible situation if the United Nations had ever come in here. Under the policies of so-called "neutrality" adopted in the Congo, they would have interposed themselves between us and the rebels, restraining us from trying to wipe them out. This would have given them a chance to consolidate themselves. We would have had a Stanleyville in Cameroun. The United Nations will come to ruin in Africa if it seeks to use military force for purposes that clash with the will of the recognized government.

Of course, the radical Lumumba said much the same thing. But that is just the point. Both the radicals and the conservatives have lined up against the U.N. Both have said that the U.N. should get out of the Congo, or at least be restricted to a minimal role; and both have accused the U.N. of imperialism. Guinea's Diallo Telli has referred to the U.N. as "the docile standard-bearer" of colonial interests. Many conservatives have condemned the February 21 resolution of the Security Council, which permits "the use of force," as an unconscionable violation of Congolese sovereignty designed to serve the imperial interests of the radicals and the Communists. Here, of course, is the difference between radical and conservative denunciation of the U.N. If the radicals are against the world organization, it is because they believe it defends a wholly unsatisfactory *status quo;* if the conservatives have reservations about the U.N., it is because they believe it may act to upset a *status quo* that, free from outside intervention, will permit a slow movement toward a settlement favorable to conservative interests.

The conservative strategy, which has decried all foreign involvement in the Congo, whether multilateral or unilateral, was summarized in a parable related to the General Assembly by the delegate from the Congo (Brazzaville): "An African adage says that it is ill-recommended to interfere in a fratricidal quarrel because the parties ultimately come together in the evening about the same campfire. . . . Let us leave the people responsible to meet around the campfire in order to prepare for what we call in our country the 'palavers' which generally meet with success."

"It is necessary . . . to wait patiently until the obstacles are overcome one by one," added Malagasy's Louis Rakotomalala, capturing the conservative mood nicely. External intervention, whether unilateral or multilateral, would only complicate the process. This is one of the reasons why Thiam has called the principle of noninterference in the domestic affairs of other states "the Golden Rule of international relations."

THE MODERATES

The new states that have assumed radical or conservative positions concerning the Congo crisis are all African, with the single exception of Indonesia, the radicals' Asian outpost in the battle against neocolonialism. The moderates, on the other hand, include many non-African postcolonial states, in addition to those African states that, for ideological, historical, or political reasons, refuse membership in any African bloc.*

Historically, Ethiopia and Liberia have remained aloof. (Their positions are changing rapidly, but they continue to be independent of present blocs.) For ideological reasons, Tunisia and Togo cannot identify with the French-speaking conservative group; nor can the Sudan and Somalia, for historical reasons. Political considerations (and possibly ideological ones, as well) prompt Tunisia, Togo, and the Sudan to keep their distance from the radicals. Togo's delicate relationship to Ghana demands this, as does the relationship of Tunisia and the Sudan to the U.A.R. Somalia has not yet been drawn into the larger African arena, since her border problem with Ethiopia is her preoccupation. Nigeria is self-possessed, content with her size and her potential, and intent, thus far, on playing an independent role. Libya, like Morocco, has at times been radical in diplomatic discourse, but conservative at home. There is a tendency to reflect the U.A.R. line, but Libya, unlike Morocco with its claim to Mauritania, has no compelling interest in sub-Saharan politics.

The African moderates, then, are an ideological and political in-between group. The non-African moderates are located in an arena sufficiently distant from the Congo to be somewhat less affected

* The Monrovia Conference, which brought together moderate and conservative states, sought to create, not a bloc, but an all-inclusive African group transcending existing blocs.

by the passions that excite the radicals and conservatives. As compared with these two extremes, there is less emotional content to the judgments of the moderates about the Congo, and greater inclination to deal with the problem in terms of institutions and procedures, rather than personalities and symbols. For the moderates, the problem of achieving order in the Congo presses slightly more heavily than does the concern to establish this group in power, or prevent that group from ascendancy. The foregoing are not bold distinctions; they are nuances, but none the less important.

For the extreme radical, and the extreme conservative, the "enemy" in the Congo crisis has been defined simply—it is neocolonialism in the one case, Communism in the other. The moderates, though there are great variations among them, tend to acknowledge that the situation is, in the words of Prime Minister Nehru, "extraordinarily complex not only for us but for everybody, and more especially for the Congo itself."

Some moderates—Ceylon, Tunisia, and Togo, most particularly —have been almost as vigorous as the radicals in their condemnation of Belgian "maneuvers, subterfuges, and crimes." But most moderates would agree with Tunisia's Ambassador Slim, who, in apportioning blame, cited also the "personal ambitions" and "regional interests" of the Congolese political leaders. Jaja Wachuku, of Nigeria, found the Belgian presence a "vital problem," but not a central one. The greatest enemy of order in the Congo was "the political conflict between the leaders, which makes it absolutely impossible even to get rid of the Belgians." Insofar as "foreign interference" has contributed to Congolese disorder, it is, in the view of many moderates, a misdemeanor committed by several states, and not by Belgium alone.[2]

As to the proper definition of the Congo, the moderates, more than either the radicals or conservatives, have tended to emphasize the legal environment of the problem. Their position has been closer to that of the radicals than of the conservatives, for they have consistently demanded a unified Congo. But this has been the case not so much for reasons of doctrine (radical doctrine concerning the threat of neocolonialism dictates a strong, unitarian regime), but because the law reads that way and because a confederation, under the Tananarive formula, for example, would end by tearing the country apart. That is to say, when moderates have insisted that "there must be no dismemberment of the Congo," they have tended to link that requirement, not with the problems of "neocolonialism" or "Balkanization," but with "the rule of law" and the necessity to preserve in law the entity known as the Congo. The *loi fondamentale* may need modifying, but modifications must be undertaken in accordance with due process; changes can be effected only by the Parliament.

The governmental crisis in the Congo found the moderates divided. Some, like Ceylon and India, supported Lumumba; others, like Tunisia and the Sudan, professed absolute noninterference.* Among the Lumumba supporters there was a subtle, but important, distinction between the radicals and moderates. The radicals championed Lumumba as a symbol of the dignity of emergent Africa and the struggle against colonialism; the moderates, however, tended to back Lumumba as the "legal Prime Minister." None of the moderates recognized the Gizenga Government in Stanleyville; Ceylon, which has been extremely close to the radicals, took the position that, following Lumumba's death, no lawful government existed in the Congo.

It is concerning the role of the United Nations that the clearest distinction arises between the moderates, on the one hand, and the radicals and conservatives, on the other. Unlike the two polar positions, the moderates consistently have supported the U.N. More and more, the U.N. operation in the Congo—the U.N. Force, the Conciliation Commission, and the principal staff members of the U.N. Mission—has depended upon the moderate camp; and concurrently, the influence of the radicals has declined. Even the Sudan, the only moderate permanently to withdraw its troops from the U.N. Force, said, when announcing that withdrawal was in prospect, "We do not mean to imply that the United Nations, led by the Secretary-General, is not doing its best."

As to the objectives of the U.N., the moderates again have been closer to the radicals than to the conservatives. The U.N. must support Congolese legal institutions, uphold the territorial integrity of the country, maintain order, and remove foreign military and political personnel not under the U.N. Command. At the point of procedures, however, the radicals and moderates have divided. While the radicals have insisted that the U.N. should be made an adjunct to the legitimate Congolese Government, adding its force to that of the government in a campaign to unify the country, the moderates have maintained the propriety of an inde-

* On the critical issue of seating the Kasavubu delegation in the General Assembly in the fall of 1960, all the African moderates, with the exception of Togo, abstained. Togo voted against Kasavubu. The Asian moderates divided; India and Ceylon voted against Kasavubu; Malaya abstained.

pendent position for the United Nations, and have consistently opposed the use of force to change the *status quo.*

More than either the radicals or conservatives, the moderates have been exercised about the general problem of disorder, the rebellious troops, and the repeated lapse of governmental authority in the Congo. Order, or at least the avoidance of civil war, has increasingly been given a higher priority by the moderates than the establishment of the consolidation of some particular regime. To cope with the problem of disorder, the moderates have urged strengthening the U.N. mandate. A corollary problem has been that of relating the authority of the U.N. to the prerogatives of the sovereign Republic of the Congo.

Ceylon, which as we have seen presumed the absence of a lawful government following Lumumba's death, advocated that the U.N. constitute the "authority" that is lacking in the Congo. Similarly, India has urged that "all Congolese armed personnel, including the Armée Nationale Congolaise and private armies, should be disarmed and neutralized. The United Nations should be entrusted with law and order functions until such time as the ANC's force with the assistance of the United Nations . . . becomes a disciplined force, subject to the authority of a constitutional government." Surely this would be neither more nor less than temporary trusteeship.

Others, including Tunisia, Nigeria, and Malaya, have said that the U.N. must beware of interference, and must, under no circumstances, establish a "trusteeship" over the Congo. Yet *all* moderates have advocated an expansion of U.N. authority, and have pressed for U.N. involvement in such tasks as "disarming" the army and "insulating it from politics"—tasks that surely imply certain governmental prerogatives for the U.N. Mission in the Congo.*

In short, the moderates have been the U.N. proponents in the Congo. Anything less than an expanded mandate for the U.N., they have argued, would perpetuate chaos and create a beachhead

---

* For Krishna Menon, however, the problem is nonexistent by definition. The U.N. Mission in the Congo, he has said, *cannot* be regarded as "foreign interference" because the U.N. entered the Congo in response to an appeal from the government of the Congo and on the basis of a voluntary agreement. But, he noted parenthetically, "once an agreement has been accepted it can be terminated *only by the consent of the parties.*" That is to say, the U.N., whose actions cannot legally be construed as interference in Congolese affairs, is also legally invulnerable to unilateral actions by the Congolese Government. The legalisms of Krishna Menon are intricate.

for great-power (or small-power) intervention. As for the problem of unilateral intervention, the moderates, with the conservatives, have insisted that all states keep hands off the Congo. The terse cable of Togo's President Olympio to the Secretary-General on the occasion of Lumumba's death sums up the moderate view: "Struggle for the influence carried on in the Congo by African and non-African States must end. . . . All assistance by States Members of the United Nations must be channeled through the United Nations, the only body which cannot be accused of political or other designs on the Congo."

How significant are those differing attitudes about the basic issues in the Congo crisis? It is easy to exaggerate. Positions have, in fact, been blurred as the protracted conflict dragged on. For example, in the round of votes cast in the General Assembly on April 15, 1961, radicals, moderates, and conservatives found themselves in the same camp concerning many of the proposals. Hard-core radicals and many conservatives, for example, agreed that Belgian political and military personnel must leave the Congo. Conservatives, who heretofore had insisted that the U.N. follow a "hands off" policy in the Congo, supported a U.N. resolution advocating the convening of Parliament and the formation of a national government. Conservatives and moderates meeting at Monrovia in the spring of 1961 "reaffirmed faith in the United Nations as the organization best adapted to achieve a real solution of the Congo problem."

The politics of postcolonial Africa are fluid. Positions are forming, but they are not fixed. Only the position of the extreme radicals has substantial ideological content. Even this position allows room for tactical maneuver. The other positions are flexible and subject to change—some of them, we may be sure, to abrupt change.

At the same time, conservative, moderate, and radical tendencies are reflections of basic suppositions concerning the core issues of postcolonial politics; how to organize a postcolonial state; how to relate that state to the former metropole; how to effect a new system of international order to take the place of the now defunct colonial order. On these issues there are cleavages—some of them serious. (The positions of the new states are summarized schematically in the accompanying table.)

In a speech before the General Assembly in April, 1961, Jaja Wachuku, head of the U.N. Conciliation Commission to the Congo and, later, Foreign Minister of Nigeria, noted the existence

TABLE

Core Positions of the New States Concerning the Basic Issues in the Congo Crisis

	Radicals	*Moderates*	*Conservatives*
	Ghana, Guinea, Indonesia, Mali, Morocco, U.A.R.	Ethiopia, Liberia, Libya, Nigeria, Somalia, Sudan, Togo, Tunisia, and all active Asian states, except Indonesia	Cameroun Republic, Chad, Congo (Brazzaville), Dahomey, Gabon, Ivory Coast, Malagasy, Mauritania, Niger, Senegal, Upper Volta
Who is the "enemy"?	A simple view: Western "neocolonialists" and their African "puppets"	A complex view: Belgium, African and non-African interventionists, and irresponsible Congolese leaders	A simple view: Communist imperialists and their African "acolytes." (Several conservative states would subscribe to the more complex view of the "moderates")
How to organize the Congo?	Establish a strong centralist government under genuinely nationalist regime closely affiliated with Pan-Africanist aspirations	Preserve the legal and territorial integrity of the Congo; support the legal Government and uphold the institutions of the Presidency and Parliament; pursue constitutional changes in strict accord with due process	Establish a decentralized government consistent with the diversity of the country; affiliate with the Brazzaville group
What role should the U.N. play?	Strong U.N. intervention should be an adjunct to the legitimate regime; short of this, no significant or legitimate role at all	Expand U.N. authority for the maintenance of law and order; assist in evacuating foreign personnel, in creating a dependable Congolese army insulated from politics, and in establishing the requisite conditions for constitutional government	A minimal role limited to barring foreign intervention and under no circumstances involving interference with Congolese settlement of the problem
How should the problem of direct aid or intervention be solved?	All direct aid necessary to defeat the imperialist plot against the Congo and to unify the Congo under a genuinely nationalist regime	No foreign intervention; all aid through the U.N.	No foreign intervention

of the three groups of African powers. "In the end," he said, "none of the three are powers at all. A house divided against itself cannot be effective. . . . If we are going to speak effectively and act effectively in the United Nations, this is the time, because to the African states the Congo is a challenge. . . . We are responsible for whatever happens. I will not blame what you call the East or the West."

The Congo is indeed a challenge to the new states and, most particularly, to those of Africa. There will be many more challenges before long. Whether the house will irrevocably divide against itself, or unite in effective action, none can say for sure. But Wachuku is surely right. Primary responsibility throughout much of the continent now rests in African hands.

IV

A CONSERVATIVE VIEW OF THE
NEW STATES

by LAURENCE W. MARTIN

THE new states derive much of their influence in the world
from Western estimates of their merits and importance, and
consequently, any suggestion that these estimates are sadly mis-
taken deserves a hearing. By the beginning of 1962, British Conservatives had grave misgivings about the conduct of the new
states and the wisdom of Western policy toward them. These fears
became vehement after the United Nations' military action against
Katanga, the Indian invasion of Goa, and the unsatisfactory neutralist response to the Russian resumption of nuclear testing. It
was this issue of nuclear testing that provoked the Foreign Secretary, Lord Home, into his now-famous denunciation of the
"double standard" by which neutralists were supposedly far more
indulgent of the activities of the East than of Western actions.

Ever since the dissolution of the Empire began, relations with
new states have been high on the British agenda. The new state
of today is the colony of yesterday, and, for Conservatives, with
their close association with the Empire, discussion of policy toward new states is never wholly extricable from debate over what
constitutes wisdom in colonial affairs.

All empires develop justification for their existence, and these
excuses become arguments for prolonging the relationship. After
independence, the same arguments almost unconsciously become
stern criteria for the subsequent performance of the new states.
Since the days of Edmund Burke, British Conservatives have justified colonial possessions as a trust to be discharged by preparing
the subordinate peoples for responsible self-government. Undoubtedly, this defense is hedged round with vested interests and a

suspicion of hypocrisy, for most Conservatives believe that Britain has derived important military, economic and financial advantages from the Empire. Much recent British defense policy, indeed, has been concerned with vanishing bases and the rising "air barrier" athwart the Middle East. Moreover, recent arguments over Central Africa have served to recall the personal stake many prominent Tories have in colonial territories. But, for all that, even the firmest critics of colonial policy would admit that the idea of trusteeship is more than a mere rationalization of self-interest, and that it has exercised a real influence on Conservative policy.

Among the conditions for responsible government and personal freedom, Conservatives give pre-eminence to the maintenance of public order, due process of law, and respect for property and the rights of minorities. As the Colonial Secretary put it in October, 1961, "I believe that without security, without respect for the rights of minorities and the feeling of security that comes from confidence in this respect, there can be no true justice and no true peace between man and man."[1] Order and sanctity of property are, of course, civic virtues that come most easily to a colonial power compelled by its nature to seek administrative rather than political progress in its colonies, so long as it is intent on supremacy. Yet these are also virtues that Conservatives genuinely prize at home as well as abroad. As for minorities, Conservatives bolster the case for a cautious approach to emancipation by asserting that the trust is held for all the people in each territory. It would therefore be wrong to mistake an articulate but often narrow and rabble-rousing group of politicians for truly representative and therefore rightful heirs to the trust.

Recent evidence of rapid decay in the constitutions of new nations has reinforced Conservative suspicion that many colonial peoples are far from ready to meet the Conservative criteria of responsibility. Many would agree with Lord Salisbury that, "in some areas of Africa, Western ideas are still only a very thin veneer over primeval savagery,"[2] and events in the Congo have been taken for confirmation of this. The growing autocratic tendencies in Ghana have come to be regarded as typical: "Africa," observed a Member of Parliament, "is littered with broken maces and disused copies of Erskine May [the guide to parliamentary procedure]."[3] It is this sense of vindicated pessimism that motivates British resistance to efforts at the United Nations to establish a timetable for decolonization.

An unfortunate but dominant complication of this argument

arises from the fact that the problems now at the top of the decolonization agenda involve sizable white minorities. These have a special claim on Conservative attention as "kith and kin," as a vital element in the economic and administrative community, and as an earnest of the possibility of avoiding a racial division of the world. The last consideration has been carried so far as to depict Katanga, Rhodesia, and Portuguese Africa as "three nonracial bastions."[4] This is an extreme view, but beyond doubt the plight of the settlers considerably stiffens the resistance of those who most doubt the wisdom of a rapid advance toward "one man, one vote."

It is not to be wondered that, at this sensitive juncture in colonial affairs, American policy is highly suspect. Conservatives generally regard the United States as deeply ignorant of colonial questions yet eagerly intent on generously giving away the possessions of its friends for the sake of a misreading of history and a naïve faith in something called self-determination. Examples of such criticism abound. Sir John Slessor entitles a chapter in his recent book, "Colonialism—the American Obsession."[5] Sir Alan Burns' *In Defence of Colonies*[6] is a prolonged diatribe against America, well laced with references to the Mexicans and Red Indians. Even calmer critics of American policy are impressed with an American tendency to overlook the complexity of the tasks that face even the most willing emancipator. Thus, Elspeth Huxley complains:

> It is one thing to express American sympathy and support for African nationalism and quite another to do so by attacking America's partners in NATO who have the practical and exceedingly delicate task of de-colonizing their vast inherited empires. American information services have played the Communist game by pursuing a propaganda line that roughly runs: "We got rid of King George's redcoats—now it's your turn."[7]

A skeptical view of the preparation of colonial territories for self-rule could be taken for an indictment of the notion of trusteeship, or of its execution by the British. Whatever the merits of past colonial policy, Conservatives naturally prefer to regard the mission as well conceived and to insist on trying to carry it to a conclusion. The simplest lesson to derive from this would be to hang on indefinitely, and this view is not without its adherents. The Conservative Government, however, while professing to resist violent demands for progress, as in Northern Rhodesia recently, has obviously decided that the remaining period of colonial rule must perforce be brief. Macmillan's famous "Wind of Change" speech is the text for this determination, and the former Colonial Secretary, Iain Macleod, was its personification. Given its determination to retire, but in good order, the government's policy is thus a series of tactical stands fought in the midst of a hasty strategic retreat. The underlying motives are apparently a lively appreciation of the material costs of hanging on, a belief that suppression is not an atmosphere conducive to education in democracy, and a certain feeling that graceful and prompt retirement, perhaps prefaced by a brief training period of condominium with nationalist leaders, is the best hope of an amicable relationship with one's successors.

Before finally dismissing the case for a continued colonial relationship as merely indicative of a certain Conservative state of mind, it must be remarked that such a relationship serves as a reminder of the functions served by colonial regimes. Insofar as there is any truth in Conservative doubt as to colonial capacities for self-rule and self-defense, it points to the probability of future internal and external instability among the new states. Many of the colonial regimes were, after all, imposed chiefly as a reluctant answer to anarchy. If this solution is removed before another has evolved, we must expect the colonial function to be assumed by other, possibly international, entities. Thus, the colonial experience drawn on by Conservative commentators may have its future relevance for whatever body takes up the, doubtless disguised, colonial role. We may expect, and indeed already have, a debate on the merits of colonial administration by the new trustees.

The hallowed Conservative prescription for not dealing with developing colonial units on a basis of full independence has been the Commonwealth. As a halfway house between independence and tutelage, as a source of continued great-power status for Britain, as a possible third force, this idea has long been dear to Conservative hearts. Insofar as the notion recognizes the impossibility of continued British dominance, the idea has its claim to realism. It has undergone alluvial stages of disillusionment; it was first a projected federation, then a free association that could be expected to act together, even going to war as one, then a merely consultative group and, latterly, a tenuous "link with the colored races." Today, the Commonwealth is taken less seriously in Britain than ever before. Despite protestations to the contrary, Britain's application to the Common Market showed where the government's head and pocket were, if not its heart. Unofficial spokesmen are less inhibited. Thus, a columnist can write that he is "certain there is no longer any justification for allowing the Commonwealth to weigh heavily in any political, economic or military decisions we have to make."[8]

True realism demands recognition that the new states will base their policies not on what the Western or the ex-colonialist nations believe desirable, but on what they conceive to be their own interests. From this point of view, it is futile and dangerously distracting to waste time trying to adapt the colonial relationship when what is required is a foreign policy to deal with the new states. Not a few Conservatives have undertaken to look for such a policy. For example, one of the most articulate, Peregrine Worsthorne, has said: "The idea that if the West gets out fast enough a grateful colored world will rally to its side is naïve. . . . The rewarding question is surely: 'How can the emerging countries of Asia and Africa be fitted into a world balance of power which does not leave the West hopelessly at a disadvantage?' "[9] The important question then becomes simply: Do the new and postcolonial nations have special characteristics that will affect their policy in ways that the West must take into special account?

For Conservatives, the first determinant of postcolonial conduct arises from their analyses of the likely performances of the new states, as states. If they are incapable of stable and efficient, let alone democratic, self-management, the resulting chaos will be a source of disturbance and Communist opportunity. Similarly, the belief that many of the new national leaders have no deep comprehension of what is entailed by democracy suggests that they also lack the ideological commitment that inhibits truly democratic national leaders from carrying diplomatic maneuver to the point of alignment with Russia. Moreover, the suspicion that these politicians will resort to totalitarian methods gives rise to fears that they will, at worst, develop an affinity for the totalitarian bloc, and, at best, testify to the questionable utility of democracy in an underdeveloped nation.

Politicians as irresponsible and vainglorious as the Conservatives fear many of the new states' leaders to be, may well develop designs against their neighbors and other schemes for self-aggrandizement, uninhibited, as is the West, by the balance of the Cold War, and abetted by the admittedly numerous territorial questions open to the "cartographic" countries. Merely the acute internal problems of the new states may, according to the supposedly classic technique of creating external distractions from domestic woes, make the new states a disturbing influence in world affairs. On this theory, leaders such as Nkrumah find it more pleasant to make sweeping plans to organize all Africa in the future than to rule Ghana competently in the present. Tunisia's revival of its claims on Bizerte, Kassim's designs on Kuwait, and Nehru's seizure of Goa at a time when Chinese incursions were allegedly a source of electoral embarrassment to the left-wing associates of Krishna Menon, have all been fitted into this pattern; and as these examples suggest, many of the likely objects of ambition are within Western spheres of interest.

From a Conservative point of view, there is a real danger that the West will uncritically extend over such new imperialist adventures the mantle of rectitude that it accorded efforts at self-determination. In reality, as a Conservative pamphlet observed some years ago, this kind of anticolonialism "is a manifestation of power politics and not a universal and praiseworthy desire to spread the idea of national freedom."[10] Having no innate innocence denied other nations, a new state pursues its interests like any other, and this naturally engenders conflict with the interests of others. With a new state, however, there is the added restlessness born of immaturity and internal problems.

In addition, though Conservatives may believe emotional anticolonialism both unjustified and irrelevant to the practical problems of the day, they are well aware that it is a real force imparting an anti-Western bias to the postcolonial states. This bias is compounded by the "salt-water" fallacy, according to which Soviet land imperialism over white peoples does not count. Nor is this emotion likely to evaporate readily. "Since colonialism," warned the London *Times,* "is a flexible concept, which can be extended to almost all relations between rich and poor countries—even when there is no political connection—it is likely to distort the thinking of poor countries for much longer than the facts warrant."[11] There seems to be little foundation for the view, voiced on occasion even by Lord Home, that, with only a few remaining colonies to liberate—but what colonies, with their white minorities!—colonialism will soon be a dead issue. The charge of neocolonialism is already freely made. Leaders of new states will see ghosts even where there is no substance, and these will be useful ghosts serving to provide a rationale for numerous adventures and an excuse for many failures.

British Conservatives have been among the first to suggest that the bias against the West, derived from historical experience, is reinforced by the nature of the two protagonists making up the prime balance of power in the contemporary world. The aim of the new nations and, indeed of most small nations, is to exploit this balance, while avoiding enlistment on either side, thereby preserving independence and playing off each side against the other to secure positive assistance. This is what *The Daily Telegraph* has called the new technique of "auctioning not favors but needs."[12] Such neutralism tends to give being in the middle precedence over interest in where the middle is. Thus, while the neutrals undoubtedly have substantive interests, they also have a tactical or "evasive" interest in being in the middle. The middle of a scale is, however, set by its ends, and to many Conservatives it seems as though the unyielding nature of the Soviet Union combines with the solicitous policies of the United States to offset the center of the scale, or even to move it steadily toward the East. Writing from the Belgrade Conference, Worsthorne applied this analysis to the Berlin crisis:

> They are quite disinterested in the rights and wrongs of the Berlin dispute. Their only concern is to make sure that peace is somehow preserved, and since they currently feel that this objective, which is uppermost in all their thinking, is more likely to be achieved by putting pressure on the moderate Americans than the immoderate Russians, this is what they are seeking to do.
> In other words, Russia's recent brutal disregard for neutralist feelings and America's recent skillful courtship of them, instead of combining to turn the unaligned nations towards the West against the East are doing precisely the opposite.[13]

This is, of course, the origin of the British complaint of a "double standard," and has become part of official British thinking. Thus, a Minister of State explained to Parliament that there are "occasions again and again when it is the West which is looked to to make concessions because of the feeling that it is no good asking the Communists to give way."[14]

The original charge of a double standard referred to the failure of the neutrals to condemn Soviet nuclear tests. After the Goan invasion, however, Conservatives charged that yet another double standard had been introduced, in respect to the new states and the West. In reality there is, of course, only a single standard, namely the self-interest of the new nations. Its discriminatory application arises from the nature of the great powers rather than from that of the postcolonial countries.

The inclination of neutralists to claim the role of peacemaker and arbiter while acting with bias against the West is partially accounted for, and at the same time rendered more dangerous, by what Conservatives would regard as massive neutralist ignorance of the true nature of the most important questions of the day. In view of their low opinion of the new states' capacity to handle their own affairs, Conservatives naturally regard them as frequently incompetent to offer an opinion even on the affairs of other underdeveloped countries. All the more, then, are they thought prone to substitute slogans and facile generalities for constructive analysis of the broader issues of international politics. This is what *The Daily Telegraph* had in mind when it dubbed the Declaration of the Belgrade Conference a "lazy document." The most serious aspect of this ignorance is failure—or refusal—to recognize the role played by the balance of power between East and West in making neutralism possible at all. Thus, as long ago as 1956, the moderate *Economist* saw Nehru, Nasser, and Tito as "three men on an ice-floe, congratulating each other on the speed with which the warmth of their bodies is thawing it, and not yet fully aware that they owe both their eminence and their close association to the ice-floe's continued existence."[15]

The danger is not so much that the neutralists consequently refuse invitations to join the West, such as those John Foster Dulles used to issue, but that, whenever they can bring influence to bear, they will actively seek to inhibit and prevent the West from playing its role in the balance of power. Here lies the most dangerous consequence of taking too seriously neutralist pretensions to insight, rectitude, and a right to arbitrate.

Neutralists wield their most conspicuous influence on worldwide affairs in the General Assembly, and it is therefore no accident that the United Nations has become the bitter focus of debate about policy toward the new states. In addition to a legal right to be concerned with remote questions, the United Nations, by its devices for debating, voting, and even acting, confers on small states an actual capacity to influence matters that would otherwise be far beyond their reach. It is, in fact, a device that makes it possible, as never before, for a nation to indulge its lesser fancies; whims for which it would never spend resources more substantial than the energies of its delegate.

The Conservative Party has always had reservations as to how far the United Nations, and in particular, the General Assembly, would serve British interests. Events in 1956 greatly reinforced these doubts and entrenched them in the internal workings of the Party. In this respect, it was perhaps unfortunate that the General Assembly dealt with the Suez crisis after the first great infusion of new states. Complaints that the United Nations has a bias that militates against a sound solution of colonial problems began, however, much earlier. "Both before and after 1950," wrote a Conservative historian and Member of Parliament, "much more of the United Nations' interest appeared to be devoted to the grievances of the smaller and newer nations or the nonindependent peoples, generally directed against the larger and older nations; and these were popular causes in which Britain was often, though not invariably, on the unpopular side."[16] By 1952, Britain's failure to get redress from the United Nations or the International Court for its grievances against Iran led the British delegate to express "restlessness, not to say indignation" at the performance. This feeling grew so that a moderate study of Britain and the United Nations, published in 1957, could observe that "there are some grounds for suspecting that the hope of United Nations intervention has tended to exacerbate rather than to relieve nationalist feeling and to put a premium on insurrection and the use of violence. . . . If the United Nations were to continue to operate in this way, Britain might be forced seriously to reconsider her whole attitude to the Organization."[17]

The recent direct involvement of the United Nations in colonial administration, as in the Congo, is the natural result of the premature removal of the former regimes. Conservatives view the consequences with alarm, foreseeing United Nations involvement in undertakings that will overtax its resources and, possibly, break it entirely. The United Nations, warned *The Daily Telegraph,* "has neither the machinery nor the staff nor the money to govern a dependency. . . . At the moment its name is a farce and its activities a tragedy."[18] "What worries me," said the Prime Minister, in a recent debate, "is that the United Nations will find itself with a province as large as France on its hands and no means at all of governing it."[19] The General Assembly, believed to be ignorant, irresponsible and attentive to the loudest voice, does not inspire confidence in Britain as a body likely to be sensitive to the subtleties of order and minority rights. For many of the British, the United Nations' use of force in Katanga, symbolized by the ill-advised request for 1,000-pound bombs, was not isolated bad judgment, but the natural result of launching a grandiose and ill-prepared operation. The accident that the immediate outcome was somewhat better than they expected does not explode the theory on which Conservatives based their objections.*

On the broader canvas of world events, United Nations' preoccupation with colonialism appears, to Conservatives, as an abandonment of the primary task of keeping the peace by serving as a lubricant between the great powers. The Conservative belief that keeping the peace has such undeniable precedence over self-determination in the theoretical purposes of the United Nations is open to question. It opens, indeed, the perennial debate over the proper balance between enforcing the peace and removing the causes of war in an international organization dedicated to pacification. Be that as it may, Conservatives have watched with anxiety the gradual rise of the General Assembly, in which the smaller powers have their greatest influence, and this anxiety has recently extended to the Secretariat. Dag Hammarskjold was under heavy Conservative fire before his death, and the election of U Thant has been interpreted by some as the formal enthronement of an anticolonial bias that had already eroded impartiality.

Conservative criticism is far from entirely negative. Official expressions of concern have all been made within the context of a desire to save the United Nations, even if from itself. Britain has loyally paid her dues, made large voluntary payments, provided logistical support to the Congo operation she criticized, and responded to the United Nations bond issue. Conservative spokesmen recognize that the record of the neutralists in the United Nations and elsewhere has not been one to justify unmixed gloom in the West. The partial rebuff to Khrushchev's troika plan for the Secretariat and to Russian efforts to support a splinter regime in the Congo, the responsible attitude of the "Lagos" states toward the Congo, the general, if perhaps temporary, emergence of these "moderate" neutrals, are all admitted as mitigating circumstances. *The Daily Telegraph,* a harsh critic, is ready to concede that the neutrals are not deliberately trying to abet Soviet domination, at

---

* In an extreme comment on early claims of United Nations success, *The Daily Telegraph* commented: "Succeeded? What standards of success does the United Nations set itself? Where law and order existed, it has destroyed them. What does it hope to put in their place? It is difficult to escape the conclusion that Katanga may now lie at the mercy of a world-body of cranks and theorists, inexperienced and ignorant, utterly irresponsible in the sense that they have no stake in the country nor any save the most temporary interest in its welfare, men seemingly as incapable of government as of allowing others to govern. After them, the deluge? On the contrary, they are themselves the deluge."

least of themselves, while *The Times* has taken Lord Home to task for the excessive gloom of his pronouncements on the United Nations.[20] For, although Lord Home's strictures have great force, it is not at all easy to see what measures he proposes to substitute in situations such as that in the Congo, where direct embroilment of the great powers is what many wish to avoid. Nevertheless, conscience, which makes the West so much more susceptible to moral pressure than the East, is peculiarly powerful in the context of the United Nations, where hopes of amicable cooperation are so readily invoked. The United Nations therefore remains a place where the bias of "evasive neutralism," tending to move the neutralists toward the Soviet position, is particularly virulent.

The Conservative view of the new states presented so far treats them, more or less, as a group. But the fundamental Conservative belief that neutral policies will be determined by the several interests of the new states, as interpreted by their current leaders, warns against regarding neutralism as a single problem. Conservatives, therefore, emphasize the degree to which the new states, far from being united, are divided by separate interests. Thus, Indian objection to alliances, suggests a writer in the *Round Table,* is explicable less in terms of liberal theory than in terms of Pakistan's membership in SEATO, and does not extend to India's own special arrangements with Nepal.[21] The rallying cries of anticolonialism and the avoidance of identification with either side in the Cold War contribute certain common elements to neutralist foreign policies, although specific interests divide them—Ghana from Togo, Morocco from Mauritania, Egypt from Syria—and may be expected to do so increasingly as experience illuminates their separate national interests. Nehru's performance at Belgrade, where he played down anticolonialism, is regarded as an example of this, as might be expected from one of the neutrals more experienced in independence and responsibility. As the process continues, the particular interests of neutrals may, therefore, be expected to be a source of divisions among them, of differentiated grievances against the West, and, presumably, of varying responses to Western policy.

It is in keeping with this, and with the general perspective of the Conservative view, that when one turns to prescriptions for policy the emphasis is on a frank recognition that relations with the new states, like all international relations, will be based on the pursuit of self-interest by both sides. For our part, it is important that we should not come to think it shameful to stand on interest.

Realization that many justifications of colonialism masked strategic interests, for example, does not make strategic matters less real. In the same way, we should not become so fascinated by the moralistic atmosphere of decolonization that we forget our own predominant material strength.

Similarly, we should abandon any illusion that neutralist policies will be based on factors other than interest; that neutralists can be won over by adopting their slogans—as in the attempt to apply the tag of self-determination to Berlin—or that a superior moral nature renders them susceptible to demonstrations of rectitude on our part. Perhaps the best expression of this warning comes from the lips of a Labour Member of Parliament, famous on both sides of the House for his Toryism, who commented:

> In looking at the uncommitted world, the Americans and the Russians have had two different theories. The Americans have thought that the uncommitted world was influenced by righteousness and the Russians have thought it was influenced by power. When, just on the eve of Belgrade, the Russians put it to the test, it seems to me that the Russians proved their point. They established that what the uncommitted world was concerned with was not righteousness but power. . . . Those in the uncommitted part of the world . . . are not fundamentally concerned with judging righteousness. They are engaged in backing winners.[22]

If testimony of an undeniable Tory is required, Lord Salisbury wrote a few years ago for an American audience, that "one thing is certain; [the uncommitted] will be greatly influenced in their final decision by the comparative material strength and resolution of the Western and Communist blocs."[23] Positive anticolonialism, observed another Conservative writer, is "an expedient of power politics, and to that there is only a power political answer."[24]

Western policy toward the new states should, therefore, be designed, as foreign policy always should, to induce them to interpret their interests in a manner as favorable as possible to the West. Pandering to anticolonial prejudices, or expecting sustained gratitude for particular favors, is a delusive policy. In the first place, such indulgence is open to all the objections to any policy of appeasement. "The appetite comes with eating," commented *The Daily Telegraph* on the prospect of Indonesian demands on Australian New Guinea after consumption of the Dutch variety. It is indeed remarkable how often Conservatives invoke the image of Hitler in discussing the more contentious neutralist leaders. Sir

Anthony Eden's obsession with this analogy for Nasser is well known, and this was amplified by the fear that in the world of postcolonialism the Egyptian leader might become "the hero of the dark-skinned races."[25] Nor could the British press refrain from the appropriate reminiscences when Nehru announced that his "patience was exhausted" in regard to Goa.

The conception of "evasive neutralism" reinforces these arguments against appeasement. If neutrals are determined to stay in the middle, Western concessions will not only encourage further demands; they will invite increased hostility stimulated by neutralist fears that friendly relations with the West will embroil them with the East.

This does not mean that "good conduct" may not be rewarded or favors bought. It does mean that it must be the West, and not the neutrals, who define good conduct, for the only "goodness" relevant must have reference to Western interests. Otherwise, the neutrals' experience of Western reactions will not guide them in directions favorable to the West. In other words, while neutralists' policies will be based on their interests, it is in our power to help define those interests by manipulating the international environment within which they must be pursued. If the double standard depends on neutralist estimates of what the market will bear, we can influence the terms of trade.

The concept of evasive neutralism suggests that a simple multiplication of favors may not always best effect this adjustment. We should not be afraid to resent injuries actively. Probably this implies willingness to be more selective among neutrals. This should not mean a return to "pactomania," for this is not our need. But it is virtually impossible for the West to remain aloof from the multitude of disputes that have already begun to break out among the neutralists themselves, and this makes equal amiability with all an unattainable goal.

Emphasis on the importance of Western power and on the need to discriminate in favor of conduct advantageous to the West brings one to the role of the Atlantic alliance. The Conservatives repeatedly insist on overriding priority for the solidarity of this league. They fear America has allowed the neutralists to distract it from the overwhelmingly superior power and reliability of Europe. Consolidating and developing the resources of the Atlantic community, they believe, would far outweigh the material or moral consequence even of losing Afro-Asia. But, in fact, such consolidation is regarded as the way to not lose the Southern Hemisphere. The

Common Market, it can be argued, is already demonstrating the powerful attractive force that growing cohesion within the West might exercise over underdeveloped countries. If, said Lord Salisbury, the neutralists "can be shown that the Western Alliance is strong, united, and resolute, they are much more likely to come down on the right side than if it appears to be weak and vacillating."[26]

Here, of course, there is some inconsistency, for the right-wing Conservatives who are most insistent on the solidarity of the alliance have been, like General de Gaulle, most reluctant to sacrifice nationalism in military affairs. Clearly, the solidarity argument is frequently a device to enlist America behind British interests rather than an open-minded effort to work out the best policy for the West. But it is rarely recognized in the United States, one of the two prime protagonists in the world balance, that it is impossible for any of her lesser associates to weigh the value of other nations and groupings to the West without a bias derived from the fact that all are competitors for limited American attention and assistance. A higher estimate of the neutralists is necessarily an implicitly lower estimate of Europe. The feeling of neglect is real, and the argument in favor of priority for the alliance is both deeply felt by Conservatives and thoroughly in keeping with their view of international politics.

As one reviews the Conservative case, it seems that the persistent demand for an abandonment of illusions can be accepted wholeheartedly only if it clearly extends to Conservative illusions. Thus one can endorse the value of the Atlantic alliance and the danger of attributing exaggerated importance to the new states. But if the European allies claim priority over the new states for American attention on the ground of their net value to the alliance, they must accept the full and consistent application of this criterion.

It is as unreasonable for an ally like Portugal to expect to retain its weight in the alliance, if it becomes a liability, as it should be for an uncommitted nation to expect favors when its policies are harmful to the West. Nor should one fall into the error of believing that the services rendered by a neutralist have to be comparable in kind to those of an ally, or that the moral value of having neutralist friends is wholly ephemeral merely because it has hitherto been exaggerated.

Once more, the danger is in swinging from one extreme to another. Hence the warning against appeasement, against excessive faith in gratitude and slogan-borrowing, is well taken; these may well have been the besetting sins of the West, requiring a careful re-examination of liberal assumptions. But the corrective can go too far. In the first place, while there is nothing to be said for generosity based on false expectations of reward, a certain benevolence is part of Western interests. If we can enhance our security by riding roughshod over the interests of others, we may well be driven to do it. Yet this is not the world we want to live in, and we must, therefore, be skeptical of any suggestion that we should stop looking for alternatives. Concessions to neutralist aspirations are not always fatal to our interest and, as *The Times* has observed, even gradualist colonial leaders must be allowed to show results: "To mistake moderation for lack of determination is to invite extremism."[27] More particularly, it would be a gross error if the reaction against uncritical benevolence led to a conviction that no deals whatsoever with neutralists could be advantageous. Conservative emphasis that neutralist policy is grounded on interest is, indeed, particularly suggestive of the possibility of working out such deals. It is true that many of the general principles, such as anti-colonialism and racial self-assertion, that the neutralists most fluently pronounce have an anti-Western bias. However, particular issues to which the principles might be applied produce a variety of specific, and necessarily fairly detailed, proposals among which the West is frequently able to inject compromises of its own design. In such cases, the new states invariably divide according to their degree of militancy and direct involvement in the issue at stake, and thereby enable the West to salvage some of its immediate interests and curb the further consolidation of the neutralists in an anti-Western posture.

The danger of overreaction seems especially acute with regard to the United Nations. In part, the present dispute as to the degree of reliance that can safely be placed in the organization is another chapter in the age-old debate between liberals and conservatives as to the merits of assuming an international order based on rights or power. But the Conservative view does not rule out the possibility that calculations of power may recommend acceptance of a constitutional framework for order based on an equipoise of strength; indeed Conservatives constantly return to the necessity of basing order on a balance of power in their criticism that the new nations ignore it. Insofar as this means anything, it is a willingness to subordinate occasional short-run preferences to the will of the majority in the expectation of long-term advantages to be secured from a general application of this principle. The difficulty at present, of course, is that even many of those willing to accept this principle are convinced that the policies of the new nations are not only inimical to present Western interests, but also destructive of the long-term purposes of the organization. This may be so—this is not the place to argue the point—but it is at least obvious that one should not confuse determination not to allow abuse of a principle with a refusal to accept the principle that is abused. The abuse may well become so grave as to remove all hope of saving the principle. But the risk of testing this by experience does not seem excessive once the West has undergone its Conservative inoculation against an uncritical drift on the tide of illusion.

The Conservative analysis puts the question of relations with neutralists back in the arena of international power politics where it belongs. What is important is the effect of the new states on our national interests; all their other affairs are secondary. Recognition that the policies of the new states will almost certainly—as ours clearly should—be based on their concept of their own national interest and pursued by what power they can muster is a salutary insulation against the fallacy of believing them amenable to mere good will and what we regard as reasonableness. But interests and power calculations do not always lead where some Conservatives believe, and we should not confuse hard-headed prescriptions with those that are merely pig-headed. The fact that some of the firmness called for by realism happens to coincide with some of the policies advocated by emotional opponents of change clearly does not mean that the latter are well advised in their other policies. Thus, if the Conservatives usefully explode some myths and facile assumptions, we must take care not to adopt new ones. Conservative principles, like anyone else's, may be useful guides, but they are no substitute for the statesmanship that must judge each case as it arises.

V

THE "THIRD PARTY": THE RATIONALE
OF NONALIGNMENT

by GEORGE LISKA

NONALIGNMENT reflects the peculiar conditions of a world in which Communist power is rising and Western colonial empires have virtually disappeared in fact if not in memory. Nonalignment poses the most arduous single problem that the West, and the United States in particular, has had to face in the area of foreign policy since it first decided to contain Communist power proper.

Neutrality versus Alliance

Nonaligned countries avoid alliances, refusing to add their power to that of others. If it were merely a matter of withholding their power from others, they would pursue a traditional policy of neutrality. In wartime, they would remain aloof, except when asked to mediate; under Cold War conditions, they would stay equally aloof. Not all the nonaligned countries have been pursuing such a neutral policy. The militant neutralists have not been content merely to withhold their power from others as the traditional neutrals have done. Among those neutrals are Switzerland and nineteenth-century Belgium; countries that have been neutralized by treaty more recently, such as Austria; and those that have tried to virtually neutralize themselves, such as Burma. The "positive" neutralists have instead engaged in an active policy of playing the great powers against each other and offering unsolicited mediation between them.

The smaller the margin of power that favors either of two contending parties, the more relevant is the total power of an intrinsically weak third party. Such power need not be greater than the net advantage favoring one of the contending major powers, and it may be incommensurate in kind. Short of—and some times even despite—its manifest abuse, third-party influence is greatest with stalemated contestants. They are more than normally inclined to show respect for the forms (independence) and the fictions (impartiality or superior morality) upon which nonbelligerent or nonaligned countries base their claims to protection, function, and authority in the international arena.

In the annals of traditional diplomacy, there are two major counterparts to contemporary neutralists. One is a league of armed neutrals that actively seeks to prevent forms of warfare, generally naval, that may injure its members' interests, principally its economic ones. The other counterpart is a former ally now bent on separate peace. The validity of this latter grouping may be affirmed or denied, depending on how one judges the post-independence "defection" of the neutralist countries from the Western system, despite continued adherence, in many cases, to the principal values and aspirations of the West. A comparison of the actual behavior of the two groupings is less controversial.

The similarity between separate peace and neutralism is quite pervasive. It bears, first, on the salient reasons for separate peace in war: reaction to inferior status within an association, material inability to cope with the adversary, and desire for a special advantage for oneself, rather than for a more successful ally. For neutralist groups in firmly aligned and manifestly threatened countries, the desire to be released from struggle, typical of separate peace under duress, is aggravated by the apparent impossibility of leaving an alliance. To neutralist regimes situated in the zone between the two major alliances, the ease and profitability of the policy magnifies the desire for special advantage, typical of separate peace under inducement. The characteristic strategy of separate peace is to demand an impossible performance by the partner to be deserted, so that the anticipated failure to comply may make defection legitimate and reduce the danger of sanctions. The principal demand of the neutralists has been for instant and complete withdrawal of all vestiges of colonial control; a secondary demand has been for disarmament and diversion of resources into economic assistance. The latter demand coincides with the separate-peacemaker's typical ambition: to pacify the general conflict in such a way as to retain and consolidate previous gains. The characteristic technique is offering unsolicited mediation. Such mediation may be undertaken in good faith, when it is "armed" with the promise of behavior favorable to the complying side; or terms may be so defined as to ensure an apparent compliance of the favored party.

The attitude of the neutralists toward presently contending "blocs" is one thing; their position toward the institution of alliance as such is another. Traditionally, there have been two kinds of policy; neutralism has added a third. The three policies indicate degrees of increasing hostility toward alliances.

The first type of antialliance policy rules out alliance with a particular country while approving or condoning policies of alliance generally. Thus France, after 1871, would not consider an alliance with Germany unless the latter returned the conquered provinces. The rejection of this particular alliance, however, only intensified France's search for allies against the German enemy.

The second type of antialliance policy favors abstention from all alliances. Such a policy may be adopted after a dispassionate weighing of the gains and liabilities that could be expected from all feasible alternatives. Abstention was the policy pursued by England and the United States in periods of "splendid isolation" and has remained the policy of traditional neutrals. Incidentally, the abstaining country need not be opposed to alliances among other countries, for these often ensure its own position of aloofness. For instance, in the period before World War I, neutral Belgium favored an Anglo-French alliance that, at different periods, served as a restraint on France or as a counterpoise to Germany, or both. And when Great Britain became antagonized by Germany's *Weltpolitik,* yet remained anxious to avoid commitments on the Continent, she stopped opposing the alliance between France and Russia, her colonial rivals. Similarly, early American statesmen did not extend their philosophy of nonentanglement to imply opposition to alliances among European powers. A change in American outlook did occur, however, in the twentieth century, as the environment and prevailing ideology changed. The United States, for a while, adopted an antialliance policy of a third type, similar in nature to that pursued or advocated by neutralists.

The third, or neutralist, antialliance policy opposes all alliances, including those among other powers. Antialliance ideology holds that competition for allies is a cause of tension and war. Alliances are concluded in anticipation of a test of strength; they increase the total power that statesmen can wield and encourage them to use it while the alliance holds together. Alliances might partially substitute for national armaments, but they also instigate an armaments race as states seek to attract new allies and to disrupt the alliance of the adversary. Armament efforts at least have the merit of absorbing national energies domestically; the race for allies takes place between countries and puts a high premium on prestige. Prestige is born of success, and the diplomatic success of one state entails the humiliation of another, which then seeks retribution. Since alliances are built on shared antagonism rather than on amity, they tend to fall apart. War is then welcomed as an alternative to disintegration of the alliance and isolation. The fear of isolation is viewed in the antialliance ideology as the *reductio ad absurdum* of the rationale for alliances. In the absence of alliances, all nations would be "isolated" and thus more amenable to universal law and its sanctions.

Nonalignment and neutralism must be viewed in a double perspective, since they result from closely interwoven responses to external factors and domestic conditions. Nonalignment can be adopted on the basis of rational estimates of the conditions required for national security and domestic stability; but a policy of militant neutralism, on the other hand, is likely to be strongly affected by nonrational ideological preoccupations and by an almost too pragmatic quest for aid and status internationally.

We have seen earlier that there is no single motive for alignment; there are also many traditional reasons for the nonalignment of smaller powers. If only one issue or conflict is dominant, and the smaller state does not wish to be identified with the policy of either power center in a bipolar structure, it may elect to rely on almost automatic protection (assuming that one power group balances the other). In such a case, the danger of provoking one side by aligning with the other may well appear greater than the need for, or possibility of, protection. When more than one issue dominates the international system, a smaller state may hesitate to determine its alignment on the basis of only one of the issues. It might make common cause with the West against the East on the issue of Communist expansion, but not with the industrial, residually imperialist North, against the formerly colonial, preindustrial South, on the other dominant issue of today—economic development and political independence for the less developed countries. Similarly, as the number of particular conflicts increases, so does the fear of the smaller states that alignment may involve them with new antagonists. The political cost of alliance becomes extravagant when it entails not only an initial compromise with the ally, but the liability of adding his enemies to one's own as well. Such considerations would suffice to keep Afghanistan or Burma out of an alliance that included Pakistan and, consequently, antagonized India.

While following traditional antialliance patterns of thoughts and action, the nonaligned states and the neutralists have stressed two new factors in contemporary international relations to justify opposition to alliances. The first concerns modern weapons of mass destruction. According to the neutralist school of thought, no individual or collective effort by small countries can significantly increase a small country's security if security means capacity for defense against a nuclear power. So-called deterrence requires actions that are indistinguishable from provocation in the eyes of the target state. To parry the provocation, each great power will try to demonstrate that its nuclear opponent is unable to protect the small ally. The safest course for a small country is, therefore, to do nothing to attract the contending giants either as allies or as enemies. It should, instead, rely on the nuclear powers' reluctance either to initiate a major conflict over a small country or to antagonize other small countries by using force against any of them. Spontaneous solidarity of nonaligned countries to oppose great-power encroachments is the most effective "alliance" in a nuclear environment available to a small country.

The second factor that is working against alliance is the alleged relationship between Western alliance policy and Western colonialism. From the anticolonial viewpoint, the West has had two kinds of alliances. The more objectionable kind associates former colonies with former metropolitan or other Western powers; the other kind does not involve ex-colonial nations. The immediate victim of neocolonialism, which perpetuates Western presence and control, is the allied small country itself. The prototype of the neocolonial alliance is the Anglo-Iraqi alliance that replaced Britain's League of Nations mandate in the 1930's. Its military and political clauses can be read simply as devices to buttress a pliant oligarchy aligned with British interests and supported by the major ally's residual presence in the country. The government of the dependent ally cannot conduct its own foreign policy, and the people are not free to change the regime by force, if need be.

According to the same view, the dangers of neocolonial alliances may be only indirect, but less real, for other countries in the region. Colonialism thrives on conflict between indigenous forces. As long as smaller countries depend on their own resources, the argument might run, conflicts are nonexistent or inconclusive. But when lesser countries align with a major outside power, even if ostensibly against another major power, the ally acquires new resources and believes, rightly or wrongly, that it has gained additional support for pressing its claims on neighboring small states. In the eyes of Nasser and his followers, the Baghdad Pact disrupted the common front of the Arab League against Israel and, under the guise of an anti-Soviet front, intensified the ambitions of the Iraqi elite with regard to Syria and Egypt. From Nehru's viewpoint, SEATO has enabled Pakistan to be tougher toward India and Afghanistan, and Thailand to press her ambitions against Cambodia. The affected states cannot but react by aligning with another power or by giving a militant slant to their nonalignment, to enhance its nuisance value, penalize the great-power ally of their local adversary, and secure countervailing outside assistance. In one way or another, the great-power adversaries secure new avenues of influence to the lesser states. By introducing arms and discord into the region, the alliance of a small state with a great power constitutes, in Nehru's words, a "reversal of the process of liberation."[1]

The other kind of Western alliance is that which does not include a former colonial dependent. NATO is such an alliance. The neutralists have objected to NATO only to the extent that, at least indirectly, it helped the metropolitan members resist the trend toward "decolonization" by reducing a colonial metropole's defense burden against the Soviet bloc in Europe. Alliances like NATO and, on the Communist side, the Warsaw Pact, are least "provocative" because they associate countries that are close to each other geographically and do not encircle the principal target state. Moreover, they are not "colonial" alliances, because they associate nations kindred in culture and color. Affinity in ideology and political organization among the members makes such groupings even more acceptable to the neutralists. They have been inclined to overlook the fact that such affinity has been forced upon the lesser allies in the Warsaw Pact, so long as the ideology can be considered "progressive" and the dominant Soviet ally manages to avoid overt repression within the alliance.

Seen from the neutralist viewpoint, the above criterion for differentiating between acceptable and unacceptable alliances has certain advantages. A big, unaligned country such as India may acceptably enter into security arrangements of her own with a small country like Nepal. And, as long as the areas included within the alliances of the major powers are kept at a minimum, the in-between or unaligned area will be large. The fly in the ointment is the Sino-Soviet alliance. At first it ran afoul of the anticolonial principle, because China was weak and racially different from Russia. After the Bandung powers failed to dissuade Peking from coveting China's former "protective" belt of dependencies, the security aspect became critical. Instead of growing, the unaligned area might be progressively reduced, and reduced near the homeland of nonalignment, at that.

Foreign Policy and Domestic Imperatives

As reconstructed so far, the neutralist position on alliances has ignored the objective requirements of international equilibrium and security. The omission is not serious if one holds that a strategic parity would remain in existence between East and West even if the West withdrew from all bases in former dependent nations. All that is necessary is that the United States retain links with Japan, Australia, Turkey, and a few small island bases; it would need neither SEATO nor CENTO. Some such beliefs may have led neutralist governments to feel that their countries could enjoy the best available protection at little cost and risk to themselves. An imaginary neutralist might go so far as to postulate a natural division of labor between nonaligned countries and the West if only the West suffered this partnership to be disguised by anti-Western tirades. The fear of adverse repercussions among nonaligned countries might restrain the Sino-Soviet bloc from small-scale military and paramilitary penetrations by land; and the fear of a Western deterrent could restrain the Communists from an all-out assault. Such a complementary politico-military deterrent, our imaginary neutralist might conclude, would reduce the Sino-Soviet bloc to truly peaceful competition. In short, flexibility in diplomacy and avoidance of provocative policies insure short-run security.

In the long run, Soviet imperialism will not replace that of the West, the neutralists seem to believe. In this way, neutralist opposition to peacetime commitments can be bolstered with assumptions about the character of the two chief contestants and about the winners in the Cold War. The neutralists have inclined to discount the Western thesis that Communism is inherently aggressive; on the contrary, they have largely adopted the theory that internal expansion will absorb Communist efforts and that the Communists' bellicosity will subside when they have attained Western levels of mass consumption.

The assumptions about the West and particularly the United States, have been, in many ways, complementary. The United States may be deemed capable of deterring all-out war even without bases or allies on the Sino-Soviet periphery; but America has not been credited with the ability to defend small countries without destroying them, especially if these countries are close to the Sino-Soviet bloc. The neutralists have also seemed to assume that within the limits of American capability and resolution, the United States is tacitly committed to defend any country that is threatened by a Communist power, regardless of that country's previous policy. Therefore, it would be absurd to undertake the material and political liabilities of alignment.

Assumptions regarding "victory" in the Cold War have likewise militated against alignment. The leaders of many nonaligned countries remember the two World Wars; their independence movements triumphed largely as a result of the second. In that conflict, the Western nations suffered initial setbacks but finally defeated the totalitarian states. Japan's totalitarian expansionism in World War II was temporarily of great service to the cause of anticolonial nationalism in Southeast Asia. For the neutralists, this recent history has set the guidelines for the long-term perspective: The West is likely to win over the Communist bloc in the end and therefore needs no assistance; and the methods used in gaining independence could be revived for consolidating it. Japan had once proved useful; the neutralist should stand ready to garner any incidental advantage from the more recent Cold War conflict.

The long-range neutralist ideal is the decline of both contending sides' power and influence relative to the new nations. This is what happened in both world wars and, unless a third destroys everything, it will, so the neutralists hope, happen again. The basic requirement is that the Cold War substitute for war be a competitive economic build-up of the less developed nations.

Meanwhile, however, concern about voicing fear has been very much a part of the universe of nonalignment and neutralism. There are nonaligned leaders who will privately admit that they fear Communist encroachments and resent Soviet "nuclear terror"; but the dogmatic neutralist rejects the very thought that he is swayed by the fear of anything and anyone. Fear makes for caution and has been a paramount reason for the nonalignment of Burma, Afghanistan, and Cambodia, countries close and vulnerable to the Sino-Soviet bloc. Absence of fear may be put forward as the reason for nonalignment when remoteness or the natural protection and vast size of a country like India apparently give a nation immunity.

Fear of an external threat often stimulates very pragmatic calculations. These may produce either alignment or nonalignment. The option will be affected by such intangibles as historical experience and political culture, as well as by specific, tangible threats. Thailand, for instance, chose alignment despite, and partly because of, her proximity to China. Burma opted for nonalignment. Unlike the Burmese, the Thai have long been independent and are impressed by the limitations of neutrality. And unlike the Cambodians, the Thai elite is familiar with the pitfalls of a playoff policy. The Thai propensity for active diplomacy led, therefore, to initiative for and within a Western alliance. The Burmese tendency toward withdrawal found political expression in nonalignment. Moreover, the specific threat to Thailand came from a "Free Thai" movement based in Communist China, while the Burmese were beset by incursions of Nationalist Chinese. The case of Iran is similar to that of Thailand. The difference between India and Pakistan is less complex. West Pakistan is a home of warlike races; more importantly, India thought of nonalignment first, thereby leading Pakistan to do the opposite. Afghanistan in turn took a line contrary to that of Pakistan. Controversy over Kashmir and Pushtoonistan loomed larger than the possible threat of either the Soviet Union or China.

Much in the neutralist ideology of international security seems based on an optimistic degree of confidence in automatic protection. But seen in a second perspective, as a politics of compensation that reflects concern with internal problems, neutralism combines deep-seated emotions about the past with crudely pragmatic methods for coping with the present.

Many new nations have instituted a priority that the liberal, democratic West has more consistently preached than practiced—that of domestic over external conditions as determinants of foreign policy. This is not surprising. Domestic concerns tend to be preponderant in societies that are free from external security dilemmas or helpless to cope with them, and whose central authority is subject to factional opposition, rather than free for action abroad because of equipoised pluralism at home. In addition, many of the new states tend toward internationalization of domestic politics; this follows the essentially feudal pattern of internal factions aligning with, and receiving moral and material support from, different outside powers. Even if the politically less developed countries manage to contain the internationalization of their internal troubles, their domestic politics still tend to resemble international politics. Factional leaders fight to survive in governing positions, and other factions strive to conquer such positions, without accepting the arbitrament of a successful performance of functions associated with the modern state.

The policies of nonalignment and neutralism are a means for counteracting these tendencies. Nonalignment presumably enhances the international status and, consequently, the domestic authority of "national" leaders. This promotes short-run stability. And the isolationist bias of nonalignment appeals to both traditionalist and nationalist factions, while it helps insulate factional and regional struggles against the strains of outside interference. The graver the internal troubles, the greater the temptation for leaders to go beyond nonalignment to militant neutralism. Indonesia's militancy has intensified as internal tensions increased. And underlying Indian "positive neutrality" is the leaders' concern with preventing the division of the country into several quarreling states.[2]

This fear of domestic division is one of the reasons for the militancy of the neutralist governments in relatively non-integrated new nations. Neutralism, as an active foreign policy, provides a focus for domestic cohesion, and silences opposition to the government. Moreover, to governing groups in many new nations militant neutralism appeals as a reaction against the passivity of former colonial status. The hallmarks of dependency—lack of a separate foreign policy and of diplomatic access to third states that could counterbalance the metropole—seems perpetuated in today's "unequal alliances." Any neutralist leader of a new nation is determined to avoid a relapse and to demonstrate his freedom and ability to create and use foreign policy alternatives.

In contrast, the neutralism of opposition groups in well-integrated societies, such as Britain and Japan, stems from different experiences. Such groups covet withdrawal and passivity in reaction to the government's active policy of alliance and involvement. They are less concerned with independence, which seems assured, than with immunity to the danger of nuclear destruction, which appears acute. Their pacifism is a delayed response to wartime exertions and deprivations, unlike the pacifism of some nonaligned countries that is influenced by their prevailing religion and world view. However, neutralists in opposition and neutralists in power share the desire to remove domestic politics from the pressures attending permanent alignment. The socialists in Japan, West Germany, and even Britain would probably fare better if, wittingly or unwittingly, the American alliance did not work in favor of the more conservative regimes. But the "protest" vote, however intense, is too small to offset the vote for continuing "protection." By the same token, the Soviet alliance helped the Communist Party electorally in Czechoslovakia in 1946.

Neutralists in and out of power are likely to develop along different lines in the future. Neutralists in well-integrated, allied countries may become increasingly militant as the level of the arms race rises. On the other hand, neutralists in positions of authority may progressively temper their militancy as they come to grips with concrete problems; and they may become less volatile as they realize that too frequent shifts in tactical alignment tend to debase their standing.

In the initial stages of independence, compensation has worked both as a psychological response to past dependence, and as a tactic to make up for present weakness. The psychological reasons for generally anti-Western policy are often quite subtly related to colonial experience. A leader may fear that alignment with the West would degrade him in the eyes of his own state and other ex-colonial nations. At Bandung, Nehru identified those favoring alliance with the West as "yes men," "hangers-on," and "camp followers." Or, a leader may adopt neutralism to make up for his Western traits and to disarm the traditionalist strata in his society.[3]

Foreign policy serves the needs of compensation best when it can be changed more easily than basic domestic policies. That is eminently the case with neutralist policy. The basic international posture of a radical or socialist regime like that of Sékou Touré, in Guinea, merely extends domestic policies abroad; but occasional moves toward the Western position can help keep Communist influence in bounds. Even more conspicuous is the utility of an anti-Western foreign-policy slant for an internally conservative government that hopes to undercut nationalist and leftist opposition, possibly with the aid of external claims known to be opposed by the West. For example, although turning to the East diplomatically for internal reasons, the royal government in Morocco stepped up its claims in the south—in Mauritania and the Spanish Sahara. Likewise, Nasser's neutralism was originally the new regime's way of making up for his predecessor's alleged deference toward the West. Subsequent Western opposition to Egypt's objectives in Israel and the Middle East generally consolidated Nasser's anti-Western policy.

In pursuing regional ambitions, the neutralists force compensatory shifts by others. Unaligned countries such as Burma, Tunisia, and even potentially powerful Nigeria have been opposed to bids for regional dominance by local states no less than by outside powers. To counter such bids, leaders of threatened countries may move toward alignment with the West, if they can; or they may try to outbid their regional competitors in the pro-Soviet line, if they dare, or must. The danger to the first line comes from radical nationalism; the risks of the latter course come from indigenous Communism. The relatively pro-Western nonalignment policy of Tunisia, and of some of the former French-African colonies, as well as of Nigeria, was originally rooted in the personalities of the leaders and in the relatively smooth accession of independence. Thereafter, the standing of the leaders and their policies has depended on their ability to steer a middle course—or to balance opposites. They have had to withstand regional ambitions of neighbors and satisfy the hunger of domestic nationalists and modernizers for prestige and progress while securing just enough Western assistance to contain and construct without being compromised.

Nonalignment and neutralism are international policies inspired largely by domestic concerns. By the same token, they are political policies largely motivated by economic needs and interests. The leaders of new and some not-so-new nations are committed to economic development as a means to the political stability that, among other things, would keep them in power. Many have come to believe that their countries cannot afford the cost in national unity or defense spending that a controversial alliance policy would entail. The main reason, however, why the policy of nonalignment is economical is that it brings in material assistance from both sides. The merely nonaligned leader seeks to demonstrate his impartiality by accepting assistance from both sides; the militant neutralist is seeking to prove his international importance in accepting such aid. When the neutralist leader has to accept the West's conditions of aid, he pays the price for extending the tripartite game into the field of economics. To have a Soviet alternative helps in relations with the West. And the existence of a Western alternative has enabled some neutralists, such as India, to put economic relations with the Soviet bloc on a sound monetary basis. Even when a neutralist country has had to put up with bilateral barter, as did the United Arab Republic, and overcommitted itself economically, a chastened regime can, as a last resort, presumably count on the West to bail it out.

To sum up, the range of policies of small countries runs from biased neutralism through strict nonalignment to outright alliance membership. Since the eclipse of the British-oriented ruling group in Ceylon, only some of the formally nonaligned French-speaking African elites have been openly critical of Sino-Soviet (and indigenous) imperialism; with such lone and, possibly, passing exceptions, the bias in neutralism has been against Western colonialism. The typical nonaligned regime is primarily concerned with internal stability and, in some cases, with security against proximate powers. The militant neutralist invokes anti-imperialist ideological precepts while working to profit from the contest between old and new imperialisms. Non-Communist Marxist that he often is, the neutralist actively seeks to employ the Soviet "antithesis" against the Western "thesis" to advance what he sees as the higher goal of his own nationalist and socialist synthesis.

VI

NEHRU, NASSER, AND NKRUMAH
ON NEUTRALISM

by ERNEST W. LEFEVER

A FABLE from sub-Saharan Africa and a proverb from Kenya illustrate the different ways in which neutralist leaders see themselves and the roles of their nations in the Cold War. Jomo Kenyatta, the veteran nationalist leader in Kenya, once said: "When two elephants fight, it is the grass that suffers; and when East and West are struggling in Africa, it is Africa that suffers." This proverb points to the undesirable impact of the bipolar struggle on the aspirations of the neutralist rulers of the emerging states.

The beneficial effect of the Cold War on small neutralist nations can be illustrated by the well-known African fable of a clever rabbit that, desiring to become king of the beasts, challenges the larger animals to a contest to establish his supremacy. He proposes a tug of war, but makes the rope so long that the contestant cannot see his opponent on the other end. The wily rabbit pits one large beast against another and then claims the victory over the loser. He repeats this until he eventually proclaims himself king of the beasts.

The object of this study is not to determine whether the Afro-Asian neutrals gain or lose because of the Cold War. It is, rather, to examine the interpretations of their international roles in the larger struggle between the Communist world and the committed nations of the free world expressed by the three leading neutralists—Prime Minister Jawaharlal Nehru of India, President Gamal Abdel Nasser of the United Arab Republic, and President Kwame Nkrumah of Ghana.

The philosophies of "positive neutralism" expounded by these advocates of nonalignment in Asia, the Middle East, and Black

93

Africa are variations on a central theme that finds expression in the lesser leaders of the emergent states throughout Asia and Africa. The top politicians of Indonesia, Burma, Ceylon, Morocco, and Guinea are, like Nehru, Nasser, and Nkrumah, all self-avowed apostles of nonalignment. They all are responding to the same historical forces—internal weakness, a recent colonial past, and global bipolarity. The differences among the neutralists are differences of emphasis and style, for each molds his public philosophy to his personality and to his political and cultural setting and each adapts his policy to changing circumstances inside and outside his country.

Since neutralism is a function of bipolarity, this study focuses on the impact of American and Sino-Soviet policies upon the emergent states of Asia and Africa. It is concerned primarily with the publicly stated philosophy of Afro-Asian neutralism as it bears upon, and adapts to, the external military policies of the major Cold War antagonists. These policies include engaging in direct and indirect military action, maintaining foreign military bases, offering foreign military aid, and joining military alliances, as well as policies on the control of nuclear weapons. Other aspects of United States, Soviet, or Red Chinese foreign policy will be referred to, but primarily as they relate to defense and military affairs.

Contemporary anticolonialism is a political and psychological reaction against European political control and economic domination. It celebrates recently acquired independence and demands freedom for all remaining subject territories. Afro-Asian neutralism, on the other hand, is a response to a political and ideological struggle so extensive and profound that no state anywhere can avoid the decision to take sides or not take sides. Although the foreign policies of the emergent states are influenced by both the colonial past and contemporary realities, there is no necessary or consistent relationship between a nation's position on the colonial question and its position in the Cold War. The mood, or philosophy, of anticolonialism may affect a nation's fundamental decision on whether to be committed or not, and, once the decision is made, it may affect the form the commitment or nonalignment takes, but it is not the determining factor. Anticolonialist but nonneutralist Pakistan is explicitly allied with the West, while anticolonialist but neutralist Guinea leans toward the Communist bloc.

Nehru, Nasser, and Nkrumah regard the Cold War as dangerous and destructive. Each has elected a policy of positive neutralism and nonalignment with either the Communist bloc or the Western coalition. Each wants to maintain political independence and freedom of action in the world of Cold War rivalries. Each maintains that nonalignment does not mean moral neutrality. "The only camp we should like to be in is the camp of peace and goodwill," said Nehru, in 1959.[1]

Nasser has said: "I will not become the stooge or satellite or pawn or hireling of anybody."

According to Nkrumah, "nonalignment can be understood only in the context of the present atomic arms race and the atmosphere of the Cold War. . . . But this attitude of nonalignment does not imply indifference to the great issues of the day. . . . It is in no way anti-Western; nor is it anti-Eastern."

Necessity, national self-interest, and high moral principle are all given as reasons for pursuing a policy of neutralism by the three leaders. Each emphasizes that the desire for nonalignment is a natural outgrowth of the peculiar history of his people. Nehru speaks of "ideals inherited from our past," including "years of conditioning by Gandhi." Nasser points to "our national aspirations, our psychological complexes, our experience with foreign powers." All three acknowledge that the necessities of world politics and a prudential regard for the national interest both point to nonalignment as the best policy.

Nonalignment, the policy of enlightened self-interest, according to Nehru, Nasser, and Nkrumah, yields six interrelated benefits to the militarily uncommitted nation:

1. Nonalignment insures political freedom and independence and contributes to national self-respect and moral integrity.

2. In contrast to alliance membership, which serves as a restraint, nonalignment permits freedom of expression and action.

3. Nonalignment keeps a small nation from getting involved in larger conflicts of no concern to it.

4. Alignment would make local problems more difficult to solve. Nehru, in particular, is convinced that almost any problem can be solved if it is not permitted to become a part of the Cold War.

5. Alliances involve military obligations that divert scarce resources from the urgent necessities of economic development.

6. Nonaligned nations are in a position to accept and, indeed, to bid for economic aid from both sides in the Cold War.

Their reluctance to acknowledge the blessings of bipolarity does not prevent neutralist leaders from claiming that their foreign policies greatly benefit the peace and welfare of mankind. In this, the neutralist statesmen are scarcely unique. Especially Nehru tends to justify his neutralist policies in terms of universal moral principles rather than in terms of national interest. Nasser and Nkrumah are less inclined to do so.

Nehru's frequently expressed confidence in the efficacy of non-alignment as a policy of peace appears to be rooted in a view of the world that ascribes a high degree of rationality and moral capacity to human nature. Our preparation for war, he said, in 1949, "is not flattering either to man's reason or to our common humanity." He maintains that the tensions and conflicts of the Cold War can be mitigated and a hot war avoided by developing greater understanding, tolerance, and patience, supported by appropriate efforts to reconcile differences peaceably. His words, at times, sound like those of a pacifist, but he has repeatedly insisted upon the need for nonnuclear military force in a world where expansionist governments still exist.

Nehru dramatically clarified his position on the relation between colonialism and coercion in December, 1961, when India seized Goa and two other Portuguese enclaves in an almost bloodless blitzkrieg. This action demonstrated that Nehru regarded acquiescence to continued colonialism as a greater evil than military invasion. Many Westerners were shocked by an attack against Goa by a man who had lectured the world on the virtues of mediation and nonviolence, but the truth is that Nehru had never disavowed the use of military force for the achievement of national objectives, although many of his public utterances tended to give this impression. On a number of occasions he rejected the use of force to "liberate" Goa, but, as long ago as 1955, he said in a statement on Goa: "As far as I can conceive, under the existing circumstances, no government can be pledged to nonviolence. If we were . . . surely we could not keep any army, navy, or air force— and possibly not even a police force."

Nehru is a complex man, and perhaps he was describing himself in 1956, when he said: "We in India appear to have a split personality; we speak unctuously about nonviolence . . . while in our daily behavior we are coming down to a level which is not a civilized level at all." If Nehru and other Indian leaders had been less unctuous, the outcry against the Goan action would not have been so great. Defense Minister V. K. Krishna Menon said he expected members of the United Nations to be jubilant about the Indian conquest of Goa. Nehru hardly expected this response, but he was clearly stung by sharp criticism in the West. He justified his action in terms of liberating a colonial area and reminded the West that India had helped save the United Nations by sending troops to strengthen the U.N. force in the Congo. He acknowledged that he had been called a hypocrite, but insisted that the Goan action was "entirely in keeping" with the principles of Ghandi.

Nasser and Nkrumah also believe that their policy of nonalignment and their support of coexistence will mitigate East-West conflicts and make nuclear war less likely, but they are more restrained than are Indian spokesmen. Nasser has said that his policies "may help the cause of peace and end the Cold War." And Nkrumah has stated that "the peace of the world is served . . . by keeping one great continent free from the strife and rivalry of military blocs."

India's theory of nonalignment has been tested in the crucible of Cold War politics for fifteen years. In 1961, Nehru said that time has "confirmed" its validity, although its implementation has been "affected by events," such as the border dispute with China. Nasser's brand of neutralism has had a shorter, but more severe, test since Egypt became a republic in 1953. He, too, believes he has chosen the wiser policy. Nkrumah likewise shows no disposition to alter his foreign policy after five years of independence. Each man remains a self-avowed, orthodox neutralist. Each believes his theory has proved resilient enough to support changing policies designed to meet rapidly shifting circumstances on the international scene. (The problem of adaptation under the impacts of events will be discussed later.)

The Neutrals as Mediators and as a "Third Force"

The Afro-Asian neutralist leaders have set for themselves four paramount objectives—consolidate their political independence; eliminate the last remnants of European colonialism; develop their national economies; and play a special role separately or jointly in efforts to ease or resolve big-power conflicts. This study is interested primarily in the fourth objective.

Nehru, for historical and psychological reasons, has been more concerned with mitigating the dangers of nuclear bipolarity than have Nkrumah and Nasser, although both of them did support his peacemaking efforts at the United Nations, in the fall of 1960. Nehru is perhaps the world's foremost advocate of mediation as the best way to solve international problems. He has felt impelled to "bring nations . . . step by step . . . to the point of peaceful discussion" and to initiate "new approaches" to facilitate the solution of Cold War differences.[2] He could be described as a man with a mission to mediate, but on at least one occasion (before the U.S. Congress, in 1949) he said India had "no desire to play a leading role in the international sphere except where we are compelled by circumstances." He added, "Our geography, our history, the present events" all force us into "a wider picture."

Whether Nehru is a reluctant mediator or an eager one may depend on the nature of the conflict in question. Considerable evidence suggests that he has actively sought a place in the "wider picture." He is proud that India has twice been asked by the United Nations to help settle Cold War conflicts, first in Korea, and later in Indochina. More recently, in March, 1961, Nehru sent an urgent and lengthy personal cable to Premier Khrushchev urging him to press for a cease-fire in Laos at the request of President Kennedy. At the United Nations in September, 1960, Nehru launched what was described as a "one-man effort to end the Cold War." In a single day he conferred with President Eisenhower, Prime Minister Macmillan, Premier Khrushchev, Canadian Prime Minister Diefenbaker, Secretary-General Hammarskjold, President Nasser, and President Nkrumah to gain support for his resolution calling for the re-establishment of contact between Mr. Eisenhower and Mr. Khrushchev. The failure of this intense mediation effort, which had the solid backing of the Afro-Asian bloc, is said to have saddened and disillusioned Nehru. This episode illustrates the limitations of neutralist initiative in mediating Cold War disputes.

If Nehru is eager to play the role of peacemaker, in the general sense of serving as a bridge or promoting quiet discussion, he seems reluctant when peacemaking requires that he make a judgment between two conflicting parties on a specific question. In 1960, on his way home from the United Nations, he stopped in Bonn, where he declined a suggestion that he serve as a mediator in the German question. "If there were two hot irons, would you touch one of them?" he was quoted as saying to Chancellor Adenauer. Nehru appears willing to be a peacemaker as long as he can stay above the battle. To take sides, he believes, violates his neutrality, increases tension, and makes a solution more difficult.

Nkrumah, though sometimes called the "African Nehru," does not emphasize Cold War mediation by neutrals. Rather, he has advocated the creation of a "nonnuclear third force" of neutral states, "a war-preventing force between the two blocs of the so-called East and West." These states would refuse to "allow their territories to be used as military bases" and would reject "any allegiance dependent upon nuclear weapons." The third bloc (to be composed of African states, or Afro-Asian states, or Afro-Asian plus other uncommitted states) would support causes that promote "world peace and security," and would "exert moral pressure on the two main blocs and prevent them from plunging all of us into the holocaust of a disastrous war." Presumably, Nkrumah's third force would contribute to peace and stability by acting as a buffer and balancer in the bipolar struggle.

Nehru, in contrast to Nkrumah, opposes the creation of an organized third force. He thinks of himself as the chief spokesman for a fluid, *ad hoc* neutral grouping, which he deliberately wants to keep vague. "If a neutral nation joins a neutral bloc it ceases to be a neutral," he has said. In 1960, Nehru successfully resisted pressure by Nasser and President Sukarno to organize another Bandung-type conference of Afro-Asian powers. He reaffirmed this position at the Belgrade Conference, in 1961, when he reminded the delegates of their "lack of strength," exemplified by the fact that they could neither agree on specific solutions nor impose any ideas they might have. Nehru does not even want organized neutral bloc support in his border dispute with the Chinese.

Nasser shows little interest in Nkrumah's third-force proposal or in Nehru's efforts at Cold War mediation because he is preoccupied with concerns closer to home. In June, 1960, he opposed the formation of a neutralist bloc because "we then would have to apply our policy of nonalignment to all three blocs." While he has shown no interest in mediating Cold War disputes, he has tried his hand at mediating between the Algerian rebels and France, in both 1956 and 1961.

Nasser's constant concern with Israel and the problems of consolidating his position at home, especially after the loss of Syria in 1961, have not completely dampened his desire to be the acknowledged spokesman for the entire Arab world. He also has ambitions that reach beyond the Arab world into Black Africa. If he pursues these ambitions seriously, he will clash head-on with the aspirations of Nkrumah and other would-be Pan-African leaders. Since Nasser's first loyalty is to the Arab states, still far from united, the chances that his larger dream will be fulfilled seem remote.[3] His 1955 statement that "the peoples of Africa will continue to look to us [Egypt], who guard their northern gate, and who constitute their link with the outside world" seems naïve and anachronistic in light of the rapid political developments in sub-Saharan Africa in the past seven years.

Nkrumah, a "continental elder statesman" at fifty-three, appears to have as solid a claim as any contender for the role of chief spokesman of an African bloc, although that bloc will probably continue to be represented by several voices. By capitalizing on his understanding of "the African personality," as he calls it, he has pursued his Pan-African political ambitions with more vigor than success. He rules what is, in effect, a one-party government in Ghana, and he bids his people to "seek ye first the political kingdom and all other things shall be added unto you." His attempt to extend his friendly "kingdom" by a merger of Ghana-Guinea-Mali has not succeeded. Even his less ambitious plan for a Ghana-Guinea federation has not made any progress because Soviet-befriended Sékou Touré of Guinea has his own ideas of how Africa should be organized.

Like all Afro-Asian neutrals, Nkrumah works constantly to keep his fences mended in both Cold War camps, but he does not overlook fence-mending nearer at hand. With one eye on Israel's increasing economic activity in Africa and the other on his possible future influence in North Africa, Nkrumah, on the very same day, in 1958, married an Egyptian girl, received a wedding gift from Nasser, and signed a $20 million trade agreement with Israel, Nasser's arch enemy.

U.S. Military Pacts, Military Aid, and Overseas Bases

Nehru, Nasser, and Nkrumah have similar interpretations of American external military activities (pacts, military aid, and bases), but their separate views reflect sharply the pressures and anxieties of local conditions and are adapted to meet changing circumstances. Nehru can never forget Pakistan or Red China. Nasser is preoccupied with Israel. And Nkrumah is devoted to building an African bloc.

MILITARY PACTS

Nehru has denounced, with indiscriminate impartiality, all military alliances—NATO, SEATO, the Baghdad, Warsaw and the Soviet-Chinese pacts—along with his general condemnations of the arms race and big-power rivalry. "This whole approach of the

Cold War and military alliances," unless abated, will "lead to final catastrophe," he said, in 1954. Pacts are bad for all parties because they increase tension and fear. He resented deeply the establishment of SEATO with Pakistan as a member and as a recipient of U.S. military aid. This penetration into India's cherished "area of peace," he said, would disturb "the entire balance of power in this region." It would probably be unfair to ascribe his indignant protests of American aid to Pakistan solely to its bearing on the Kashmir issue. He did use the occasion to invoke larger moral considerations, insisting that such aid spreads the "climate-of-war" mentality and thus endangers the peace.

In 1956, Nasser said that the "policy of military blocs and pacts inevitably results in a suicidal arms race, causes misunderstanding . . . and tensions." More than a year before, he implied that mutual defense pacts between the Arab world and Western powers would be desirable after the Arabs had overcome their residual suspicions of Western designs in the Middle East. At the same time, he warned that "this hammering, hammering, hammering for pacts will only keep alive the old suspicions." When the Baghdad Pact was formed in 1955, tying two Middle Eastern states—Iraq and Turkey—to the West, Nasser said that he was disillusioned, and accused the U.S. and Britain of violating a "gentleman's agreement" to permit Egypt to create a purely Arab defense alliance. "If defensive pacts are necessary in the Arab world," he said in 1959, "they should be formed by Arab countries alone, for the people must feel . . . they are defending their own families . . . not British or American interests."

Nkrumah insists that "blocs and rivalries exacerbate" international disputes. In 1960, he warned the new African states that defense pacts with outside powers will endanger "African unity" and "bring the Cold War to Africa." Later, he said, "A military alliance with any atomic power is . . . a threat to the security of Africa and world peace."

MILITARY ASSISTANCE

The three neutralist leaders appear to have spoken out against U.S. military assistance only when an adversary or rival power was the beneficiary.

Nehru, who relies primarily upon Britain for weapons, has been particularly disturbed about U.S. military aid to Pakistan. In 1957, he said: "It goes against the grain to indulge in an armaments race, but we can no longer ignore the rate" at which the "latest and deadliest weapons are pouring into Pakistan"; presumably, he assumed Pakistan was arming against India. In August, 1961, Nehru said he was considering the purchase of supersonic jet fighters to match those supplied to Pakistan by the U.S. In spite of the Pakistan problem, and even though Chinese troops occupy 12,000 square miles of Indian territory (according to traditional boundaries), Nehru continues to refuse U.S. military aid, although he does welcome moral support from America. Since the end of 1959, Indian opinion generally sees Communist China as a much greater threat than Pakistan, and apparently Nehru now shares this view. While India does not accept direct American military aid, she has received indirect assistance. The $3 billion in economic aid from the U.S. has helped India develop heavy industry essential to the manufacture of modern weapons and has released a substantial portion of domestic resources for national defense. India has bought a small amount of military equipment from Washington on a commercial basis.

In 1954, three weeks after signing the agreement for the withdrawal of British troops from Suez, Nasser said that the Middle East needs, and will accept arms from the West. A year later, shortly after his arms deal with the Soviet bloc, he accused the United States of a "deliberate attempt to maintain the military superiority of Israel over the Arabs," and complained that, after trying for three years, he was unable to get a single piece of armament from the U.S. He has continued to receive a substantial amount of arms from the Soviet orbit.

Nkrumah secures his weapons and other forms of military assistance mainly from Britain, but in November, 1961, he announced that he would buy an undisclosed amount of Soviet bloc military equipment to supplement British arms. He has had little to say for or against U.S. military aid. In his *Foreign Affairs* article, in 1958, he made a general statement deploring "the use of the sale of arms as a means of influencing other nations' diplomacy."

U.S. OVERSEAS BASES

The views of neutralist leaders about U.S. bases, like their views on American military aid, are expressed almost exclusively in terms of their national interests, although Nehru frequently invokes universal values.

Nehru's persistent opposition to American military bases falls under his general condemnation of all tension-producing elements in the East-West struggle. Overseas bases, in particular, he has said on various occasions, give the Soviet Union a feeling of being encircled. This frightens the Russians and leads to further tension and, thus, is a threat to peace. Nehru has shown considerable reluctance to make critical reference to the Soviet moves that prompted the United States to establish bases in the first place; his recent troubles with China may have modified his outlook on this point.

Nasser has spoken out against atomic-missile bases in Turkey and has called for the liquidation of all foreign military bases, recalling that in 1956, Egypt was "attacked from military bases in Cyprus and Malta."

Nkrumah's views on military bases are focused on the problem of keeping Africa free of nuclear weapons. He has urged the United Nations to "prevent any state having nuclear weapons from possessing military bases on the African continent."

Nuclear Weapons and Arms Control

The neutralist leaders are virtually unanimous in their opposition to nuclear weapons, and in their support of disarmament proposals. In the United Nations, the emergent states have voted as a bloc in support of efforts to stop nuclear testing, to prevent the spread of nuclear weapons, and to reduce and control arms generally. On these issues, the Afro-Asian states almost always vote with the Soviet Union and against the United States when there is a difference between the two, which there often is, and which usually involves verification or control. The mild censure of the U.S.S.R. for unilaterally resuming nuclear tests in the atmosphere, in 1961, was a notable exception. The Soviet Union makes sweeping proposals for "general and complete" disarmament, and the United States insists on proceeding in stages, with appropriate verification procedures at each stage.

This persistent pattern before September, 1961, was illustrated in 1960 at the Fifteenth General Assembly of the U.N., when the neutralists enabled the U.S.S.R. to get three arms-control resolutions passed by comfortable majorities. The U.S. abstained on all three votes. The balloting, in which no negative votes were cast, was as follows: The Assembly called upon all governments, nuclear and nonnuclear, to prevent wider dissemination of nuclear weapons (sixty-eight voted yes, twenty-six abstained); it urged the states concerned to conclude an agreement on the prohibition of nuclear weapons tests and to continue the then-existing voluntary suspension of such tests (eighty-eight voted yes; five abstained); and it urged these states to reach agreement on the cessation of tests "under proper international control" (eighty-three voted yes; eleven abstained). Acknowledging its sympathy for the "spirit which prompted" these resolutions, the U.S. spokesman said his government abstained because they involved unverified commitments of an indefinite duration which are "an unacceptable substitute for verified agreements."

While the disarmament views expressed by Nehru, Nasser, and Nkrumah at the 1960 session of the General Assembly are generally consistent with their previously stated positions, there has been a gradual shift in Nehru's views toward a greater appreciation for the complexities of the arms-control problem, and hence a greater sympathy for the U.S. position.[4] In his October 3, 1960, speech, Nehru supported an early agreement on banning weapons tests. Though such a ban is not really disarmament, he said, it would "bring a large measure of relief to the world." "Disarmament must include the prohibition of the manufacture, storage and use of weapons of mass destruction, as well as the progressive limitation of conventional weapons," and it "should take place in stages . . . to maintain broadly the balance of armed power." Disarmament without controls, he added, "is not a feasible proposition. It is even more clear that controls without disarmament have no meaning . . . both questions should be tackled simultaneously." In October, 1961, Nehru said the explosion of the 30-megaton Soviet bomb was "regrettable."

Nasser's comments on arms control in his September 27, 1960, speech before the United Nations were vague and admonitory. He demanded "that an end be put to nuclear weapons tests and that the big powers get rid of the huge piles of nuclear weapons," urged "a system of controls conducive to tranquility and security," and called for a "continuous reduction of the armaments budgets."

In his Assembly speech of September 23, 1960, Nkrumah emphasized the economic implications of the arms race and the role of neutrals in arms control. Armaments, he said, "threaten the future of mankind," and divert resources that should be devoted to closing the gap between the "developed and underdeveloped countries." He urged that this problem be studied, along with the technical aspects of controlling nuclear weapons. Disarmament would be facilitated, he added, if the great powers agreed on a control system in which the inspection teams would be composed of only "certain members of the small uncommitted nations. This would eliminate all suspicion, create confidence in the inspection method." A week later he endorsed Khrushchev's proposal that a group of "uncommitted" nations be added to the existing ten-nation East-West disarmament committee. Two years before, he had called for the representation of African states "on all international bodies concerned with disarmament."

Except for Nehru's increasing sophistication on the arms control question, the approach of the three leaders has been almost identical. Primarily concerned with eliminating or reducing nuclear weapons, they have said little or nothing about arms control among the small powers. Since they have been more interested in inveighing against the nuclear-arms race than in examining concrete proposals for tackling the control problem, they have almost always endorsed, tacitly or explicitly, the Soviet propaganda position in the United Nations and outside. Often, they have seemed to confuse devious Soviet disarmament propaganda with a genuine desire for peace, and American candor and concern for control with a lack of interest in peace. Their views at the Belgrade Conference, which convened the day after the Soviet Union unilaterally resumed nuclear tests in the atmosphere, reflected a change toward the Western position, a change for which Nehru can take some of the credit. The three leaders supported the Conference declaration, which called for a test moratorium, a ban on all nuclear tests, and a "general and complete disarmament" treaty "guaranteed by an effective system of inspection and control" under an international team.

Nehru, Communism, and the United States

Nehru's neutralism has sometimes been criticized as naïve, inconsistent, one-sided, and even "immoral" by American spokesmen. He has been accused of using a more generous standard in judging Communist behavior than in judging the behavior of the West. His response to certain international issues during the past decade has lent credence to these charges of inconsistency. How could this urbane, Cambridge-educated gentleman, dedicated to Western democratic values and human rights, repeatedly seem to condone Communist brutality and, at the same time, criticize the lesser evils of the Western democracies?

Nehru's response to the Hungarian revolt in 1956 is the most vivid illustration of the problem. In three key United Nations resolutions condemning the Soviet suppression of the revolt, each of which passed the General Assembly with a substantial majority, India abstained. In each case, the Soviet bloc voted against the resolution. The votes were as follows: *Nov. 4, 1956:* On a resolution calling upon the U.S.S.R. to desist from armed attack against the people of Hungary and to withdraw its forces, fifty voted yes, eight voted no, fifteen abstained; *Dec. 12, 1956:* On a resolution condemning Soviet action in depriving Hungary of its freedom and independence, fifty-five voted yes, eight voted no, thirteen abstained; *Jan. 10, 1957:* On a resolution calling for establishing a committee of five nations to investigate conditions in Hungary, fifty-nine voted yes, eight voted no, ten abstained.

In a speech on November 9, 1956, Nehru justified India's abstention on the November 4 resolution by labeling the military action in Hungary as "civil conflict" and the situation as "very confusing." In the same speech, he is reported to have given "in detail and without a trace of counterbalance" the justification for the Soviet attack that he had received from Bulganin.

In sharp contrast to his efforts to excuse or explain the Soviet repression in Hungary, Nehru repeatedly and in the strongest terms attacked the Anglo-French invasion of Egypt in October, 1956. He promptly dispatched a vigorous message to Secretary-General Hammarskjold saying that India was profoundly shocked and urging the United Nations to take "strong" measures. The Hungarian crisis, which had been developing since October 23, brought no public statement from Nehru or any other Indian leader until November 5, when Nehru employed the phrase "a plague on both houses": "We see today in Egypt, as well as in Hungary, both human dignity and freedom outraged by the force of arms to suppress peoples and to gain political objectives." This statement appears to contradict his speech four days later, when he called the Hungarian war a "civil conflict."

Nehru has not hesitated to condemn the violation of human rights in South Africa and in all the colonial countries of Asia and Africa. But he has been reluctant to criticize the suppression of fundamental rights in Eastern Europe. During the United Nations debates on Communist violations of human rights in the Assembly sessions of 1949 and 1950, for example, India remained silent and abstained on every resolution.

This lopsided public concern for human rights, which seems to provide a moral sanction for Soviet violations and moral condemnation for Western sins, can be explained, at least in part, by a cardinal principle in Nehru's philosophy—his conviction that peace is the primary objective of foreign policy—and, in part, by his deep-seated anticolonialism. His single-minded dedication to peace (for big powers) provides him with a larger consistency underlying his smaller inconsistencies. For him there is no double standard. He has one yardstick, which might be called his "climate-of-peace" theory. All acts of states are judged by whether they contribute to a "climate of peace" or a "climate of war." According to this flexible yardstick, "colonialism," the overlordship of subject peoples, is morally wrong because it violates human rights and politically inadmissible because it leads to tension and tension makes for a "climate of war." The Anglo-French attack on Suez, the French war against the Algerian nationalists, and South Africa's policy of apartheid all violate his anticolonial principles and poison the "climate of peace."

Soviet suppression of the Hungarian "freedom fighters," on the other hand, did not fall under Nehru's anticolonial strictures. Further, the Western-sponsored condemnation of Soviet behavior at the U.N., according to his view, was ineffectual and served only to increase Cold War tension, and, thus, militated against the "climate of peace." Nehru's strong emphasis on avoiding tension at times prompts him to condemn, not the party guilty of rocking the boat, but rather the party criticizing the guilty party. He whips the horse that pulls.

Nehru's relationship to any Cold War issue cannot be understood apart from this intense preoccupation with the problem of how to create a psychological climate conducive to the relaxation of tensions and the peaceful solution of conflicts. This explains why he has sought to nurture an environment of negotiation and mediation. He seems to believe that fear, mutual suspicion, and misunderstanding, rather than the substantive conflicts of interest and irreconcilable demands that divide nations, are the fundamental roots of war. The primary peacemaking task, therefore, is to create an atmosphere of trust and understanding. His publicly expressed confidence in the rationality and moral capacity of men and nations is almost indistinguishable from the faith of the nineteenth-century idealists in the West.

But Nehru's political behavior is not fully consistent with his public philosophy, and there are signs that his philosophy itself is gradually changing under the impact of events at home and abroad. His emphasis on method rather than on substance in confronting Cold War conflicts tends to be reversed when he deals with issues of vital concern to India, such as his disputes with Pakistan over Kashmir and with Portugal over Goa. Here he focuses on substance, on conflicting demands; and ironically, the great powers have emphasized method—negotiation, plebiscites, and mediation. Nehru's approach to Kashmir, is, to say the least, a pragmatic adaptation of this climate-of-peace doctrine. The Goan invasion, although not a direct Cold War issue, also illustrates the centrality of the national interest over instrumental values such as mediation or nonviolence.

As a champion of peaceful coexistence, Nehru attempts to get along with both camps in the Cold War. He has no basic ideological dispute with democratic America. Concerning Communism, he has said that "Marx is out of date," Communism as a system is oppressive and cruel, and that the U.S.S.R. and Red China are "monolithic states." He has also said he prefers Communism to Fascism because "at least it aims at something better." Further, Nehru believes that the Communist regimes in Russia and China will probably become more moderate with the passage of time, because history shows that a "proselytizing creed" is gradually "toned down" and, eventually, learns to coexist peacefully.

Nehru's disinclination to acknowledge the element of threat in world Communism has been challenged by a series of actions starting with the Hungarian revolt, in 1956. Two years later came the revolt in Tibet, which, in 1959, was followed by the violation of the generally accepted northern frontier of India by the Red Chinese. In that year, also, came the revolt against the Communist government of India's Kerala state. In every case, with the possible exception of Kerala, Nehru reacted more slowly and more moderately than did important sectors of articulate opinion in India.

Nehru's mild response to Peking's harassment of Indians in Tibet in 1959 drew sharp criticism from some journalists and politicians. *The Times* of India commented: "Is there no limit to the humiliation we are prepared to accept at China's hands?" One correspondent said that, for the first time since 1937, when Nehru became India's foreign-affairs expert, "Indian opinion affirmed itself instead of waiting" to hear from Nehru. He added: "Indians are fed up with China and weary of Nehru's wisdom."

When China violated the traditional border of India, Nehru announced a "dual policy" of "defense and negotiation." His response was criticized by Parliament and the press. Opposition members accused him of appeasement. A *New York Times* correspondent said on September 5, 1959: "A study of leading Indian newspapers suggests that Mr. Nehru has been so far behind public opinion on Communist China in recent months that he may have to run to catch up." Six days later, Nehru told Parliament that China's claim for huge areas along India's Tibetan border "is quite impossible for any Indian to discuss, whatever the consequences." This strong statement drew loud cheers. He has pursued his policy of "defense and negotiation" ever since. After his talks with Premier Chou En-lai in April, 1960, Nehru said there was "no meeting ground at all" between them and expressed doubt about the value of projected talks between India and China. Toward the end of 1961, he stepped up his criticism of China as an aggressor, sent military reinforcements to the frontier territory, and said India may eventually be compelled to use force to defend its rights.

Of all the Communist challenges he responded to, Nehru acted most forthrightly in dealing with the Kerala problem. He expelled the elected Communist administration in Kerala and said that the Indian Communists were the "real reactionaries" clutching outdated economic theories. He and other Indians were outraged when the local Communists justified China's border violations.

What all this adds up to in terms of a revision of Nehru's views toward Communism, coexistence, or nonalignment is open to debate. He still clings to the slogans of coexistence and nonalignment, but there may be a deeper change in his outlook and, perhaps, in his foreign policy. Some observers have said that Russia's betrayal of Hungary and China's betrayal of India have brought India to the end of neutralism, the end of ambiguity. This new orientation, said one Indian commentator, was proclaimed to the world on December 9, 1959, when the Indians received President Eisenhower in New Delhi: "On that day, many onlookers agree, even the mirage of Indian neutrality was swept into the ash can of history. . . . While technically there has been no change in official policy, Indian public opinion has veered sharply even from military noninvolvement. . . . The Five Principles of Coexistence (Panch Shila) have been turned by China into another scrap of paper."

Without probing into deeper changes Nehru may have experienced, his present public statements do reveal a greater understanding for the American position in the Cold War struggle, than they did at any previous time. This was true of his statements on the Berlin crisis in 1961, but only after some straight talking by

U.S. Ambassador John Kenneth Galbraith. He also showed an understanding of U.S. policies in his behavior at the Belgrade Conference.

Philosophically and politically, except for the "colonial" issue, he has been with the West all along. Just as he has become increasingly concerned with the substantive aspects of the disarmament dialogue between the U.S.S.R. and the U.S., he may now see more clearly that India has a stake in the issues that divide the world. If this is true, he will be less concerned with creating a climate of negotiation and more concerned with the merits of the conflicting positions. *The Times* of India observed in October, 1960:

> On Berlin, disarmament, atomic control and on other issues, both the Soviet Union and the West have submitted proposals; to these the Asian-African powers must react unequivocally without taking refuge in vague resolutions containing nothing more original than a proposal that the Soviet leader and the U.S. President should contact each other.

Nasser, the Aswan Dam, and the Communists

Using *Life* magazine as a platform, Nasser, in July, 1959, complained that he had been bitterly attacked by both the Communists and the West. The Communists had criticized him "all the way from *The Daily Worker* in London to *The Red Flag* in Peking," and Khrushchev had recently called him a "hotheaded young man." On the other hand, Nasser added, "my critics in the West assert that I am responsible for opening the Middle East to Communism."

The ambiguity of the major Cold War protagonists toward Nasser is largely a reflection of Nasser's ambiguity toward them. This ambivalence is rooted in Nasser's brand of neutralism, which has been less aloof and less correct than the neutralism of Nehru. Nehru maintains that he has attempted to stand above the battle, to remain uninvolved in strictly Cold War issues, except as a mediator. Nasser has shown little interest in mediation. In fact, he has tended to use the Cold War to advance his own political objectives. His policy of capitalizing on the bipolar struggle has involved risks and he has been buffeted from one side to the other.

For Nasser, as for Nehru, the Cold War is a secondary concern. His primary interest is to advance Arab nationalism under his leadership and to destroy the influence of Israel. His attitude toward the United States and the Soviet Union tends to be determined more by the policies of these countries toward Israel, than by all their other foreign policies combined. "So long as Moscow and Peking oppose Israel, they are regarded through a rosy lens," said C. L. Sulzberger in 1961.

Nasser's intense concentration on Arab interests, and his willingness to exploit Cold War rivalries to advance these interests, account for his vacillation and contradictions on the Communist issue. In 1954, he said that if there is aggression in the Middle East, it will come from "the Communist world." On April 3, 1955, he reaffirmed this view, just five months before it was learned that Egypt had received a large shipment of heavy arms from the Soviet bloc. Nasser's growing criticism of the West, spurred by his failure to get Western arms and by the inclusion of Turkey and Iraq in the Baghdad Pact, appeared to be temporarily assuaged in the aura of good will following the departure of the last British troops from the Suez Canal zone in June, 1956. A month later, he expressed deep bitterness when Secretary of State John Foster Dulles abruptly withdrew the U.S. offer to help build the Aswan High Dam. Mr. Dulles cited the weakness of the Egyptian economy as the reason for his action, although he was motivated chiefly by Cairo's arms deal with the Communists. Nasser immediately accused Washington of lying about Egypt's economy and exclaimed: "May you choke to death on your fury!" He asserted that Egypt would build the High Dam without Western assistance and retaliated by nationalizing the Suez Canal. He had been studying the question of nationalization for some time, he said, but Dulles' abrupt withdrawal "made up our minds for us." This led directly to the Anglo-French attack on Egypt in October, 1956, which Nasser interpreted as an untimely and brutal reassertion of Western imperialism.

Nasser's growing economic and military dependence upon the Soviet bloc, stimulated by the Suez crisis, was accompanied by increasing political cordiality with the U.S.S.R. and increasing estrangement from the United States. In March, 1957, Nasser said that America was trying to starve his people by refusing them wheat, whereas Russia had sent Egypt 600,000 tons the previous year. In an interview with William Atwood of *Look* three months later, Nasser made these points: (1) Soviet-bloc aid comes without strings; U.S. aid carries unacceptable conditions amounting to control. (2) Communist aid "helped us survive" and to "escape domination of the West." (3) Egypt did not vote for any of the ten U.N. resolutions criticizing Soviet military action in Hungary because "the Soviet Union was the only country in the Security Council that supported us in our dispute over the Suez Canal. We abstained out of gratitude." (4) "We were attacked by your British and French allies. We were threatened by Dulles. I read what they call me in the American press. . . . It is hard for me to trust you." (5) In 1954, Egypt was on friendly terms with America. "But you refused us the weapons we needed; you organized the Baghdad Pact aimed at dividing the Arabs; you withdrew your offer to help us build the Aswan High Dam. So we drifted apart."

In the same interview, Nasser also expressed some distrust of "local Communist parties" because they "always work to seize power. . . . Their objectives are dangerous—and that is why the Communist Party is illegal in Egypt. But our people do not have to like Communism to feel sympathy and friendship for Russia." In September, 1957, he said: "The Soviet Union has helped us in all our crises. When we faced starvation after last year's attack, the Soviets sold us wheat and petroleum and the United States refused." In November, 1958, on the day that six Soviet experts arrived to work out the details of a 400-million-ruble loan for the Aswan Dam, Nasser reaffirmed his policy of nonalignment and praised Soviet–U.A.R. friendship.

Nasser's friendship for Russia suffered a sharp setback in March, 1959, after the revolt in Iraq, when he accused the Soviet Union of trying to destroy the United Arab Republic. Premier Kassim and Arab Communists, he declared, were "agents of a foreign power" trying to split the U.A.R. "The Communists, who think they can march against us from Baghdad, will, with the help of Allah, be the losers. The banner of Arab nationalism will be raised over Baghdad also, as it was when the Tartars were routed. . . . As we crushed the imperialist agents, we will also crush the Communist agents. . . . We believed at the beginning of our Revolution that the Communists were independent, but they proved to be agents of Moscow. . . . The Soviet Union interfered in our internal affairs."

Premier Khrushchev replied by saying that Nasser's anti-Communist policy was "doomed to failure" and that Nasser was a "rather hotheaded young man" who "took upon himself more than his stature permitted."

Nasser said he was subsequently attacked by "Communist radios and newspapers . . . from Bulgaria to China." Two months later, he reported that Mr. Khrushchev had given him renewed assurances of nonintervention in Arab affairs, but that Nasser had adopted a wait-and-see attitude.

Throughout 1960 and 1961, Nasser's ambiguity toward Communism persisted. In February, 1960, he renewed his anti-Communist campaign and said that Communist agents in Bulgaria were still plotting against the U.A.R. But two months later, in sharp contrast, he said Chinese Communist volunteers would not worry him if they fought with Moslem nationalists for independence in Algeria. Acknowledging "the clouds which overshadowed our friendly relations with the Soviet Union in the past," Nasser in May, 1960, said the Soviets did not threaten the U.A.R. with economic blockade and, in general, pursued a "wise and noble policy toward us." This "noble policy" has not precluded attacks on Nasser for his treatment of domestic Communists in Egypt. In March, a Communist theoretical journal published in Prague declared that "more than 200 Communists and democrats have been thrown into prison" and treated worse than "vicious criminals." In June, Egyptian and Soviet papers engaged in a vigorous exchange.

Nasser still claims that he is ideologically neutral and politically unaligned, that he is pragmatic rather than dogmatic about big-power issues. He shows little interest in substantive Cold War questions. He has tried to use the Cold War rather than permit himself to be used by it. Most of his outside assistance has come from the Communist camp, although the U.S. is still helping the U.A.R. On April 7, 1961, for example, President Kennedy asked Congress to appropriate $10 million to help salvage historic monuments that would be submerged by the waters of the new Aswan High Dam. In the following month, the U.S. agreed to "sell" the U.A.R. $36.4 million worth of wheat and invest the counterpart funds earned thereby in Egyptian development projects. It was reported in January, 1962, that Nasser had made a new arms deal with Russia, primarily involving ships. Nasser welcomes assistance when it serves his ends and condemns it when it interferes with his purposes. The key to his attitude toward Communism and the United States is his dedication to Arab nationalism and his ambition to be its chief leader and spokesman. "By military solidarity and by voluntary cooperation in economics, culture, and foreign policy, the Arab nations can grow strong in their own right." How independent and neutral Nasser really is, is a question that cannot be answered from a study of his public utterances alone. But he certainly leans toward the Communist camp.

Nkrumah Between East and West

If Nasser's neutralism has leaned toward the East, Nkrumah's neutralism, at least in the past, has leaned slightly toward the West. Except where the colonial problem is directly at issue, Nkrumah's relations with Ghana's former colonial master, Britain, have been cordial, in contrast to the strained relations between the U.A.R. and the United Kingdom. Like Nehru and Nasser, Nkrumah is primarily concerned with domestic and regional problems and only secondarily with Cold War issues.

Nkrumah is flexible and pragmatic. Twenty years ago, he called himself an "orthodox Marxist," ten years later a "Marxist social-ist," and more recently a "Christian Marxist." In consolidating his political position, he has drawn upon Marxist analysis and Western democratic experience and has adapted both to the "African per-sonality." Ghana has no Communist Party.

As early as 1953, Nkrumah said: "As we would not have British masters, so we would not have Russian masters." Addressing the All-African Peoples' Conference in December, 1958, he warned that "colonialism and imperialism may come to us yet in a differ-ent guise, not necessarily from Europe." This statement was under-stood variously to refer to Soviet expansion, to Communist pene-tration through Egypt, and to direct Egyptian expansion. A week earlier, Nkrumah said that Nasser had corrupted the noninterfer-ence principles of the Bandung Conference and had intruded Asian and Communist influences into African affairs. More recently, Nkrumah has attempted to develop a concert of views with the U.A.R. and Morocco.

After talking with President Kennedy in March, 1961, Nkrumah voiced his preference for the United States over the Communist camp and warned Americans not to equate anticolonialism with Communism. Cordial Ghana–U.S. relations were jarred by Nkru-mah's message to Premier Fidel Castro in April, 1961: "Please accept my personal congratulations on the news of the successful crushing of the recent invasion of Cuba." Nkrumah did not regard this expression of anticolonialism as a violation of his neutrality on Cold War issues. In July, 1961, he told the workers at a Budapest factory that Ghana has chosen "the same direction of development as you have chosen."

Nkrumah has gladly accepted nonmilitary assistance from both sides. In 1958, he said that Ghana will develop "with the interest and support of the West, or . . . be compelled to turn elsewhere.

This is not a warning or a threat, but a straight statement of political reality." Ghana's trade and aid ties have been mainly with Britain and the United States. America has been providing technical assistance at a rate of about $1 million a year and, since 1958, has been helping Ghana design a large hydroelectric dam for the Volta River. In the latter half of 1961, Nkrumah ran into serious economic and political trouble at home. In August, Peking announced a $19-million, five-year, development loan, without interest. In October, when Nkrumah returned from a nine-week trip to the Soviet Union, Red China, and Eastern Europe, during which he attended the Belgrade Conference, he promptly dismissed his British chief of staff and all other British officers from command posts and announced that he would augment his British arms by purchasing Soviet weapons. About seventy Ghanaian cadets were flown to Moscow for military training and hundreds more were scheduled to follow. The trickle of Soviet-bloc technicians began to increase. Concurrently, Nkrumah cracked down on his political opponents with an authoritarian whip.

In spite of these developments and Nkrumah's pro-Soviet posture at Belgrade, the United States, after a last-minute reappraisal, decided to go ahead with its offer of $133 million in loans to help build the Volta River Dam and an aluminum-smelter project in Ghana. The Soviet Union is presently designing another hydroelectric dam further upstream on the Volta River. Nkrumah openly acknowledged his help from the Communist bloc in a statement on November 27, 1961, at the opening of the U.S. trade fair in Accra: "We make no apology . . . for the steps we have taken recently to strengthen our trade and economic relations with the Soviet Union, Eastern European countries, and China." Reaffirming his "positive neutralism and nonalignment," he warned Americans not to be misled by recent press reports that "put the worst possible construction on everything we do."

Nkrumah's neutralism, like the neutralism of Nehru and Nasser, is a logical outgrowth of a foreign policy based upon a shrewd calculation of the national interest combined with a crusading anticolonialism. This strong anticolonial bias sometimes leads to less-than-prudent pronouncements and policies.

Conclusions

This study of the views of Nehru, Nasser, and Nkrumah on neutralism yields certain general observations that apply equally to India, the United Arab Republic, and Ghana, as well as to other neutralist states of Asia and Africa. Qualifications of any of the observations will be indicated.

1. The primary concern of all the neutralist states is *not* neutralism but nationalism. Their first task is to build a viable nation-state, to consolidate their newly gained political independence, and to develop economically. Anticolonialism, the desire to gain or maintain independence from former European colonial powers, is the strongest psychological-political force. Nationalism and anticolonialism are two expressions of the same force.

For neutralist states, therefore, the primary struggle in world politics is the conflict between nationalism and colonialism, not the conflict between the Communist world and the free world, or between the Soviet Union and the United States, or between Communism as a political system and Western democracy. The main threat to their interests and aspirations, as they see it, is colonialism, not Communism, although we can expect a gradual lessening of interest in the classic colonial issue during the decade ahead.

2. Neutralism, or nonalignment, as the neutrals all prefer to call it, is primarily a response to the Cold War, and only in part a product of rising nationalism. It takes three to make a neutral. Afro-Asian neutralism is a function of bipolarity. The foreign policies of the new states are influenced by both the colonial past and the Cold War, but there is no necessary or consistent relation between the two. Some new states clearly lean toward the Communist bloc, and others toward the West; two such states, Pakistan and the Philippines, are aligned militarily with the U.S.

3. The leaders of the emergent states who have chosen nonalignment believe that this position best serves their national interests. Though they admit that prudence and necessity dictate a neutralist policy, the three leaders often interpret and justify their nonalignment at home and abroad in terms of high moral principles. Sometimes they say their policy is an outgrowth of the national character or tradition, and sometimes they claim that it is the best way for their country to contribute to world peace. Of the three men, Nehru is the most inclined to interpret his policies in terms of moral principle, and Nasser the least. In this dichotomous justification for their foreign policy, the neutralists are little different from the leaders of aligned states, great and small, who seek to interpret their policies in the most acceptable terms.

If a prudent regard for the national interest is the determining consideration, it follows that the neutralist leaders pursue a strictly neutral course only when it serves their interests, and depart from it when it does not. Under the pressure of serving the national interest, their attachment to neutralism is pragmatic rather than doctrinaire; instrumental rather than absolute; and transitory rather than permanent.

4. Because they represent countries that are small and relatively uninvolved in the Cold War conflicts, Afro-Asian neutralist leaders tend to feel morally superior to the leaders of aligned states. They sometimes feel that they are uncorrupted by power and that they possess an innocence and detachment that qualifies them to speak for reason and humanity—a role denied to powerful and guilty nations. In a speech before the U.N. Assembly in 1960, Premier Saeb Salaam of Lebanon expressed this view: "We, the small, uncommitted nations, can perhaps take a more objective view of the world situation. We can judge international issues with comparatively greater detachment and impartiality; in a sense, the small uncommitted nations can be said to represent the unbiased conscience of humanity." Nehru reflects this mood more fully than either Nasser or Nkrumah, and he has in this spirit attempted to serve as a mediator between the Cold War adversaries. With this conception of his mission, Nehru must have been shocked when Nepal, in 1960, pointedly included India, along with the U.S., the U.S.S.R. and Communist China, among the countries that should not interfere in its affairs. And he did not enjoy being called a hypocrite and aggressor because of his attack on Goa by the very nations he had so often criticized for using, or threatening to use, force.

All three men have supported efforts for the elimination or reduction of nuclear weapons with humanitarian arguments, but they have shown little concern for the merits of alternative proposals for dealing with the problem.

5. The neutralist nations both suffer and profit from the existence of the Cold War, but they probably profit more, at least in the short run, than they suffer. By playing one side against the other, consciously or unconsciously, Nehru, Nasser, and Nkrumah have each received economic aid from both. The great bulk of India's aid has come from the United States, the preponderance of Egypt's aid from the Communist bloc. If there were no Cold War, these and other Afro-Asian neutrals would probably be getting less outside help. They enjoy an additional economic advantage because of their military uninvolvement in either camp; by remaining unaligned, their defense budget may be smaller than it otherwise

would be. As a result, they can devote a larger portion of their national resources to economic development.

To put it another way, the relative balance of power between the chief Cold War antagonists has produced a degree of military stability in the world. Both the U.S. and the U.S.S.R. tend to deter each other from attacking independent states. This "extended deterrence" provides a measure of security for the uncommitted states, security they would otherwise have to buy through membership in an alliance, through a bigger defense establishment, or through both. In short, neutrals are protected as well as endangered by the Cold War. In the long run, the Cold War may, of course, erupt into a hot nuclear war in which the whole world, including the neutrals, would suffer.

6. The contribution of the neutrals to the preservation of international peace and stability is severely limited. Their efforts to mediate big-power disputes are effective only when the big powers are willing to compromise their differences. If that willingness is present, an agreement can probably be reached through normal diplomatic channels, without mediation. When the big powers do agree, neutrals can often make an instrumental contribution by providing personnel or armed forces for an impartial observation team or a U.N. police force.

Theoretically, one neutral state, or a bloc of neutrals, could play a role as a balancer, but in the present situation of nuclear bipolarity, with the great disparity between nuclear and nonnuclear powers, this role is not feasible. Furthermore, the neutrals do not possess enough unity to form a coherent and viable bloc.

The Times of India, in 1960, pointed out that "the Afro-Asian bloc has tended to overestimate its capacity for peacemaking largely as a result of the misplaced enthusiasm" of certain Western and Soviet spokesmen for "the so-called third bloc," and added: "It is necessary to reject such fulsome flattery in favor of a less idealized version of what the Asian-African powers can do to promote world peace."

7. Since neutralism is not rooted in an absolute principle, but rather is an outgrowth of circumstances, we may expect constant adaptation in the foreign policies of neutralist states in response to changing conditions. There have been small but significant modifications in India's policies as a result of Communist China's expansion into Tibet and her penetration of India's northern frontier. Nasser has also modified his policies in response to Communist pressures in the Middle East. Neutralist leaders, like political lead-

ers of other states, are responsive to the changing interpretation of the sources and natures of primary and secondary threats to the security of their nation. Neutralism as a position or a policy will be discarded when it no longer serves the national purpose.

8. While it is relatively easy for an Afro-Asian state to pursue a neutralist foreign policy, it is difficult, if not impossible, for it to be objectively neutral in a world torn by a profound struggle between the West and the Communist bloc. Secretary of State Dean Rusk, in March, 1961, after he had talked with Nehru, was asked what the United States meant by a neutral government in Laos. He replied: "A country which is not committed in any military sense to any side, that is not a base of penetrational operations for anyone, that is, a country not under the domination of outsiders, a country whose own leaders can order its affairs, including its own foreign policy."

Few Afro-Asian nations qualify for membership in the neutral club according to this definition. Moreover, even an objectively neutral nation will cease to be so if its vital interests demand temporary alignment in a time of crisis. In short, neutrality tends to be an ephemeral luxury enjoyed by certain states blessed by a favorable combination of geographic, economic, military, and political factors. In a bipolar situation, neutrality is a viable posture only when the nation's vital interests are not threatened by either side. Today, when national interest is at stake, a responsible neutralist statesman cannot avoid the burden of deciding between competing alternatives offered by the West and the Communist bloc.

9. The degree of foreign policy unity within the Afro-Asian neutralist bloc depends upon the issue in question. At the United Nations, these states have usually voted as a bloc because they were responding either to the colonial problem or to general resolutions on peace. This unity based on either anticolonialism or a vague desire for world peace tends to give way to differences when local interests and conflicts are involved. One American official observed: "They may all vote together for the big generalities of peace and disarmament, but when it comes to dividing up aid, they're at each other's throats." This is to be expected, because these countries are by no means identical in history, culture, or economic development, and there are many rival political interests that divide them. In spite of this diversity, the African heads of government at the twenty-nation conference in Monrovia, in May, 1961, passed a resolution declaring that they will, in the future, vote as a single bloc at the United Nations. This declaratory statement really

means that on general issues of peace, disarmament, and colonialism, they will probably vote as a unit. It hardly means they will vote as a bloc on an issue involving a dispute between two or more of their own members. At Belgrade, Nehru sounded a more realistic note when he warned his fellow neutrals to weigh correctly "both our actual and potential strength and lack of strength," pointing out that the unaligned nations possess neither the prerequisite unity for a consensus on specific world issues nor the power to impose such a consensus if they could reach it.

VII

THE NONALIGNED STATES AND
THE UNITED NATIONS

by FRANCIS O. WILCOX*

IN the minds of many people, the United Nations is once again going through a period of agonizing reappraisal. This stems from a number of factors, but in large part it is due to the actual and potential impact of the Afro-Asian nations—and particularly the nonaligned countries—upon the organization.

The United Nations is not merely passing through a normal period of growing pains. Rather, it is in the far more painful throes of a profound transformation that transcends anything the framers of its Charter had in mind. Whether it will survive is not the question. Just how, and in what form, it will survive is of great interest to all mankind.

In 1945, when the United Nations was launched in San Francisco it emerged from the deliberations largely as a creation of the Western world. Its rationale was Western; it was deeply rooted in the values and cultural patterns of the West; and it was based upon Western legal concepts and Western ways of doing things.

Its membership, too, reflected the predominantly Western character of the organization. The roll at San Francisco was made up chiefly of countries from Latin America, Western Europe, and the British Commonwealth. It included only four countries from the African continent—Egypt, Ethiopia, Liberia, and the Union of South Africa—and only thirteen states from the entire Afro-Asian land mass stretching from Japan to Morocco were represented.

In these circumstances, it is quite understandable why the West-

* I wish to express my appreciation to Donald E. Weatherbee, of The Johns Hopkins School of Advanced International Studies, for research assistance in the preparation of this material.

ern point of view has usually prevailed in the United Nations. It was a Western organization, guided by Western parliamentary practices and procedures, and led, for the most part, by staff members and diplomats from Western countries. Despite Soviet obstructionism, the United Nations by and large did what the Western world wanted it to do.

Today, all this is changing. The United Nations is no longer Western, in either membership or outlook. Of the 104 members of the United Nations in the spring of 1962, 29 came from the African continent—the largest single regional group of states in the organization. Fifty-one, or almost half the total membership, belonged to the Afro-Asian group.

It should be emphasized at the outset that the nonaligned states are by no means identical with the Afro-Asian group. Forty-three of the fifty-one countries referred to above may be classed as nonaligned, because they are not involved in regional or other alliances of the Western world or the Soviet bloc. In addition to this number, one must add the seven non–Afro-Asian states of neutralist persuasion: Austria, Cyprus, Finland, Ireland, Israel, Sweden, and Yugoslavia. The degree of nonalignment in the neutral states varies greatly, of course. Some countries, like Guinea, Mali, and Indonesia, lean toward the Soviet Union. Others, like Malaya, Liberia, and Cameroun, lean toward the West. Still others sit rather solidly on the fence.

It is always difficult to measure intangibles in mathematical terms. Influence is qualitative as well as quantitative. But certainly the nonaligned countries have brought new customs, new ideas, new voting patterns, and new problems to the United Nations. In both number and outlook, they are making a significant impact upon the U.N. The organization is going through profound physical and ideological changes whose real significance may not be definitely evaluated for years to come.

It may well be true that the nonaligned countries now hold in their hands the future and destiny of the organization. They can make it or break it. The direction that the U.N. takes, and the vigor with which it acts, will depend to a large extent upon the kind and quality of support given to it by the nonaligned countries.

This chapter will examine the impact the nonaligned countries have had on the United Nations. In doing this, we should note their own conception of their evolving role in the U.N., review the various contributions they are making to the work of the organization, survey the main criticisms that have been launched against them, analyze their voting record in the General Assembly, and evaluate briefly the significance of these developments for the United States and the United Nations.

The Attitude of the Nonaligned States Toward the U.N.

It is natural that the nonaligned states, like the small states generally, should pay lip service to the importance of the United Nations in their approach to world affairs. This attitude stems not only from their posture as weak nations anxious to preserve their independence in a disjointed and turbulent world, but also from their deep concern over the possible outbreak of nuclear war. It can be argued that the great powers do not need the United Nations; at any rate, they can defend themselves in time of peril. Similarly, the aligned countries, associated with the Soviet Union in the Warsaw Pact and other pacts, and with the Western powers in NATO, CENTO, SEATO, the Rio Pact and other defense agreements, have certain assurances against aggression and are less inclined to turn to the United Nations for protection. But the nonaligned countries, without the protective umbrella of the United Nations, would be standing relatively unshielded and alone in a world where aggressors could often take their toll.

To the smaller nations, and the nonaligned countries in particular, the United Nations has tremendous value. It was designed to protect their independence and integrity and to help them raise their standards of living. It is also a center where a small state, without much status or prestige, can greatly enhance its influence by joining with other states to realize common policy objectives. Even more important, membership in the U.N. is a symbol of each country's standing and dignity as a sovereign entity. For nonaligned nations, with the sole exception of Switzerland, the advantages of participating in the activities of the United Nations have proved compelling.

Many of the public statements of the leaders of these states strike a strong note of approval and support for the United Nations. "These last years of difficulty and crisis," said Prime Minister Nehru of India, when he addressed the Assembly on November 10, 1961, "have brought out more than ever before the importance of this organization. Indeed one wonders what the world would be like if the United Nations ceased to be or did not function. Therefore it is of the highest importance that this great organization would not only function but should function with effectiveness and with the support of the countries represented here."[1]

As for the role of most of the uncommitted countries in the United Nations, their leaders are quick to point out that neutralism does not mean noninvolvement in the great issues of war and peace. It does not, and must not, mean passivity toward, or disengagement from, difficult world problems. It does not mean, in their view, fence-sitting or attempting to escape international responsibilities. Rather, it means that nonaligned nations have not chosen sides in the East-West struggle and remain uncommitted about any such allegiance.

As the Foreign Minister of the United Arab Republic pointed out to the Assembly in 1961:

> It is obvious that nonalignment, as intended, refers only to antagonistic blocs, and is a counterbalance to their disagreements which seriously endanger world peace and security. It is not intended to be a passive attitude of indifference to what is going on in the world, or a mere protest against the upsurge of antagonistic blocs where cold war quarrels . . . shake the foundations of peace.[2]

The frequent use of such terms as "dynamic neutralism" and "positive neutralism" to describe their policies suggests the mood in which many nonaligned nations find themselves in connection with their role in world affairs. They look upon themselves as a kind of bridge between two competing camps, a third party whose unique position enables them to view with objectivity the issues and tensions of the Cold War. With such a detached view, they believe they are able, either through the United Nations or otherwise, to anticipate, and perhaps prevent, situations from developing that might lead to serious conflict between the great powers. Thus, the Minister of Foreign Affairs of Iraq, Hashim Jawad, told the Sixteenth General Assembly that the nonaligned countries represented at the Belgrade conference had shown a desire "not to remain aloof from the great struggle between East and West but to assert their influence in the defense of peace and justice without being committed."[3]

It is open to question, however, whether this professed detachment is either real or possible in the modern world. It is also a debatable question whether the policy of nonalignment in the U.N. actually strengthens the cause of peace. In any event, the nonaligned countries recognize the obvious truth that the United Nations is not powerful enough to keep the peace in any real confrontation of the great powers. At the same time, they also realize that very few disputes in the U.N. are completely devoid of Cold War overtones. Accordingly, many of them have been willing to proffer their political and even their military support to the U.N., in those situations where they believe such assistance would help keep the Cold War out or prevent a Cold War confrontation between the great powers. The Suez, Lebanese, and Congo crises appear to be cases in point. In both situations, the nonaligned states preferred small-power intervention under the U.N. flag as an alternative to great-power intervention and competition.

This does not mean that the nonaligned states have any great enthusiasm for the prospect of developing a strong United Nations, equipped with the kind of armed forces contemplated under Article 43 of the Charter, and capable of maintaining world peace. On this point their pragmatism, like that of most U.N. members, outruns their idealism. Most of them remain quite willing to vote for a modest strengthening of the United Nations staff charged with planning collective action to meet future emergencies; many of them also have shown themselves willing to furnish small contingents of troops for U.N. peace-keeping activities on an *ad hoc* basis. But few, if any of them, have any illusions about the possibility of creating a permanent U.N. peace force in the foreseeable future.

Neutralist attitudes toward the peaceful-settlement procedures of the United Nations follow somewhat the same pattern, and are designed to achieve the same general objectives. Newly developing areas abound with budding disputes that usually involve two or more of the small states. In order to stabilize potentially dangerous situations and prevent great power intrusions, the nonaligned countries tend to support the peaceful procedures of the United Nations, including the concept of a "U.N. presence" in troubled areas. In practice, this pronounced allegiance has been sporadic and wobbly. In particular, one must distinguish between great-power conflicts and localized disputes that affect the national interests of the non-aligned countries—especially those disputes that involve their territorial ambitions. As relatively weak states they have frequently turned to the U.N. for protection. Thus Iran gained Security Council support to speed the withdrawal of Soviet troops in 1946; South Korea obtained U.N. military assistance following the invasion from North Korea in 1950; and Egypt secured U.N. intervention during the Suez crisis. Various nonaligned countries have resented and opposed U.N. intervention, however, when they believed such intervention might prove inimical to their national interests—India with respect to Kashmir and Goa; Indonesia with respect to West Irian; Morocco with respect to Mauritania.

Although neutralist nations may disagree somewhat over the kind of United Nations they want to see develop, and their precise role in it, they stand together in their opinion of the proper functions of the organization. On this point, there can be no doubt: the principal function—and the most urgent one—is to rid the world of the last vestiges of Western colonialism. The most compelling factors in international relations are the continued existence of colonialism and imperialism, and the threat of neocolonialism. It follows that the major efforts of the United Nations should be directed toward eliminating these evils.

To be sure, the nonaligned nations are willing to admit that other great problems confront the United Nations—problems like disarmament, economic development and the maintenance of world peace. But in a way even these issues are secondary in that they are either directly related to colonialism or find their roots in the evils of colonialism. As N. Ako-Adjei of Ghana pointed out on September 26, 1961:

> In our view, colonialism is the greatest evil of the modern world, the source of all the troubles which presently affect mankind. It is the root cause of the desire to possess arms and therefore the root cause of the arms race and the problem of disarmament. Colonialism and neocolonialism are a perpetual threat to the peace and security of the world.[4]

It is easy enough to dismiss this approach to world affairs as naïve, inaccurate and illogical. But no amount of sweeping can possibly brush the colonialism problem under the rug. Those who have not had the privilege of listening to the never-ending flow of words in New York, and feeling the hot winds of independence blowing through Africa, cannot possibly comprehend the great emotion and the depth of feeling that exist with respect to this issue. Above all else, it is the factor that shapes the attitudes and conditions the behavior of the nonaligned countries in the United Nations.

How the Nonaligned States Vote

Much has been written in recent years about the mathematics of the new United Nations.[5] Many critics in our country have seriously questioned whether this rapidly expanding world organization can remain a useful instrument for promoting either the national interests of the United States or the cause of world peace.

"With the states of Asia and Africa now constituting almost 50 per cent of the total membership," the argument runs, "won't the United States inevitably find itself in an embarrassing minority in the General Assembly? Isn't there a real danger that the Afro-Asian group, and the nonaligned countries in particular, will be inclined to vote as a bloc against the interests of the free world? Can we possibly trust the future of world peace to the whims and the caprices of an unwieldy organ like the General Assembly?"

Questions like these are based on several interesting assumptions about the nature of the nonaligned countries in the United Nations. One is that they have a solid enough ideological base to enable them to vote as a bloc on important issues. Another is that their interests, in the light of present world conditions, tend to be antithetic to those of the United States and the free world. Still a third assumption is that, because of their inexperience and their lack of knowledge about world affairs, they might become an irresponsible and uncontrollable element in the Assembly. These assumptions, which will have to be tested by time, are at present based more on fear than on fact.

"Prejudice," someone has said, "is a great timesaver. It enables us to form opinions on important issues without bothering to learn the facts." With this admonition in mind, I have yielded to the lure of the numbers game and have completed an analysis of eighty of the most important roll-call votes in the Fifteenth and Sixteenth General Assemblies. Included are key votes in both plenary and committee sessions. Although this analysis does not reveal any startlingly new facts, it does underline some interesting trends.

SOME VOTING STATISTICS

First and foremost, the figures do not reveal either extensive bloc voting or overwhelming pro-Soviet voting on the part of the nonaligned states. In those instances where the United States and the Soviet Union voted differently, 26.1 per cent of the votes cast by the fifty nonaligned countries coincided with those of the United States, and 29.2 per cent with those of the Soviet Union. A regional analysis of the figures reveals that the voting pattern of the seven non–Afro-Asian states—Austria, Finland, Ireland, Sweden, Yugoslavia, Cyprus, and Israel—coincided with that of the United States most frequently (43.5 per cent with the U.S.; 19.3 per cent with the U.S.S.R.), whereas the coincidence of the eleven Arab states was the lowest (11.6 per cent with the U.S.; 40.5 per cent with the U.S.S.R.). The twenty-three African countries voted with the United States 30.7 per cent of the time and supported the Soviet position 24.4 per cent of the time. The figures for the nine Asian states were 19 per cent for the United States position, and 34.2 per cent for the Soviet position. Most significant, the votes of all the states differed from both the Soviet Union and the United States nearly one-third of the time, or 31.3 per cent.

So far as individual states are concerned, the following countries had the highest voting coincidence with the Soviet Union: Guinea, 59.4 per cent; Mali, 53.7; Indonesia, 53.7; Iraq, 52.5; Afghanistan, 46.2; Morocco, 46.1; U.A.R., 45; Yemen, 43.6; Saudi Arabia, 43; Ceylon, 41.8. Those having the highest coincidence with the United States include: Malaya, 47.5 per cent; Dahomey, 47.4; Niger, 47; Gabon, 45.6; Ivory Coast, 45; Malagasy Republic, 44.7; Laos, 42.4; Chad, 39.4; Mauritania, 39.4; Upper Volta, 39.1. India's votes coincided with those of the United States 10 per cent of the time and with those of the Soviet Union 41.2 per cent of the time.

As these figures stand, they obviously give an oversimplified picture of the position of nonaligned countries. In many instances where the votes of the nonaligned countries happened to coincide with those of the Soviet Union, it is misleading to say that they have supported the U.S.S.R. It would be more correct to say that the Soviet Union, usually quick to seize an opportunity to curry favor with the nonaligned states, identified itself with their position to further its own political purposes.

The relatively low voting coincidence of the Arab countries with our own voting record deserves special comment. It was due, in part, to the fact that the eighty votes tabulated included six votes on resolutions dealing with Arab-Israeli relations and the Palestinian-refugee problem, where deep differences exist between the United States and its Arab friends. These differences make the improvement of our general position in the Middle East extremely difficult. Indeed, I am confident, from what many Arab leaders have told me, that if we could find a solution to the Palestinian refugee problem this would do much to facilitate Arab support for our positions on other important questions before the United Nations.

Concerning the role of Afro-Asian countries generally, it should also be noted that the statistics above do not include those states allied to the free world in some type of regional or security arrangement. These countries—including China, Iran, Japan, Pakistan, Philippines, Thailand, and Turkey—often exert a moderating influence upon the other members of the Afro-Asian group. Moreover, with the possible exception of their stands on certain colonial issues, they tend to support the Western position much more consistently than do most of the other Afro-Asian countries.

GROWING NUMBER OF ABSTENTIONS

Among other things, the voting statistics underline the growing strategic importance of abstentions in General Assembly voting procedures. During the Sixteenth General Assembly, there were twenty-eight abstentions on the Korean resolution; thirty-one on the Hungarian resolution; twenty-nine on the Tibetan issue; and thirty-seven on two of the Palestinian refugee resolutions. The great majority of these abstentions were from nonaligned countries. Twenty-nine of these countries abstained twenty times or more during the eighty votes tabulated.* Despite nonaligned claims that they are deeply concerned with the great issues of our time, it is a startling fact that in a good many instances the nonaligned states—with sufficient voting strength to swing the decision either way—were unwilling to take a stand on the issues involved.†

In such situations, of course, the nonaligned countries find themselves confronted with a very difficult dilemma in the United Nations. On the one hand, they are anxious to influence world events and take whatever action they consider appropriate to help prevent the outbreak of war. This they believe they can do by helping to reduce tensions and Cold War conflicts through the simple device of encouraging a greater spirit of understanding and tolerance among the great powers, and by occasionally attempting to reconcile differences by peaceful means. At times, they can accomplish this objective by supporting U.N. resolutions and bringing real, if limited, pressure to bear upon issues that do not directly involve them.

On the other hand, in keeping with their pronounced desire not to take sides in the East-West struggle, some of the nonaligned

---

* Cambodia abstained thirty-eight times; Togo, thirty-four; Finland, thirty-one; Laos, twenty-eight; Afghanistan, twenty-seven. In addition, there were a good many absences among the new nonaligned states.

† The December 20, 1960, resolution on the Congo is a good case in point. The vote was forty-three to twenty-two, with thirty-two (twenty-six nonaligned states) abstentions. Since a two-thirds majority was required for passage, even a slight shift might have changed the result.

countries are equally anxious to avoid becoming so heavily enmeshed in Cold War issues that they might be called upon to support one camp or the other. Accordingly, they tend to resent any
attempt on the part of the Soviet Union or the United States to
use the U.N. for Cold War purposes. Moreover, they often deplore
the consideration of embarrassing Cold War issues, like those involving Tibet or Hungary, where they might be required to stand
up and be counted. In such cases, their desire to play a dynamic
role in world affairs may be offset by their reluctance to offend the
sensitivities of the Soviet Union—or perhaps, in some instances,
the United States—by publicly voting against one of the great
powers. When that happens, their only alternative is to abstain.
This they have done more and more frequently.

SOME DIVISIVE FACTORS

The voting statistics also illustrate vividly the many divisive
factors that operate within the nonaligned group of countries. For
example, the Casablanca Five—Ghana, Guinea, Mali, Morocco,
and the U.A.R.—had a voting coincidence of only 7.9 per cent
with the United States, while comparable figures for the twelve
French African states ranged from 36.9 per cent, in the case of the
Central African Republic, to 47.5 per cent in the case of Dahomey.
Or, to cut the pie the other way, the Soviet resolution to seat Communist China offers a classic example. In the General Assembly,
thirty-six voted for admission and forty-eight against the proposal,
with twenty abstaining; a tally of the votes of the nonaligned
countries showed nineteen yes votes, twelve no, and fifteen abstentions, and the vote among the African countries was nine for admission, nine against, and eleven abstentions. In much the same
way, the nonaligned vote was divided on the resolutions on Palestinian refugees (twenty-five to eleven to eleven), West New Guinea
(twenty-six to fourteen to six), Mauritania (twenty-six to twelve to
eight), and many other issues.

These figures suggest a high degree of political fluidity within
the Afro-Asian group. Again, a good case in point is the African
continent, where competing blocs and groups of states are being
formed with bewildering rapidity. In addition to the five Arab
states of North Africa, which have their special loyalties, there is
the Casablanca Five, which has Morocco and the U.A.R. within its
fold. South of the Sahara, six of the former French colonies remain
within the French Community. Four others make up a loose confederation—the Council of the Entente—and twelve have formed

the African-Malagasy Union. Three countries—Guinea, Ghana, and Mali—are members of the Union of African States. Finally, there is the Monrovia group of twenty African states. Obviously, with political alignments so fluid and so constantly evolving, any analytical attempt to force them into a pattern now would be quite premature.

In some respects, it can be argued that the nonaligned nations exercise an influence on world affairs far out of proportion to their economic and military strength. From a military point of view, they are all relatively weak. Even if they were inclined to join forces, pooling their weaknesses would not make them strong. As one Asian diplomat remarked when asked about the possibility of effective collective-defense pacts in the area, "Zero plus zero plus zero still equals zero."

In addition, there are vast differences among the nonaligned states—differences in geography, history, race, culture, language, religion, and political and economic institutions—that make agreement on fundamentals exceedingly difficult. One has only to compare Indonesia with Tunisia, India with Somalia, or Iraq with Nigeria or Senegal to appreciate just how vast these differences are. As Hamilton Fish Armstrong rightly points out, any agreement reached by the nonaligned states can be only on general issues expressed in very general terms.[6]

This is not to say that they do not share common concerns and common aspirations. As new countries, they want recognition and they want to be accepted as equal members of the international community. They are against colonialism. They are in favor of economic development. They are opposed to racial discrimination. But, beyond these issues and a few moral platitudes, they have not been able to evolve anything like a real ideological basis for cooperation or a common core of ideals that might bind them together in their mutual efforts to promote the cause of peace.

It follows that the impact of the nonaligned countries is more potential than real. When they vote together in the Assembly, they can prevent the passage of any resolution that they consider adverse to their interests. In other instances, by joining hands with other Afro-Asian countries and attracting some additional support from the West or the Communist world, they could form the nucleus of a solid two-thirds majority. In practice, however, they do not usually vote as a bloc; ordinarily, they split on important issues—some voting with the Western countries, some with the Communist bloc, and a good many joining the abstainers.

Since it lies within their power to swing votes on critical questions, they do have what has been referred to as a nose-counting importance, and their votes carry with them certain political and propagandistic overtones. Moreover, it is obvious that the presence of the nonaligned countries in the Assembly has a definite effect upon the whole U.N. program. Certainly the very existence of a bloc of neutralist votes "in being" has often deterred delegations from submitting proposals that might otherwise have carried the necessary majority.

THE TENDENCY TO COMPROMISE

It is true, too, that in the setting of the United Nations, the tendency of the neutralist countries to tread the path of compromise can have an adverse effect upon both the organization and the cause of peace. It seems to many people that some neutralist delegations, at least, are heavily involved in a constant search for a middle ground. There seems to be an unceasing attempt to please both sides to a controversy, in the apparent belief that there is virtue in compromise.

Edmund Burke once said that "All Government . . . every virtue and every prudent act—is founded on compromise and barter."[7] Burke, of course, was writing in the spirit of the Western tradition that, when differences between states arise, both sides should be willing to make some concessions to achieve an acceptable solution. But this is a sound principle only if the parties in the controversy are motivated by a genuine desire to find a solution to their differences. Such a situation does not normally prevail in the United Nations. Neutralist countries seeking a middle ground between the United States and the U.S.S.R. usually find that the United States delegation is made up of reasonable men who take a rational approach toward world affairs and have some flexibility in their negotiating position. Similarly, they normally find the Soviet delegation relatively rigid and inflexible and unwilling to make very many meaningful concessions. It follows that compromises worked out by go-between countries are likely to be compromises favoring the Soviet Union.

On occasion, nonaligned countries can play a useful role in reconciling divergent views. Before assuming the role of the great compromiser, however, they should have the negotiating techniques of the Soviet Union clearly in mind. Otherwise, they may find themselves engaged in the dubious procedure of encouraging the West to trade an orchard for an apple to win agreement with the U.S.S.R.

The result may be either a bad bargain for the West or a watered down resolution that has little practical value.

The Charge of Irresponsible Action

Another criticism often directed against the nonaligned countries is that they have discharged their duties as members of the United Nations in an irresponsible manner. The British Foreign Secretary, the Earl of Home, for example, in a speech delivered late in 1961, took the new states to task for sponsoring the resolution of December 14, 1960, urging immediate independence for non–self-governing territories. "Such a resolution and others like it," said Lord Home, "reveal an almost total lack of responsibility and certainly pay no heed to the main purpose of the United Nations which is to insure order and security of peace."[8]

EXAMPLES OF IRRESPONSIBLE ACTION

One need not search very deeply into the annals of the United Nations to find disturbing examples of what some people refer to as irresponsible action on the part of the new nations. One action widely criticized as irresponsible was the sixty-seven–to–one vote of the Sixteenth General Assembly to censure the remarks of South African Foreign Minister Louw after he had made some comments in the general debate that were displeasing to other African countries. This was clearly an emotional response to a parliamentary situation, one that is hard to justify in terms of either precedent or logic. Whether the content of Mr. Louw's charges were entirely accurate is quite beside the point. The important fact is that the Assembly, led by an angry majority, cast reason to the winds and took a dangerous step toward undermining the principle of free speech, which has always characterized the debates in that body.

Another example, perhaps equally susceptible to the charge of irresponsibility, came when the Assembly adopted a series of resolutions dealing with nuclear tests and nuclear weapons. To any reasonable human being, the resolution calling upon the Soviet Union not to explode its 50-megaton bomb seemed quite justifiable. But the resolution sponsored by India and five other nonaligned countries urging a moratorium on nuclear testing pending the conclusion of a test-ban treaty clearly worked to the disadvantage of the free world, in view of the fact that the Soviet Union had just completed a series of some fifty nuclear tests. In a similar way, the resolution outlawing the use of nuclear weapons in war, proposed by Indonesia, Ceylon, and ten African states, played into the hands of the Soviet Union by underlining the frequently repeated Soviet demand to "ban the bomb."

Were these resolutions the result of a deliberate decision on the part of certain nonaligned countries to side with the Soviet Union in the great power struggle that enmeshes the world? Were they the result of political naïveté, or perhaps a lack of understanding of the basic factors that affect the power balance in the world today? Or did they stem primarily from the deep concern of many United Nations members, following the collapse of the nuclear-test talks in Geneva, over the dangers from increasing fallout and the possibility of nuclear war?

To critical observers in the United States it makes little difference whether the resolutions in question resulted from an honest mistake in judgment, a difference of opinion, or just plain irresponsibility. Nor does it help very much to point out that many of the new countries have long been motivated by a deep-rooted opposition to both nuclear testing and the use of nuclear weapons. The point is that the issues involved go to the heart of our national defense and of free-world survival, and should be dealt with by the Assembly not emotionally but only after a calm and careful consideration of all the facts.

THE OTHER SIDE OF THE LEDGER

On the other side of the ledger, one can find many indications of responsible action on the part of the nonaligned countries. It is of course obvious that a nation—whether it is aligned or nonaligned —should not be charged with irresponsible behavior merely because it does not support the United States on a particular policy issue. Unless one starts with the dubious assumption that we are always in the right, any attempt on the part of the United States or the West to identify responsibility with support for our position in the United Nations is bound to end in failure.

With some notable exceptions, the nonaligned countries have acted with commendable moderation and responsibility with regard to the Congo. It is true that a few of them engaged in questionable intrigues to keep Patrice Lumumba in power. It is true, too, that some of them refuse to comprehend the nature of United Nations objectives in the Congo. Yet one needs only to recall the resolution of September 20, 1960, which was sponsored by seventeen Afro-Asian countries and which put the Assembly squarely behind the Secretary-General's program in the Congo at a very critical period, to realize how helpful they have been. Similarly, the Security Council resolution of February 21, 1961, sponsored by Ceylon, Liberia, and the United Arab Republic, authorizing the United Nations to use force, if necessary, to prevent civil war in the Congo, gave encouraging vitality to the United Nations at a very important juncture. The Soviet Union, in spite of its persistent efforts, has never been able to enlist the support of enough nonaligned countries to thwart the work of the United Nations in the Congo.

There were some very dark days, to be sure, in January, 1961, when five nonaligned African states—Ghana, Guinea, Mali, Morocco, and the United Arab Republic—announced their intention to withdraw their contingents from the U.N. Congo force. Fortunately, Prime Minister Nehru pulled the United Nations from the brink of despair by volunteering several thousand Indian troops. This vote of confidence not only underlined India's support for United Nations objectives in the Congo; it also did much to help stimulate a more positive response from the other countries of Asia and Africa. Secretary-General Hammarskjold would seem to have been justified in writing, as he apparently did, shortly before his death, to "thank God for India" for saving the U.N. position in the Congo.[9]

Another case in point is the resolution adopted by the Sixteenth General Assembly approving the $200 million bond issue. Confronted with the serious prospect that the United Nations might go bankrupt, the nonaligned nations did not reflect the fiscal irresponsibility that some people associate with them. Although they realized that, in the long run, the bond issue, as a means of financing the Congo operation, would cost the smaller nations more than they would otherwise be required to pay, they accepted it realistically as an extraordinary step to keep the United Nations afloat. Four of these countries—Ethiopia, Malaya, Tunisia, and Yugoslavia—took the lead with Canada, Denmark, the Netherlands, Norway, and Pakistan, in sponsoring the measure against the opposition of the Soviet bloc. The final vote was fifty-eight to thirteen (with twenty-four abstentions), with twenty-nine of the nonaligned countries supporting the bond issue.

THE ROLE OF THE SECRETARY-GENERAL

One very helpful demonstration of good judgment on the part of the smaller nations came when the Assembly confronted the difficult task of finding a successor to Dag Hammarskjold. Faced with almost solid opposition from the smaller states, the Soviet Union withdrew its troika proposal. It continued, however, to insist upon other arrangements having to do with the Secretary-General and his deputies that were obviously designed to give the U.S.S.R. a veto over top-level decisions in the Secretariat. But the smaller states stood their ground in favor of an effective United Nations with an effective Secretary-General.

As a result of many weeks of negotiations, U Thant assumed his post as Acting Secretary-General without any limitation on his power of making decisions and appointing his deputies and chief advisers. Thus the principle that the Secretary-General should remain in full charge of the Secretariat, with the right to select his staff members, was upheld. The integrity of the Secretary-General's office was preserved—at least for the time being.

This experience should have taught all U.N. supporters an important lesson about decision-making in the United Nations. Ambassador Adlai Stevenson turned in a remarkable negotiating performance partly because he knew—and the Soviet delegate knew—that he had the full support of an overwhelming majority of the Assembly every step of the way. If the Soviet Union had proved unduly stubborn at any stage of the negotiations, he could have taken the matter to the Assembly, confident of securing the necessary two-thirds majority to uphold his position. Reason may not be a Soviet virtue, but with this kind of opposition solidly arrayed against him, the Soviet delegate had no alternative but to assume a fairly reasonable position.

The lesson here is obvious, but the point cannot be made too often. If the small nations have the courage of their convictions, if they will stand up for the United Nations, if they will support with enthusiasm and dedication the principles and purposes of the Charter, they will have a magnificent opportunity to give vitality and direction to the United Nations. But if they are weak and divided, if they are hesitant, if they are unwilling to stand up for what is right, then the cause of world peace will suffer a serious setback.

OTHER ISSUES

Even in the field of colonialism, where feelings run so high that anything can be expected, wiser counsel often exerts its helpful influence. During the Sixteenth Assembly, on two occasions when the Soviet Union attempted to take the lead on colonialism with extreme proposals, the Afro-Asian states rejected Soviet overtures and presented their own resolution setting up a seventeen-nation committee to recommend steps for a speedy end to colonialism. With the passive support of thirty-six abstentions from the non-aligned states, the Assembly voted down a Soviet amendment that would have proclaimed 1962 to be "the year of the elimination of colonialism."

In this connection, the reaction of the African states to the Algerian problem also deserves special mention. In 1961, the French-African nations simply refused to permit the Assembly to take any steps that would hamper in any way direct talks between the French and the Algerian leaders. As a result, the relatively innocuous resolution that emerged was approved by the Assembly in a sixty-two to zero vote, with thirty-eight abstaining.

As I pointed out earlier, some of the African countries have also made many positive contributions to stability in the Congo. One of the best examples came in January, 1961, when the Adoula-Tshombe negotiations for the unification of the Congo were making rather promising progress. At this point, the Soviet Union demanded that appropriate action be taken against Tshombe and that a meeting of the Security Council be held to consider the matter.

Nothing could have been more harmful to the Adoula-Tshombe talks than a meeting of the Council at that particular juncture, and Adoula did not hesitate to point this out. Some twenty African heads of state, meeting in Lagos, immediately supported Adoula's protest. They cabled the United Nations that it would be "unwise and prejudicial to the interest of the Congo" for the Security Council to muddy the waters with the kind of intervention proposed by the Soviet Union. Ignoring Valerian Zorin's protest that the African leaders had not properly understood the issues involved, the Council met and quickly adjourned.

All in all, in spite of dismal predictions by many prophets of gloom, the record of the Sixteenth General Assembly was not a bad one. In fact, it was surprisingly good when one considers the almost insuperable obstacles that faced the Assembly when it convened on September 19, 1961. The bitter Communist attacks upon the Secretary-General, the deepening crisis in the Congo, the increased pressures to seat Communist China, the serious financial straits in which the organization found itself, and finally, the tragic and untimely death of Dag Hammarskjold—all these unfavorable developments suggested that the future of the United Nations was in grave jeopardy.

These crises were met satisfactorily. In addition, the Assembly laid the groundwork for the resumption of disarmament negotiations, reactivated the moribund U.N. Committee on the Peaceful Uses of Outer Space, gave encouraging impetus to economic development and dealt appropriately with such old Cold War issues as Korea, Tibet, Cuba, and Hungary. These problems were handled with a commendable amount of restraint and moderation. Those who had predicted the speedy demise of the organization began to make some adjustments in their timetables.

The Double Standard

Another criticism often directed against the United Nations and the nonaligned countries is the so-called double standard. This criticism has many facets and cannot be simply put, but in general, it may be summarized as follows: As the United Nations has increased in size, there has been evolving within it a double standard of justice and morality, one for the West and one for the Communist bloc and other members. In this development, the neutralist influence of the nonaligned countries has been a heavy contributing factor.

SUEZ AND HUNGARY

There is much merit to this criticism. I have never believed, however, that the reaction of the United Nations toward the Suez and Hungarian crises constituted a double standard of justice favoring the position of the Soviet Union. Actually, the Assembly resolutions condemning the actions of the Soviet Union and the Hungarian regime were more vigorously worded than those addressed to the guilty parties in the Suez crisis. If there was anything like a double standard in the United Nations, it did not stem from the unwillingness of that organization to take comparable action against those who violated the Charter. Rather, it stemmed from the totally different response the parties involved gave to the judgment of the Assembly. France, Israel, and the United Kingdom agreed to a cease-fire and withdrew their forces from Egypt partly, in the words of President Eisenhower, because they had a "decent respect for the opinions of mankind." The Soviet Union did not.

Nor is it true that the nonaligned countries have demonstrated a conspicuous lack of moral fiber on the Hungarian issue. To be sure, a few of them—notably Afghanistan, Ceylon, Indonesia,

India, Saudi Arabia, the U.A.R., and Yemen—have consistently abstained from voting on resolutions relating to Hungary, and they will have to answer before the bar of history for their attitude. On the other hand, a substantial majority of the nonaligned states have been willing to stand up and be counted on the side of the Western world.

That this majority is dwindling with the passage of time has been a matter of some concern in Western chancelleries. In the Sixteenth General Assembly, only seven of the nonaligned countries were willing to vote for a condemnatory resolution. States like Burma, Cambodia, Tunisia, and Liberia, which had supported the Western position on Hungary for a number of years, abstained from the vote. Others, including Ceylon, Indonesia, Guinea, Iraq, and Mali even voted against the resolution. If this trend continues, it will be increasingly difficult in the future to muster the two-thirds majority necessary for passage of condemnatory resolutions of this kind.

It should be apparent that the growing tendency of the nonaligned states to abstain on the Hungarian issue does not reflect approval of the Soviet Union's ruthless action in suppressing the Hungarian uprising in 1956; what was wrong in 1956 is, presumably, still wrong in 1962 or 1963. It does suggest, however, that the nonaligned states now look upon this issue, and Western efforts to keep it alive, as a Cold War maneuver designed not to alleviate conditions in Hungary, but to elicit further disapproval of the Soviet Union. Right or wrong, they believe that no further good can come from a policy that is now outmoded and can serve only to embitter relationships between East and West.

I believe, also, that too many people tend to belittle the United Nations for its alleged timidity in dealing with the Hungarian crisis. We should not underestimate the profound impact that Assembly debate on Hungary has had upon the uncommitted countries and their understanding of the nature of Soviet imperialism. Delegates who were present will long remember the dramatic remarks of the Burmese delegate, during the Eleventh General Assembly, when he announced that he was prepared to vote for a condemnation of the U.S.S.R. "We do this to keep our self-respect," he said. "After all responsible waiting for action has passed, we can do no less."

"There," he said, speaking of Hungary, "but for the Grace of God, go we."[10]

SOVIET COLONIALISM

A better example of the double standard lies in the willingness of many of the nonaligned countries to oppose Western colonialism vigorously and to tend to close their eyes to the Soviet brand of colonialism. This represents a difference in moral standards which most Americans find extremely difficult to explain.

Obviously, on the face of it, the record does not justify such an approach. Since World War II, many new countries have come of age and gained their independence. Nearly a billion people, involving some forty nations, have earned the right to govern themselves and become members of the United Nations. This development, which resulted from the rapid liquidation of the Western colonial system, and which has been relatively peaceful, represents the greatest move toward freedom and independence the world has ever known.

During this period, the opposite was occurring on the Soviet periphery. State after state lost its independence. With the help of Communist armies, over 800 million people were drawn behind the Iron Curtain. As the Western colonial system approached its end, the Soviet brand of colonialism, with its tyranny and deprivation of human freedom, moved onto the world stage.

Since the nonaligned countries are presumably aware of these facts and figures, why do they behave as they do? One can understand why they might bitterly attack Western colonialism, but if they are really interested in supporting the cause of freedom in the world, why do they tend to ignore the Soviet brand of colonialism which, in many ways, may be far more objectionable than its western counterpart? It would appear to many critics that either they do not understand the issues involved or they are deliberately supporting the Soviet line.

Over the years, I have heard Krishna Menon deliver many speeches in the Assembly. All too often, he has had unkind things to say about Western countries and Western colonialism. Yet, I do not recall that I ever heard him utter any real words of criticism against the Soviet Union or the Soviet brand of colonialism.

It is far easier to explain this phenomenon than it is to justify it. Some states may find it prudent to soft-pedal their criticism of the Soviet Union for domestic political reasons; others, in close geographical proximity to the Soviet Union, may be afraid of retaliatory measures. To these countries, discretion is still the better part of valor.

But the more obvious fact is that most of the nonaligned nations are new states—nonwhite and non-European—that have emerged only recently from a long period of Western colonial rule. In some cases, their independence has been won by force. And very often, the scars of Western colonialism—envy, resentment, bitterness, and hurt pride—remain deeply imbedded in the mores of the people. Colonialism is an experience which is very near and real to them.

On the other hand, they have had little or no practical experience with the Soviet brand of colonialism. Hungary, Rumania, Bulgaria, and Czechoslovakia are far-away places, and what goes on there would appear to have no immediate impact upon the people or the national objectives of most nonaligned nations. Why should they become involved in Cold War issues whose focal points are thousands of miles away, when they have difficult problems in their own front yards to resolve?

One further observation may be pertinent in this connection. Although the representatives of certain nonaligned nations are quite willing privately to admit the evils of Soviet colonialism, they sometimes prefer not to debate such issues in the Assembly for tactical reasons. "We hope the United States will not insist on injecting charges about Soviet imperialism into the debate on our resolution on colonialism," several delegates from nonaligned countries told me during the Fifteenth General Assembly. "To do so," they argued, "would only confuse the issue and make it much more difficult for us to secure an overwhelming vote on our resolution."

Western strategy now seems to be directed toward laying the foundations for a long-range educational program in the United Nations designed to convince the nonaligned countries that Soviet colonialism constitutes a real threat to world peace and to the cause of human freedom. During the heated debates of the past few years, the nonaligned countries have learned a good many important lessons about the nature of the Soviet system. Free-world leaders hope they will be willing to learn a great deal more once the problem of Western colonialism is resolved.

THE GOA INCIDENT

The Goa incident represents an interesting and, in some ways, perhaps even more significant use of the double standard. In this case, the United Nations failed to take any action at all, largely because the nonaligned states on the Security Council were reluctant to condemn India for the use of military force against Goa.

This they appeared to justify on the ground that Portugal's ouster from Goa did not constitute aggression, as the Portuguese charged, but was a justifiable act taken in the name of anticolonialism.

Thus Ambassador C. S. Jha, of India, in presenting the Indian case before the Council, argued that the seizure of Goa was not a question of aggression, but "of getting rid of the last vestiges of colonialism in India." He further declared that this "was a matter of faith for us, whatever anyone else may think, Charter or no Charter, Council or no Council."[11] Two days later, Krishna Menon, the Indian Defense Minister, pushed the Indian contention one step further. "We consider colonialism is permanent aggression," he said. "We did not commit aggression. Colonialism collapsed."[12]

Without examining in detail the factors involved in the Goa incident, it is clear that the nonaligned countries and the Western nations looked at this problem from decidedly different points of view. It may be that Portugal's retention of a tiny enclave like Goa on Indian soil was an anachronism that should have ended with the age of colonialism. It may be that Portugal should have seen the handwriting on the wall and made the necessary arrangements to depart peacefully while there was time. Yet, in the eyes of many people, the end could not justify the means. Members of the United Nations have pledged themselves to settle their disputes by peaceful methods, and the existence of injustices in the world does not entitle them to resort to violence in defiance of the principles of their Charter.

The Indian position on Goa raises some very interesting questions about the future of the United Nations. Are disputes arising from colonial issues to be treated differently under the Charter from other types of disputes? Are all colonial powers to be considered aggressors because "colonialism is permanent aggression"? And are all new states, without regard to their commitments under the Charter, free to use force to rectify any evils of colonialism that, in their judgment, need to be rectified?

Ambassador Adlai Stevenson put the issue well when he said:

There can be only one law of the Charter, applying equally to all of its members. Any effort to apply one law in one part of the world, or towards one group of states and a different law to others will surely have the most serious consequences for the future of the Organization. If the use of force against territory under the control of other states is to be condoned for anticolonial reasons, it can be condoned for other reasons and we will have here opened Pandora's box. The end of that road is chaos.[13]

When the Charter was drafted, most delegations were in complete agreement that the primary objective of the United Nations should be the maintenance of world peace and security. Is it possible that we are entering a new phase of the organization's history when many members consider that its primary objective centers about liquidation of the Western colonial system? If there is a real cleavage here, and the Charter is in the process of being rewritten, it could presage very serious results for the future of the United Nations.

In this connection, it is highly significant that, when the Security Council found it impossible to take any action on Goa, the issue was shelved. Under the Uniting for Peace Resolution of 1950, the Western powers might have taken the matter to the Assembly after the Soviet veto of an American cease-fire proposal. They apparently discarded the idea, however, in the belief that the support given India by the U.A.R., Liberia, and Ceylon, in the Council, reflected the attitude of the Afro-Asian group, as a whole.

Some critics might call this cowardice; I prefer to characterize it as a prudent decision. Bad cases do not ordinarily establish sound precedents for future action, and for a variety of reasons, Goa was not a good case. If the Assembly had been convened, the Afro-Asian countries might have been pushed into an emotional reaction not responsive to the legal and moral issues involved. At least, the Assembly has not given status to what might have been a very dubious precedent.

As Assistant Secretary of State Harlan Cleveland points out, there is something rather grotesque about the double standard when it is applied to real problems in the real world.[14] Thus high officials from other lands may lambaste the United States in the Assembly for the denial of civil liberties in the South, while conveniently overlooking the gross violation of human rights taking place in their own countries. Our own conduct is certainly not above reproach, and we should be able to forgive and forget some of the things our nonaligned friends do. But if rules are to apply, then the same rules should apply for everyone. The nonaligned nations as well as the great powers should appreciate the logic of this principle. For it points to the wisest way of establishing a world of law in which the interests of all nations would be best safeguarded.

Impact on American Policy

There are some who might consider the preceding pages an apologia for the nonaligned countries. I did not intend them to be such; I merely wanted to look at both sides of the ledger. The neutralist countries, it seems to me, have been more maligned than aligned.

At the same time, supporters of the United Nations cannot afford to be naïve or Pollyanna-like about the future. We must look at the record in a hard-headed, realistic fashion if we are to avoid the pitfalls that misguided hope or sentiment might put in our way.

FUTURE ROLE OF NONALIGNED STATES

With respect to the future, it appears fairly certain that the nonaligned nations will continue to enjoy an increasingly important role in the United Nations. One significant straw in the wind is the decision of the Sixteenth General Assembly to set up a new disarmament negotiating group of eighteen members, adding Burma, India, the U.A.R., Sweden, Ethiopia, Nigeria, Brazil, and Mexico to the original group of five Communist and five Western countries. This decision prompted the Soviet delegate, Valerian A. Zorin, to comment that one of the major results of the Sixteenth General Assembly was recognition of the principle of equal representation for the "three principal groups of states."[15] Whether the composition of the new disarmament group constitutes any recognition of merit in the Soviet troika concept, or whether it is based on the principle of geographic representation, as the Western powers contend, is beside the point. The fact is that six fairly important nonaligned states now have a new vantage point and new influence in the United Nations.

Whether they will be helpful in encouraging the moribund disarmament talks toward more fruitful ends is problematic. If they can inject a new sense of urgency—and a few new ideas—into the negotiating group, they might be instrumental in ending the stalemate. In any event, their presence on the group has implications that reach far wider than the disarmament field. Khrushchev's suggestion, made early in 1962, that the eighteen members convene as a summit conference is illustrative. The crack may not yet be very wide, but the nonaligned states already have their feet in the big door.

At any rate, experience during the spring of 1962 would suggest that the participation of the nonaligned countries in the new disarmament group may prove quite helpful to the Western position. Disarmament is certainly one area where a little learning can be a dangerous thing, and the discussions thus far have given the newcomers an excellent opportunity to learn much about the relative merits of the Soviet and American policies and tactics. This is all to the good. The nonaligned members of the group are, after all, leaders in the geographic areas they represent. So long as they are going to exercise considerable influence, it is far better that they should know enough about the subject matter to enable them to act intelligently and constructively.

Certain other factors should be kept in mind. For some time, the states of Asia and Africa have sought to enlarge the Security Council and the Economic and Social Council to gain adequate representation on these important organs of the United Nations. Up to the present, this has not been done, because of the determined opposition of the U.S.S.R. But these changes are bound to come about, and when they do, the nonaligned countries will add considerably to their prestige and influence in the United Nations.

Similarly, the Secretariat of the future will reflect, much more heavily than it has in the past, the influence of staff members from the nonaligned countries. The first generation of U.N. staff members are rapidly reaching the retirement age. New posts, too, are opening up. More and more, these vacancies will be filled by qualified personnel from Asia and Africa. Names like Thant of Burma, Narasimhan of India, Amachree of Nigeria, and Gardiner of Ghana at the top levels are illustrative of what will be taking place in the middle and lower echelons of the Secretariat during the 1960's.

The question is whether the nonaligned states *as a group* will be able to capitalize on these developments. Will the spirit of unison that they are endeavoring to generate counteract the divisive tendencies that are pulling them apart and fragmenting many of their votes in the General Assembly? Will they be able to develop a common program of action in world affairs that goes beyond mere platitudes?

Two points may be made in this connection. During the next few years, such identity of interest as ties these countries together will be undergoing rather drastic changes. Today, the main basis for an identity of interest is the fervent desire of all of them to wipe colonialism from the face of the earth. When this common objective has been accomplished, their domestic problems, their individual needs, and their national aspirations may emerge as more important motives in their foreign policies.

Secondly, it is not only possible, but probable, that some of the nonaligned nations will become more moderate in their points of view with the passage of time. New states, especially those emerging from revolutionary situations, sometimes tend to assert themselves emotionally and vigorously with respect to world affairs. But once revolutionary ardor begins to cool and the domestic political scene becomes more stable, the governments in charge may fall into a more relaxed pattern of behavior.

Actually, most of the irritation and ill-will the United States has encountered with the nonaligned countries in the United Nations can be boiled down to our differences—or rather the differences of our allies—over colonial issues. The sooner our Western European allies can responsibly complete the complex task of liquidating the remnants of their colonial empires, the better off we all shall be. Certainly our voting position in the Assembly will be vastly improved when we no longer have to bear this cross with our allies. Yet, we know that if we encourage them to move ahead too rapidly, and generate a few more problems like the Congo in the process, the price in bitterness, ill-will and danger to peace will be even higher than it has been.

It would be, of course, a tragic thing if the liquidation of Western colonialism were to proceed from this point on without a rational program of action. What is to happen to the many non–self-governing territories that might aspire to independence although lacking the resources for it? How many of these will be set up as independent entities, and how many will be encouraged, as "sovereign states," to apply for membership in the United Nations? How are new Congos to be averted? These are burning questions for which all of us—especially the nonaligned countries—must try to find responsible answers. If some reasonable definition is not found for the word "independence," and if a host of nonviable states are loosed upon the international community, then incalculable harm will be done to the United Nations and the cause of peace.

U.N. VOTES AND FOREIGN AID

In these circumstances, one may logically inquire whether United States interests can best be served by bringing pressure to bear upon the nonaligned countries to win their support for our policies and programs in the United Nations. Or does it serve our national interests better to lean over backwards in making every reasonable effort to accommodate neutral interests, and, perhaps, even neutral prejudices?

This question has arisen most persistently in connection with our mutual aid program. Some members of Congress, and particularly the opponents of foreign aid, have argued that countries should be entitled to receive assistance from the United States only if they clearly demonstrate, by their words and their deeds, that they support the free-world position. "They cannot be neutral," the argument runs. "They are either for us or against us. They should stand up and be counted. They should either cast their lot with the free world or take their place in the Communist camp and get their assistance from the Soviet Union."

The strength of this argument was vividly illustrated again during the spring of 1962, when steps were taken in the Congress to place embarrassing limitations on economic assistance to India and to stop further aid to Yugoslavia and Poland. The debate revealed a definite hardening of Congressional sentiment *vis-à-vis* neutralism, partly because of the Goa incident and partly because of the passive attitude the nonaligned countries had displayed at the Belgrade conference with respect to the resumption of nuclear testing by the Soviet Union.

It can be assumed, if the voting position of the United States becomes more difficult in the U.N., that this tendency to relate foreign aid to voting support will increase rather than diminish. The principal purpose of the mutual aid program is to extend assistance to those countries who wish to move ahead on the difficult road of freedom through stability and progress. It is a debatable question whether any special consideration should be given to the needs of our loyal friends who, as Congress has put it, "share our view of the world crisis" and normally vote with us, in contradistinction to those who frequently vote against us.

Although we certainly do not want to reward anti-Westernism, neither would it be desirable to allocate our foreign aid on a *quid pro quo* basis. In view of our repugnance to the idea of buying votes in our national elections, our government cannot be put in the untenable and embarrassing position of trying to resort to such practices in an international organization. Moreover, the new states are fully aware of the strategic importance of their votes, and they rightly resent pressure of any kind by the great powers. They insist on being free to vote, in each instance, on the merits of the case as they see them.

This has been the policy of the United States in the United Nations from the beginning. We do not seek satellites and we certainly want to avoid leaving the impression that we are trying to create a bloc of states within the United Nations. We have always been proud of the strength that comes from diversity of views and independence of action. Generally speaking, we have proceeded on the assumption that, in the market place of ideas which the United Nations affords, the logic of our position and the justice of our own cause would win out.

By and large, the United States has fared exceedingly well in the United Nations. This is partly because the great objectives outlined in the Charter are virtually identical with the over-all objectives of American foreign policy. This identity of interests has worked out well from a practical point of view. Even during the past few years, when a few of the Assembly resolutions have been objectionable to us, the great preponderance of them have been quite in harmony with the national interests of the United States.

In the long run, the nonaligned countries will tend to be most responsive to the influences of those states that can best help them achieve their national destiny. Sincere and honest efforts to help, without ulterior motives on our part, are bound to pay rich dividends. In this connection, we must do everything we can to understand their problems and sympathize with their aspirations. Above all, we must make unmistakably clear to them our ideas about the kind of world order we believe in.

In November, 1961, Secretary of State Dean Rusk said about the neutralist nations:

> They will say things from time to time which will annoy us. They will take points of view in particular questions which differ from ours. They will criticize us specifically on certain points, sometimes in the most vigorous terms. But the test is whether they are determined to be independent, whether they are trying to live out their own lives in the way in which their own people would like to have them shape it.[16]

If this is the test, the record would seem to be fairly good. At least during the past few years, no nonaligned country has lost its independence. Nor has there been any decided shift of loyalties from the nonaligned group to the Communist camp. Indeed, if current reports from Guinea, the U.A.R., and other nonaligned countries are useful indications, these nations appear to be increasingly realistic in their dealings with the Soviet Union.

It is often pointed out that the nonaligned nations need the

United States. It is equally true that we need the nonaligned nations. They can be useful in mediating disputes when the great powers are in the mood to compromise. They are often helpful—when the great powers agree—in furnishing both troops and observation teams to U.N. peace-keeping operations. And the darker the world situation becomes, the greater the need will be for countries and leaders not aligned with either side in the Cold War. If they use their influence wisely and well, they might even prevent nuclear war.

THE POSITION OF THE U.S. IN THE U.N.

Clearly, we should not cast our votes in the United Nations merely to curry favor with our friends from Asia and Africa. There are a number of steps the United States might take, however, to improve its Assembly position *vis-à-vis* the nonaligned countries. In addition to a constant re-evaluation of our policy on colonial questions, I would, among other things, suggest the following:

1. We should strongly support the move to bring about a thorough review of the organization and procedures of the General Assembly. The sheer size of the United Nations—and it will continue to grow with the years—makes such a review essential. If this is postponed very much longer, or if certain remedial steps are not taken, the Assembly will degenerate into a huge debating society incapable of dealing effectively with the critical problems of our time.

2. We must not confuse temporary diplomatic victories in the Assembly with solid progress in matters that really count. Very often in the past, when we had our own way, we were inclined to waste our substance on relatively unimportant matters like the precise wording of resolutions, and elections to certain U.N. posts. In insisting on having our way, we needlessly consumed precious bargaining power. The time has come for us to take a more relaxed attitude with respect to lesser issues so that we can concentrate more effectively on matters of real substance.

3. We should continue to give our enthusiastic support to the demands of the Afro-Asian countries for more equitable representation on the various organs and agencies of the United Nations. Although the United Nations has more than doubled its membership since 1945, the Security Council and the Economic and Social Council have remained exactly the same size. This is an anachronism that must be remedied if the Afro-Asian countries are not to become second-class citizens in the world community.

4. We must encourage a greater spirit of unity and teamwork among our free-world partners, both in support of the United Nations and in behalf of a bold, imaginative program for the economic development of the underdeveloped areas. Up to this point, we have taken some pride from the fact that freedom thrives on diversity, and that independence of action does not necessarily result in disunity and discord. But the persistent challenge of the Soviet Union confronts us with new and serious problems. If we are to preserve the integrity of the United Nations, and if we are to achieve free-world objectives with respect to the newly emerging countries, then we will need far more help than we have received from our allies in recent years.

5. It is almost trite now to say that we must do our utmost to improve race relations here in the United States and to extend to diplomats from Asia and Africa the kind of hospitality to which they are entitled. Yet this issue, in Afro-Asian eyes, is just as important as colonialism. Indeed, to diplomats who are refused service in restaurants or who have trouble finding adequate housing because of the color of their skin, it becomes even more important. Unless we can demonstrate by our deeds that we mean what we say about equality, our diplomatic efforts are going to labor under serious handicaps in the United Nations.

Concluding Comment

It remains to be seen precisely how the presence of a growing number of nonaligned nations will alter the basic nature of the United Nations. The situation could get worse before it gets better. It is clear that these countries should have a vital interest in maintaining a strong and effective organization. One leading authority points out, however, that "escape from the risks of collective U.N. action, under the banner of pacifist neutralism, was the bedrock of their foreign policy. . . ."[17] Since the Assembly will be incapacitated by the unwillingness of the nonaligned states to act in moments of crisis, it is contended, the principle of collective security has, in fact, been negated as a real basis for U.N. action.

This reasoning, it seems to me, is only partly valid. If another large-scale, overt aggression, similar to the Korean and Suez crises, were to take place, there is a very good chance that a substantial majority of United Nations members would support collective action in order to preserve world peace. The real danger lies in indirect aggression—subversive tactics and guerrilla warfare—

where the guilty parties cannot be seen and where responsibility is hard to fix. Unless new procedures are devised, the United Nations will find itself woefully unable to cope with threats of this kind to the peace.

Another real danger lies in the continued influx of new members. So far, the situation in the United Nations, though difficult, is manageable. But if the stream of small, weak entities continues to pour out into the international community without any rational criteria for statehood, U.N. membership could be diluted to the point where the Assembly, at least, might lose its capacity to act.

There are not many signs that the nonaligned nations, in the foreseeable future, will be able to agree upon any meaningful ideological basis or evolve any genuine spirit of unity or common purpose in world affairs. There is one thing, however, that they should be able to agree upon: the relationship of the United Nations to their own security and well-being. Loyal support for an effective United Nations is the greatest contribution they can make to their own progress and the cause of world peace. Although it is still too early to predict, there are some hopeful signs that such support may be forthcoming.

VIII

ALLIES, NEUTRALS, AND NEUTRALISTS IN THE CONTEXT OF U.S. DEFENSE POLICY*

by ARNOLD WOLFERS

IT IS frequently said that Soviet conduct in international affairs has undergone a radical change since Stalin's death. Allegedly, the Soviet leaders have transferred the struggle with the West from the military plane to the economic and ideological sphere. If this is true, such a change in Soviet policy would relieve the United States of much of its concern about its military position, and permit it to concentrate on competition with the Soviets for the support of the uncommitted countries. It would be a comforting thought if a bid for the friendship of the world's less favored peoples could be substituted for the distasteful preoccupation with military power and policy.

I shall not attempt to judge how much of a shift has taken place in Soviet foreign policy. The apparent recognition by Soviet leaders that a nuclear war would destroy not merely the "capitalist" nations but the "socialist" countries as well, makes plausible the belief that they would prefer, more than ever, to attain their objectives without resorting to military force. In any case, they seem to attach great importance to the success they expect to gain by non-military means, particularly in the areas presently neutral or neutralist. What matters here is that such success, even if attained by economic, propagandistic or subversive means, might have a very serious impact on the world balance of military power and may, in fact, be directed toward this end. If that were the case, "peaceful competition" would make the military task incumbent

* First presented as a Benjamin F. Shambaugh Lecture at the State University of Iowa in a series on "Problems of National Defense."

upon the United States and its allies more burdensome, rather than less.

It is easy to see how the Western defense position could be weakened, nibbled away, or undermined, by means short of military force. A switch of any one of America's major European allies from alliance to neutrality might make NATO untenable. Therefore, if the Soviets should ever succeed—for instance by propaganda pointed at the dangers of nuclear armaments and alignment with the U.S.—in bringing about such a switch, they could achieve, thereby, a major military victory without firing a shot. Similar success might result for them if they induced uncommitted countries to align themselves with the Soviet bloc. One can hardly assume that the Soviet leaders are unaware that such potentialities are inherent in what they label peaceful competition.

The divergent attitudes of three categories of nations lying between the U.S. and the Soviet bloc and changes in attitude peculiar to each of them deserve attention here for the impact they can have on the U.S. defense position. The first category comprises the allies of the United States, countries committed to support the U.S. collective defense effort. In the second category are the genuinely neutral countries that do not support the U.S. but, simultaneously, withhold support from the other camp. Finally there are the "neutralists" whose more or less marked anti-Western stance tends to interfere with U.S. defense policies. In terms of changes of attitude, the Soviets stand to profit from any transfer of U.S. allies to the category of neutrals, of neutrals to the category of neutralists, of neutralists to the category of allies or satellites of the Soviet Union or of Red China. Whatever the Soviets can do to encourage and promote such transfers serves their interests and might at any point tip the world balance of military power in their favor.

It would be a distortion of the facts to assert that over the last fifteen years the trend has been consistently away from the positions relatively more favorably to the United States. No country, except Cuba and Iraq—the latter never directly allied with the United States—has deliberately switched from alliance to either neutrality or neutralism, though large areas of the world formerly part of allied territory, having freed themselves from Western rule, are now inside the neutralist camp. The countries that chose to remain neutral from the start have adhered to this position. Of the new neutralist states, with the probable exception of Cuba, it is still an open question whether any of them can properly be said to have joined the Soviet bloc.

However, though it would be defeatist to create an image of a definite trend against the U.S. in the position of the "in-between countries," deterioration has taken place in the U.S. defense position compared to what it was, or was expected to become, at the close of World War II, and even at later dates. At the end of the war, it was anticipated that a concert of the major powers, the victors of the war, would police the world in the name of the United Nations. Since this meant enforcing the peace merely against the then disarmed Axis powers, and against minor members of the world community if they turned aggressors, there was no reason why the U.S. as a member of the powerful "policing group" would have to meet heavy defense requirements.

Conditions underwent a radical change when, after roughly two years, the "one-world" concept had to give way to the "two-world" realities of the Cold War. The U.S. found itself burdened with the chief responsibility of establishing and maintaining a reasonable balance of power between two hostile camps to protect itself and the rest of the world against further Communist expansion. In view of the actual or potential military power of the opponent, and the military weakness of most of the non-Communist world, the defense requirements of the U.S. were bound to increase greatly.

Yet, even this was not the end of the process of deterioration. The outbreak of the Korean war revealed the extent of U.S. military responsibilities. At the beginning it also served to reinforce the comforting illusion that the world had in fact split into two parts only, one of which could properly be conceived as the "Free World," a community prepared to defend itself collectively against Communist aggression. The United for Peace resolution expressed the view that the United Nations could be made to serve as a kind of general alliance among all the members of the Free World, committing them to any collective defense action recommended by the General Assembly. However, before the war was over, the Free World community proved to be a myth. The world had been divided not into two, but into three parts, one of which consisted of nations determined to remain uncommitted to either of what they called the military blocs and to take no share, therefore, in the U.S. collective defense effort. The additional difficulties for the U.S. caused by such "noncommitment" will be discussed later.

Soon after the U.S. had accepted the fact that the world was divided into three groups, another vexing problem presented itself. Not all of the noncommitted nations turned out to be neutrals in the traditional sense of the term. Instead, many of the new states in Asia and Africa which call themselves neutralists showed a more or less pronounced partiality, if not against the United States itself, then at least against some of the basic tenets of U.S. defense strategy. As a result, their attitude and behavior—which might be termed "unneutral neutrality"—placed further strains on this strategy. Obviously, if a country goes further and accepts Soviet assistance against "U.S. aggression," as Cuba has done, or permits its territory to become a staging area for Soviet military operations, as it once appeared that Syria might do, neutralism has ceased and given way to alignment with the Soviets. So far, however, earlier expectations that some neutralists such as Egypt, Indonesia, or Iraq would in time join the Soviet camp have not materialized.

It is not always appreciated abroad why the United States set out to establish a widespread alliance system and why it stands to suffer if additional areas of the world come under neutral rather than allied control. It is rightly pointed out that few countries are less in need of allies for the defense of their own territory than the United States. When NATO was established, the danger of a direct attack on the United States did not exist at all, because the Soviets did not have the means at that time to strike at the American homeland. By the time they did acquire this capacity, the U.S. strategy of nuclear deterrence, which was the only means of countering the threat, was soon to become virtually independent of overseas bases and did not have to rely on allied military contributions. Yet, allies continued to be indispensable to the United States if the Soviet bloc was to be prevented from gaining a dominant position in the world. Should this occur, it will threaten the survival of the United States as a free and independent nation.

In order to be able to contain the Sino-Soviet bloc inside the Eurasian land mass, the United States must be able to project its military power across the great oceans. It can do so only if given adequate opportunity for the deployment of American forces and facilities overseas, and if assured of military cooperation by local allied forces stationed in the Eurasian danger zones. Thanks to its geographic location, the Soviet Union has no similar need— whether for its own protection or for that of its allies—of engaging in peacetime deployment of forces beyond the borders of the bloc. This asymmetry in the geographic positions of the two great powers gives the Soviet Union a marked propagandistic advantage. It has nothing to fear and much to gain from arousing hostility against "military blocs" and the stationing of troops on foreign soil.

From what has just been said about the need of having allies, it should not be inferred that the United States would profit if all non-Communist nations were prepared to join its alliance system. Even some of the present members may be a military liability rather than an asset. If a country has little to offer, militarily, and is so exposed that an effort to protect it exceeds U.S. capabilities, there is danger that failure to live up to a commitment to defend it may have the much-feared "domino effect" of driving other allies into the arms of the Soviets. Moreover, efforts to protect such a country may be so costly or provocative that the U.S. would be worse off as a result of the alignment than it would have been had the country in question remained uncommitted.

Any appeal of nonalignment or neutrality to peoples within allied countries is a threat to the U.S. collective-defense system. Unfortunately, forces are at work, quite aside from Soviet propaganda, that tend to enhance this appeal. The realization that a strategic nuclear stalemate is in the making, if it does not already exist, undermines allied confidence in American military protection, which for years has rested on faith in the deterrent power of the U.S. strategic force. At the same time, growing public awareness of the potential destructiveness of war in the nuclear age is increasing fear of involvement in such a war and playing into the hands of those who advocate neutrality as, allegedly, the safest means of avoiding such involvement.

Whether the U.S. approves of neutrality or not, it has little choice but to resign itself to it where it is espoused by other nations. No nation can be forced into becoming an ally, least of all a reliable ally. But it should also be stressed that, from an American point of view, genuine neutrality is the least disadvantageous choice that countries can make if they decide to remain outside the U.S. collective-defense system. This was not realized when Secretary Dulles branded neutrality as downright immoral. At that time, the illusion prevailed of a kind of predestined solidarity among all free nations. In the case of the new states today, the alternative to neutrality is either some degree of neutralist unneutrality or outright alignment with the Soviet bloc. However, it remains true that every increase in the area outside the alliance system narrows the opportunities for U.S. military deployment overseas. The liquidation of European colonial empires has already cut deeply into the territory once available for American and allied overseas bases and staging areas, which are indispensable for effective local deterrence and limited war. A point might be reached at which American support for limited war operations, particularly on the fringes of Red China, would be rendered almost impossible, with consequences easy to imagine.

The refusal of neutral countries to offer military support and opportunities for deployment thus tends to hurt the defense effort of a country that has to rely on the cooperation of others. Yet, the attitude and behavior of countries adhering to the traditional rules of neutrality compare very favorably with those of neutralist countries, not to speak of countries aligned with the Sino-Soviet bloc. The chief concern of the old-time neutrals is to avoid involvement in any future hot wars of other nations. They hope to achieve this goal by maintaining strict impartiality in peacetime. By persuading future belligerents that they will not play favorites, they expect that their neutrality will be respected by both sides in time of war, as it often has in the past. The desire to arouse no suspicion of partiality—and to have no occasion for being partial—leads them to exercise the utmost restraint in their external dealings. Any activity in international politics—even in the relatively harmless form of taking sides in the voting process at the U.N.—may arouse doubts about their impartiality. Therefore, their policy is one of passivity and abstention.

This policy is in sharp contrast to that of the neutralists. The behavior of the noncommitted states in Asia and Africa—or at least of their more radical "leaders"—deviates drastically from passivity and restraint. They insist themselves that their "neutralism" is "active" or "positive." They obviously seek to play a role in world affairs. Such departure from the age-old rules of neutral behavior calls for an explanation. When it occurs, it presents new problems to U.S. defense policy and justifies the distinction between the new neutralism and traditional neutrality.

Before identifying typical traits of neutralist behavior, it must be stressed that wide divergencies exist in the attitudes of the new Afro-Asian states. They range from a marked benevolence toward the French Community, to outspoken partisanship for the Sino-Soviet bloc, as in the case of Guinea or Mali, where it becomes extremely difficult to decide at which point neutralism ends and alignment with the Sino-Soviet bloc begins. The difficulty encountered by neutralist leaders who would like to form a neutralist "third force" stems, to a considerable extent, from their differences concerning the attitude to be taken toward the East and the West. It also reflects direct conflict or tension between the new states themselves. If one of them infringes upon the interests of another, it may drive the other into closer alignment with the West or the East, depending on the circumstances. More important, if the Soviet Union overstepped its bounds by imposing its controls overtly on one of the neutralists, it might drive others into closer ties with the West. In view of these divergencies, and the fluidity of the attitudes involved, neutralism must be understood not as conformity with a fixed pattern of behavior but rather as a current tendency toward a pattern peculiar to the states involved and one that may be weakened or reversed in time.

The new neutralism stems from circumstances and motivations substantially different from those underlying traditional neutrality and its quest for respect for neutral rights by belligerent powers. This is not to say that the neutralists are not concerned, too, with preventing involvement of their countries in the wars of others. But even when it comes to protecting themselves against such involvement, they will be shown to rely upon means different from those employed by neutrals of the traditional type. What chiefly distinguishes neutralists from neutrals, however, is the primary concern of the former, not with future war, but with objectives to be pursued under present Cold War conditions. The old-time neutrals are *status quo* powers that have no urgent demands to make on others. By contrast, the new states—and especially those that are under radical or revolutionary leadership—have their eyes fixed on peacetime opportunities and dangers that call for action in the name of both nationalist and universalist objectives, two sets of objectives not always compatible with each other.

Their nationalist objective is the attainment, or the consolidation, of sovereign national independence. Once emancipation from colonial rule—or of what is considered its equivalent—has been achieved, consolidation becomes the dominant nationalist concern. There are two facets to the process of consolidation, both of which affect the attitude of the neutralists toward international affairs; one concerns the position of the new states in the world community, the other, the position of the new leaders and elites within the national communities.

In order to gain stability, the new states need as much international respect for their sovereign independence as they can obtain. They seek, therefore, to bolster their international prestige. Passivity of the kind practiced by traditional neutrals is not the road to such prestige. Instead, the neutralists try to make themselves heard and to play a role among the nations of the world. In addition, the more dynamic members seek to mold the group into a united "third force." On occasion, they even attempt to demonstrate their ability to influence the policy of the two superpowers, as they did when they appealed to President Eisenhower and Prime Minister Khrushchev to meet and settle their differences. The United Nations has provided an ideal forum for weak nations in search of international prominence; it permits them to compete in the battle of words and votes at a time when they lack the means for other, more demanding, forms of competition.

But consolidation of independence in the eyes of the world goes hand in hand with efforts of nationalist leaders and ruling elites to consolidate their positions on the home front. A reputation for being important in the world arena may spell victory in the fierce struggle with domestic rivals, particularly with indigenous Communist factions. Here, again, only an activist foreign policy can promise rewards. What matters most in this connection is to be courted by the two major powers and, possibly by playing them against each other, to receive support and economic aid from both of them.

The United States has little reason to be disturbed about the passion for independence that possesses all neutralist countries. The trouble is that so few neutralist leaders seem to recognize that adequate American counterpower to Soviet power is the best safeguard of their countries' independence. If they do recognize it, they don't dare to say so publicly. As a consequence, there is little to check them from condemning measures of U.S. defense policy such as the deployment of forces overseas that, by serving to maintain the world balance of power, offer protection to the independence of weak countries. Such independence might also be lost if a neutralist country like Guinea came to lean so heavily on Soviet support that, inadvertently perhaps, it might find itself subjected to Soviet control. Leaders of neutralist countries whose nationalism is sincere are obviously far more sensitive to this danger than their domestic Communist rivals who prefer the unity of world Communism to national independence, even if it means subservience to Moscow or Peking; the latter cannot be expected to be deterred from going all out in their quest for Sino-Soviet support if other neutralist countries are being sucked from the neutralist camp into the Sino-Soviet orbit.

The nationalist craving for self-determination and sovereign independence continues to be a powerful force, even in those postcolonial areas where liberation has already occurred; it may burst into flames if provoked by any act that can be interpreted as outside interference or infringement of sovereign rights. Yet, a second objective, universalist in character, competes with nationalism for the prime allegiance of the neutralist leaders and peoples. It is well to remember that most of these peoples become nations in any meaningful sense of the term only after emancipation from colonial rule is accomplished and the beginnings of independent statehood have been made. Prior to that, what prods them toward their goal of liberation and carries the battle cry of liberation across Asia and Africa into the Western Hemisphere is a revolutionary ideology and movement that transcends parochial nationalist interests and, by its universal claims, appeals to all "victims of Western colonialism and imperialism." It has been the tragic fate of the West that all of the new states and would-be nations that are presently capable of affecting the course of world events recognize out of experience none but Western colonialism and imperialism, just as the followers of Marx and Lenin see economic exploitation and social injustice only where it can be labeled as capitalist. As a result, present-day neutralist ideology has a kind of built-in anti-Western bias, particularly marked where anticolonial zeal goes hand in hand with strong socialist aversion against the capitalist system of free enterprise.

Because of their anti-imperialist ideology, the more radical leaders in neutralist countries consider it their mission, even after their own countries have attained independence, to continue the fight against all remnants of European colonialism, as well as against all forms of what they conceive to be American imperialism. So popular is this cause that statesmen in the neutralist world who appreciate the dangers to national independence arising from an acute anti-Western attitude frequently dare not oppose it; there are enough domestic aspirants to power to take advantage of any lack of zeal for the revolutionary cause.

Unless more resistance develops among moderate neutralist leaders against the extremists who see their countries virtually at war with the Western "imperialist cliques" and their "stooges," the prospects for neutral impartiality on the part of the bulk of the presently neutralist states must remain dim. This means that, on many vital issues, the United States and its allies have to contend with a marked degree of ideological affinity and solidarity between the Communist camp and the partisan or unneutral neutralists within the camp of the uncommitted states. This solidarity shows itself on issues such as disarmament, the dismantling of foreign bases and the relaxation of tensions through East-West negotiations.

Disarmament offers a good illustration of how the neutralist ideology may, intentionally or unintentionally, lead to a position unfavorable to the West. It was mentioned earlier that the neutralists share the desire of the neutrals to stay out of future wars that might arise from the East-West struggle. According to their spokesmen, they also wish to keep out of the Cold War, although it cannot escape them that they have everything to gain from the East-West competition for their favor. What distinguishes the neutralists from the traditional neutrals with respect to war is that the neutralists seek to escape war not through impartiality and abstention in foreign affairs, but through active promotion of specific peace strategies, to which they are ideologically committed, and which, in their opinion, will lead to enduring peace in the world.

One such strategy, according to them, is a strategy of total disarmament, starting with the withdrawal of all military forces and facilities from foreign soil and including the abolition of nuclear weapons. Because these are also the measures advocated by the Soviets, the United States and its allies are placed at a grave disadvantage. They seem to be hedging when they insist on careful inspection schemes as part of any disarmament agreement, although inspection is indispensable to them, in view of the closed character of Soviet society. America and her allies also appear to reflect bad faith when they oppose the liquidation of all American military positions overseas, although their liquidation might irreparably tip the world balance of power to the Soviet side. As mentioned earlier, lack of concern for the balance of power characterizes many neutralist ideological predilections and attitudes. Promotion of peace through a relaxation of tensions brought about by East-West negotiations is a case in point. The tendency among the neutralists has been to regard any compromise arising from such negotiations as a gain for peace, irrespective of whether it is reached by a genuine "give and take" or results, instead, from unilateral Western concessions involving a loss in relative Western strength and counterpower.

Obviously, ideological partiality for the Soviets expressed merely through verbal pressures on the West is not the most virulent form of neutralist unneutrality, although it may affect the American defense position adversely. Discriminations in favor of Soviet military assistance, if they occur, are much more serious in their effects. They could reach a point where the Soviets would gain a military foothold in the country receiving aid and turn it into a Soviet ally or staging area. Some of the more revolutionary nationalist leaders may not be aware of the dangers to their countries' independence that could arise from a lack of restraint in ideological fervor or they may not be able to recognize in advance precisely at what point they risk forfeiting their countries' independence. It would be ironic, however, if any of the new states, out of resentment against even mild forms of Western "imperialist" control, were led into new captivity, and a captivity more painful than that which they have suffered in the past. In any case, while the United States can afford to be tolerant about many neutralist moves and attitudes with which it disagrees, it could not afford to remain passive if incursions of hostile military power into vital defense positions were to result, either from partiality of neutralist governments toward the Soviet bloc or from neutralist indifference to the prerequisites of international equilibrium.

The preceding discussion has dealt with the impact on the American defense position of the respective attitudes and policies of allied, neutral, and neutralist members of the non-Communist world. Each of the three groups was found to present special problems to those who make American foreign and defense policies. These problems are rendered more delicate by the fact that policies directed at any one of the three groups necessarily affects the two others. A policy modeled exclusively to improving relations with allies, for instance, may greatly increase the difficulties encountered in dealing with neutralists, as the United States has experienced again and again when faced with the struggle between colonialist allies and anticolonialist neutralists. Because each of the three groups may be led, under grave provocation, to switch to a group less favorable to vital American defense interests, the United States cannot afford to ignore the reactions to its policies of any of the three groups, though it may at times have to choose among them, or place priorities on its concern for their respective allegiance.

The neutrals, one might presume, raise no particular problems. The United States has ceased to condemn them for their refusal to participate in collective-defense efforts, and profits from the role genuinely neutral countries play as international mediators and conciliators.* Moreover, American benevolence toward nations that maintain a position of strict impartiality, and American respect for their right to act independently, may help attract neutralist countries toward a position of traditional neutrality. However, favors extended to neutral nations may adversely affect United States relations with its allies, either by increasing the appeal of neutrality to their peoples or by causing resentment of the favorable treatment accorded countries that bear no share of the burden of collective defense. The United States must avoid, therefore, adding to the lures of neutrality, while at the same time rewarding it where it replaces "neutralist unneutrality."

The allies of the United States rank second only to the American armed forces as pillars of American security. It might be tempting to conclude, therefore, that in viewing the three groups of countries from the point of view of American defense interests, the allied group would always merit priority over the others. In many instances, this is the case. If a choice had to be made between a move to keep France in NATO, and one that would prevent one or more neutralist countries from becoming hostile to the United States, it is hard to imagine circumstances under which the preservation of NATO would not have a primary claim on American policy. But not all cases fall into this extreme category. The way in which allies or neutralists react to similar moves by the United States may vary widely, and the weight to be accorded a specific ally or neutralist group is not the same in every instance. What matters most is to minimize the chances of having to make the kind of invidious choice mentioned above. In view of the prevailing concern about the attitudes of the new states and their revolutionary leaders, it is necessary to remind oneself of the indispensable contributions to the common defense effort that only allied countries are ready to make.

Fortunately, their own self-interest will usually suffice to hold allied countries in the alliance, provided that faith in the protective value of alignment with the United States rests on strong

* Referring to a statement ascribed to Khrushchev by Walter Lippmann that "there are no neutral men," Secretary Rusk was quoted by *The New York Times* of April 18, 1961, as saying that Khrushchev's statement "strikes at the heart of the possibilities of international organization and mediation and would set the world back a very long way indeed in settling disputes by peaceful means." I know of no greater compliment paid to genuine neutrality, but also no clearer indication of the danger that the search for men acceptable as impartial to both sides in the Cold War may run into increasing, if not insuperable, difficulties.

foundations. Similarly, national self-interest, if recognized by the leaders of neutralist states, will tend to restrain them from allowing antagonism against the United States to carry them beyond a point at which they might lose the benefits they derive from being able to choose between two camps and to obtain support from both of them.

The danger remains that some ally, or some neutralist country, may be blinded to its own best interests by fear or resentment and turn its back on the United States and the West. But if such cases can be kept at a minimum, the United States should be capable of taking the loss, if it occurs, or of compensating for it elsewhere. Whereas it would be folly to ignore the value of allied solidarity and the usefulness of neutralist benevolence, it would be defeatist, and expose the United States to dangerous blackmail, if it were assumed that the American defense position is dependent on a favorable attitude on the part of each and every American ally or each and every group of neutralist states. Moreover, only when vital U.S. defense positions are endangered by the inimical behavior of countries unmistakably allied with the Sino-Soviet bloc should it be necessary to consider direct interference, and, possibly, to take military action against them.

IX

REVOLUTIONARY CHANGE AND THE STRATEGY OF THE *STATUS QUO*

by VERNON V. ASPATURIAN

ONE of the great ideological battlegrounds between the Western world and the Sino-Soviet nations is the universe of underdeveloped countries scattered across Africa, Asia, and North and South America.'Whether the ideological allegiances of these countries will be attracted toward the West or toward the Communist world may determine the fate of Western civilization and the social and political systems that it has developed. As the world becomes trifurcated into distinct, if somewhat nebulously organized, ideosocial consensus systems, a triangular pattern of tension and conflict takes shape and demands release and resolution. These tensions and conflicts originated first in the Bolshevik Revolution of 1917 and the challenges that it represented, and later, in the disintegration of the Western colonial systems and the resultant clash between the aspirations of the emerging states and the vestigial bastions of Western rule and domination.

In short, the underdeveloped world is convulsed by social upheaval and seething with revolutionary passion for a place in the sun, long denied them by the dark shadow of colonialism. The Western world, on the other hand, seeks to arrest the social revolution that is sweeping the underdeveloped world, whether in colonial territories, newly emancipated states, or countries with ancient credentials of independence and sovereignty. This revolutionary assault is directed against two distinct targets: (1) the indigenous feudal or quasi-feudal social relics of medievalism; and (2) colonial or foreign domination, be it political or economic in character—that is, opposed to Western imperialism. Thus, the revolutions in underdeveloped countries are directed against the *status quo,* both in their internal social orders and their external relationships with the Western powers. Since the underdeveloped countries are against what is supported by the Western world and the United States, the latter emerge as the main bulwarks of the *status quo,* which is under attack.

Since this *status quo* has been under siege from the Soviet Union since the Bolshevik Revolution of 1917, the underdeveloped world and the Soviet Union find themselves tactically united, while American policy, in its zeal to preserve the *status quo* everywhere, emerges as both anti-Soviet and antirevolutionary in general. Moreover, since the *status quo* has a single defender—the West—and two challengers—Soviet Communism and native revolutionary movements—the two challengers are forced into a marriage of tactical convenience. This, all too frequently, results in their being lumped together as a single force in American foreign-policy calculations.

However, it should be made clear from the outset that this tactical alliance between Soviet Communism and the nationalist revolutionary movements in underdeveloped countries is essentially ephemeral and transitory in character because its common goals are limited to the destruction of feudalism (internally) and imperialism (externally). Soviet Communists consider support for the achievement of these objectives to be a necessary preliminary to subsequent Communist revolutions, but the underdeveloped world does not reciprocate with absolute support for Soviet foreign policy or ideological goals. Although the underdeveloped world is opposed to the *status quo,* it does not wish to replace that *status quo* with a Communist social system. Instead, it seeks to achieve the social order of the Western world. In this lie both irony and tragedy for the West, for a submerged common denominator of interests and action exists between the preservation of the *status quo* in the Western world and revolutionary change in the underdeveloped countries. The tremendous social and political energies released by one part of the world in revolution against its *status quo* could be tapped by the West to stabilize, expand, and strengthen the *status quo* in the West against the transcendental pretensions of Soviet Communism. Instead, skillful Soviet exploitation of the conflicts between the West and the underdeveloped countries may tap these energies to both subvert the *status quo* in the West and abort the social order that the underdeveloped countries seek to establish.

Although the main revolutionary tide in the underdeveloped

world is neither Communist nor Communist-inspired, it soon becomes Soviet-encouraged and supported. The more implacable and unyielding the forces of the *status quo* against these non-Communist forces, the more they are impelled toward Moscow, and the greater the danger that they may fall under its control. In this way, the Soviet Union hopes to emerge as the champion not only of Communism, but of revolutionary change and progress in general. Indeed, the new program of the Communist Party of the Soviet Union arrogantly boasts that all revolutionary roads lead to Communism. The multiple revolutions of the mid-twentieth century are merged into a single force dedicated to annihilating the bastions of the *status quo:*

> Socialist revolutions, national liberation and anti-imperialist revolutions, people's democratic revolutions, broad peasants' movements, the struggle of the masses for the overthrow of fascism and other despotic regimes, and general democratic movements against national oppression are all being merged into a single world revolutionary process undermining and destroying capitalism.[1]

Thus, in a world charged with revolutionary passion, the Western world and the United States are being trapped into becoming the gendarmes of a reactionary *status quo,* since American policy increasingly assumes the pattern of desperately preserving the *status quo,* wherever and whatever it might be, whether under attack from Communists or from nationalist revolutionary movements. Simultaneously, American statesmen, and much of the American public, frequently imagine the United States to be in the vanguard of the very revolutionary surge that its policies and instruments appear to thwart. While the image of the United States in most of the world is increasingly that of the mainstay of the *status quo,* America has recalled its colonial past in an orgy of revolutionary verbalism, although its actions remain implacably conservative. In a desperate attempt to preserve its revolutionary image while simultaneously opposing revolutions, American policy often identifies purely indigenous non-Communist revolutionary movements as Communist-inspired, directed, or infiltrated. This identification is enthusiastically welcomed by Moscow, since, instead of discrediting non-Communist revolutionary movements, it has the unfortunate effect of identifying Communism with popular causes. Thus, at the Twenty-second Party Congress, Khrushchev almost exultantly observed:

Attempts are made to blame us Communists for any action by the masses against their oppressors. When the working people of any capitalist or colonial country rise in struggle, the imperialists begin to cry: "This is the handiwork of the Communists" or the "hand of Moscow." Of course, we are glad to have the imperialists ascribe to Communists all the good actions of peoples. By so doing, the imperialists are involuntarily helping the masses to gain a better understanding of Communist ideas.[2]

This dangerous discrepancy between the self-image of the United States as revolutionary, and its image in the revolutionary world as conservative, even reactionary, requires critical investigation. The usual American response is to call for "a better selling job" or "propaganda effort," or to contrast the weekly hours the Communists spend on radio broadcasts with the puny response of the Voice of America. Characteristically, there is never any investigation of the content of American propaganda efforts, as if it were self-evident that what is said is unimportant when compared with how it is said and how often. Americans are rightly bewildered that the "land of the free," with the highest standard of living in the world, and a material culture second to none, should be represented as opposing progress. Yet, the reason is simple. Most Americans are satisfied with their *status quo* and resent the pretensions of Soviet Communism to liberate them from an imaginary oppressor; they fail to realize, however, the intensity with which any movement opposed to the *status quo* is greeted, whether or not it is Communist. There is no passion against Communism in the underdeveloped countries, because Communism is not a threat, to them, but to conditions that they detest and refuse to defend. In defending a popularly accepted *status quo* against the Soviet threat, the United States has been trapped into defending it everywhere against all revolutionary forces.

The so-called great debates on American foreign policy have never clearly presented the issues in terms of revolution versus *status quo;* the American public has never been asked whether the national interest, as distinguished from the special vested interest of some American corporations, requires that the *status quo* be preserved on four continents against popular revolutionary movements. Indeed, the American public has not even been told that a *status quo* is being defended, or what the ideological and geographical definition of the *status quo* that is being defended is. Yet there is a *status quo* that must be defended, and defended against the Soviet threat. What is required is a general theoretical definition of this *status quo* and a strategy for the most effective way of preserving it. Such strategy would reveal that, historically and logically, defending a given *status quo* is not incompatible with supporting revolutions against *status quos* elsewhere, for often one can best defend a given *status quo* in one part of the world by supporting revolutions against another elsewhere. Correspondingly, a *status quo* may actually be weakened and subverted if *status quos* are indiscriminately supported everywhere.

In answering the challenges of a revolutionary world, and the Soviet threat to exploit it, one of the obvious points requiring attention is the degree of validity and effectiveness of the Western system of social analysis, for an effective strategy of action must rest upon a sound foundation of analysis. Does the West have an accurate idea of the social and political realities in a revolutionary world, or has it been distorted by factors that have not received sufficient attention from scholars? To what extent have Western analyses of social and political forces been subverted by propaganda clichés and sanctimonious proclamations? Even more important, is it possible that the Soviet system of analyzing forces and events in the underdeveloped world in terms of social classes and class conflict gives a more accurate appraisal than the Western system—which sedulously avoids resorting to a class analysis? To what extent are Western distortions of social and international realities due to faulty perception and self-deception, resulting from the employment of imperfect analytical categories; and to what degree are they a result of calculated deception on the part of powerful pressure groups and influential cliques that have a stake in distorting and concealing realities? As concrete illustrations of tensions that might exist between vested interests and social realities: (1) How "real" are the "free" institutions of Laos, Jordan, and South Vietnam, which the United States has committed itself to defend against revolutionary insurrections, as compared with the realities of outside vested interests and the interests of local feudal landowning classes? (2) How "real" is the claim that the commitment to destroy "Castroism" in Cuba reflects the American passion to preserve the "democratic" institutions of Guatemala, Honduras, Nicaragua, Haiti, El Salvador, Panama, Peru, and Paraguay, as compared with the realities of the huge financial investments that American companies and corporations have in Latin America?

To ask these questions is not always to answer them, but it is indisputable that wrong answers, whether by calculation or through ignorance, will provide a poor foundation for a successful policy of defending the *status quo* in the Western world. An effective framework for analysis and strategy of action demands: (1) a realistic appraisal of forces and events in the underdeveloped world; (2) a knowledge of how the Soviet Union analyzes these forces and events, and how it arrives at assumptions concerning Western response and behavior; (3) a bold, unevasive, and realistic definition of the *status quo* that is to be preserved and extended, as well as of the *status quo* that must be abandoned, not to the mercies of Soviet Communism, but to the innovating and invigorating shock of bourgeois-nationalist revolutions; (4) a precise appraisal of the social forces that can be relied upon to defend a given *status quo,* and a plan as to how these forces can be broadened and strengthened; and (5) an equally precise appraisal of those social forces that are irrevocably committed to the destruction of the *status quo* that the West wishes to maintain, and a plan for preventing these forces from recruiting additional adherents among dissatisfied and frustrated populations.

What, then, is the *status quo* that the United States should be committed to preserve and strengthen? It is an ideosocial system that the Communists call "capitalist-imperialist," and which Americans variously refer to as "Western," "the free world," "the democratic world," or "capitalism," not always being certain which has priority, since they are not always compatible with one another. Clearly, there is a "free world," a "democratic world," and a "capitalist world," but they bear little relation to the "free world" of the propaganda clichés, which includes some of the most despotic, venal, and feudalistic systems on the globe. The United States finds itself supporting regimes whose vices often exceed those ascribed to Soviet totalitarianism. The vices against which the United States is committed are similarly distorted; they include "dictatorship," "the slave-world" and "totalitarianism."

The current *status quo* policy is anti-Communism, which has become an increasingly elastic and arbitrary concept, since it constitutes the ideological standard against which American objectives are measured. Reduced to their operational level, the shop-worn clichés of "freedom" and "free world" refer to freedom from Soviet (or Sino-Soviet) Communism, irrespective of any other conception of freedom that might be violated. Similarly, the vices to be resisted, "tyranny," "despotism," and "slavery," have operational relevance only with respect to Communist "slavery," "despotism," and "tyranny." Otherwise, how can one explain the zeal with which the United States defends despotism and tyranny in Iran, Saudi Arabia, Yemen, South Vietnam, and elsewhere, as opposed to the totalitarian systems in the Soviet circle, which, at least, are mitigated by accelerated cultural, economic, and technological progress? Can one maintain that life in the despotic and socially retrograde regimes of the feudal Middle East is really more free and more bountiful than in the Communist countries? If so, one must ask, "More free and bountiful *for whom?*" And when this question is answered, one begins to understand the concrete meaning of freedom.

It is indisputable that there exists a free world to defend, but it has little resemblance to the "free world" of the propaganda cliché. It is also incontestable that this free world must be defended against Soviet Communism. But there is a larger world that is neither free nor Communist, and in order that it might be defended more effectively, it should be made "free" rather than be preserved in its current state. Thus, one key to an effective *status quo* policy is not simply to defend it, but also to extend it.

The revolutionary ferment in the underdeveloped world is also motivated by a pursuit of "freedom"—freedom from colonial domination, foreign economic exploitation, and indigenous feudal ruling classes. The beneficiaries of the *status quo* in the underdeveloped countries coalesce to preserve a reactionary system from which they benefit while keeping in social bondage millions who ache for the very freedoms that the West vows to preserve, but often helps to deny.

Revolutions are not impersonal forces, but movements designed to serve the interests of distinct social groups and classes, just as a given *status quo* does. Movements aiming for the destruction of social systems that benefit some classes, in order to build other systems that reflect the interests of other classes, are authentic revolutionary movements. The wider the spectrum of classes that benefit from a given social order, the more "progressive" the system and the wider the ambit of "freedom" that characterizes the social system. Although a certain social system may have been established in the interests of a definite class, its class *origin* is not necessarily identical with the social interests it serves, for a social order originally designed to serve the interests of a given class may be gradually transformed into a social system from which all classes benefit.

The social *status quo* that should be defended, and extended, is an outgrowth of the great bourgeois revolutions that swept across Western Europe and the Thirteen Colonies in the seventeenth, eighteenth, and nineteenth centuries. These revolutions unleashed invigorating and innovating forces that fashioned a distinct civilization or ideosocial system whose benefits were diffused among all classes in society, transcending those of the bourgeoisie, or middle class, whose values and aspirations have become not merely the values of a particular nation, but those of an entire community of states we call the Western world. The middle-class social orders of the West are a system with a certain fluid, dynamic equilibrium of social, economic, and political power. The more the class interests of the social class that brought the order into being is transcended, the more "classless" the society becomes, in the sense that all classes of society become gradually "bourgeoified" as they adopt the middle-class values. In some countries, notably France and Italy, where the diffusion of interests has been fragmentary, class distinctions prevail, as the working class is denied the opportunity to become "bourgeois." Hence the substantial support that the Communist Party of each of these countries enjoys.

The revolutions that are imminent or temporarily arrested in Latin America, the Middle East, and Africa, as well as those already consummated or in the process of stabilization, are essentially a resumption of the great revolutionary flood unleashed by the French and American revolutions. Such revolutions were aborted in Eastern Europe by Soviet Communism, and arrested in Asia, Africa, and Latin America by the intrusion of Western colonialism and the unholy alliance between Western capitalism and local feudal classes in Latin America and Asia. In the African regions south of the Sahara, most of which were tribal, preliterate and even prefeudal in character, feudalism was arrested, and a landowning aristocracy did not take shape at all. The colonial authority moved in and, where European settlement was possible, white colonists became surrogates for a landowning aristocracy. This situation led to the development of a caste system rather than a class social order, a development that reached its consummate evolution in South Africa, and, to a lesser degree, in Kenya, the Congo, Southern Rhodesia, and the Portuguese colonies. In Central America and in the Caribbean area, large foreign-owned latifundian enterprises further complicated the socioeconomic system. In general, a symbiotic relationship, which still persists, was established between foreign investors and the local landowning classes. Both groups had a common interest in frustrating the emergence of an indigenous capitalist class; the landowners were afraid that a powerful capitalist class would threaten their dominant power position, and foreign economic interests feared local competition.

Consequently, the development of the middle class was first arrested and then reshaped within the socioeconomic mold created by the alliance between the local landowners and the foreign economic interests. There emerged a new type of middle class—a class whose social locus of power was not material wealth or ownership of factories, but the possession of special skills and the ability to perform certain functions—a group that might be called the bureaucratic intelligentsia. Thus, the European middle class, which created a new civilization in Europe and the United States from which all classes now benefit, aided in the preservation of feudal despotism and barbarism in the underdeveloped world and, indeed, intensified the exploitation of the population.

The distinguishing characteristic of an ideosocial system is to be found in the equilibrium of power that has been established among the social classes. The distribution of power among these classes can vary considerably, from the extreme of the Marxist-Leninist image of a "ruling class," which remains a valid approximation of social reality in many of the underdeveloped countries, to an informal graduated structure of power in which different classes share in the distribution of power, not necessarily in equal proportions, but usually in a structural hierarchy that is, to a greater or lesser degree, mobile and dynamic.

A given ideosocial system might also be defined in terms of the social class that constitutes the center of gravity in the system, whether it is the "ruling class," the most powerful class, the most numerous class, or the social class that acts as a bond between the social groups above and below it. Within this context, the ideological *status quo* the West is committed to defend is the middle-class social order, which is the dominant, but not universal, social system outside the Soviet orbit. A middle-class social system is not necessarily conterminous with a capitalist economic order, but includes "socialist" states like the Nordic countries, Great Britain, and others as well. In these countries, public ownership of economic enterprises is carried out by the middle classes, who continue to provide the social and political leadership in their countries. These countries are usually described as "democratic-socialist" systems, but they could more properly be called "middle-class socialist" systems, as opposed to the proletarian-socialist systems within the Soviet orbit. While it is true that the former are democratic and the latter authoritarian, the "socialist" systems emerging in the underdeveloped countries are also "middle class" in character, but nondemocratic. The fundamental factor is the character of the system rather than the political or economic forms by which the pivotal class exercises its power and radiates its influence.

Any ideosocial system allows considerable latitude for variation in institutions, processes, and social equilibrium. As a general rule, the more mature the system, the more variegated the internal mutations and permutations become; the newer the system, the more rigid and uniform it tends to be. In mature ideosocial systems, whose dominance has long been unchallenged, internal variations and differences are exaggerated and appear to be fundamentally incompatible until confronted with the challenge of a totally new ideosocial system.

Concepts like "democracy," "freedom," and "authoritarianism" have relevance only when they relate to a given ideosocial system, which inevitably provides their substantive definition and operational character. Therefore, authoritarian and democratic systems within a common ideosocial order are more congenial to each other than to their counterparts in another ideosocial framework, and dichotomies between "dictatorships" and "democracies," or "free systems" and "slave orders" are superficial and deceptive. The current struggle between East and West is neither a struggle between "democracy" and "despotism," nor between "freedom" and "slavery." It is a more profound struggle between ideosocial systems whose substantive definitions of common platitudes like "justice," "freedom," "democracy," "peace," and "justice," are intrinsically incompatible because their reference points are two conflicting social equilibriums.

In the revolutionary transfer of power from one class to another, the new ruling class may perpetuate itself, or it may create conditions in which class rule is transformed into a distinct culture and way of life whose social and ethical values are diffused and imparted to all classes in society. This enables a class civilization to assume political forms ranging from democracy to despotism, and economic orders ranging from "rugged individualism" to a wide measure of public ownership. It is neither the political nor the economic system that imparts to a system its distinctive flavor, but rather the class origin of its way of life. Soviet society represents a proletarian culture, not because the proletariat rules, but because the values and goals of the proletariat have become the values and goals of society as a whole.

An effective *status quo* policy consequently depends upon a clear definition of the *status quo,* of which an ideological, rather than geographical, definition appears to be least ambiguous and most defensible morally, militarily, and psychologically. Furthermore, such a definition imparts both consistency and uniformity over a wide range of possibilities. A *status quo* policy defined in this manner would be dynamic rather than static and would aim to preserve middle-class rule wherever it exists and to support its rise to power in the residual feudal communities wherever it does not exist; each middle class, however, must select the political and economic systems that it considers most appropriate for the stabilization of its authority.

Since, in most of the residual feudal countries of the world, the indigenous middle class has already come to power, or is spontaneously being catapulted in that direction, the question of outside imposition is not involved. The West is not foisting middle-class rule upon the emerging countries; this is taking place spontaneously. Indeed, the greatest danger is that the West will intervene to thwart middle-class revolutions and support the privileged position of the landowning classes. This policy, instead of supporting the ideological *status quo,* in fact subverts it. The most reliable instrument for supporting a middle-class ideosocial order is the middle class itself. Instead of relying upon a rising revolutionary middle class, which is bound to come to power and which would contribute to the stabilization of an expanding middle-class international system, American policy undermines the *status quo* by thwarting the aspirations of the middle classes. This forces their orientation toward the main reservoir of social revolution, the Soviet Union.

In analyzing the complex revolutionary patterns in the underdeveloped world, a modified class analysis is likely to be more accurate and, therefore, to offer a sounder foundation for policy than would an analysis within the context of categories like "poverty," "ignorance," "misery," and "hunger," or irrelevent platitudes like "freedom versus slavery" and "democracy versus dictatorship." Since the fundamental ideological issues have been more or less resolved in the United States and Western Europe (except in France, Italy, Spain, and Portugal) into a broad ideological consensus, Americans lose sight of the fact that, in the underde-

veloped world, the most immediate and pressing issues to be resolved are concerned with the fundamental nature of the social
order itself.

Thus, in the underdeveloped world, leaders and intellectuals
analyze social and political issues in terms of class categories, not
because they are Marxists, but because the social and political
realities of a world searching for an ideological consensus can be
better understood and analyzed in these terms. In many Middle
Eastern and Latin American countries, approximations of the
Marxist conception of a "ruling class" are realities, not figments of
the Soviet imagination. For millions, class conflict and the exploitation of classes in the underdeveloped world is a real experience.

American society has gradually "bourgeoified" into a quasi-
classless society. Class categories as tools of social and political
analysis have become suspect and, as they have become increasingly irrelevant to the American social scene, have fallen into disrepute. A vast vacuum in the sphere of social analysis has been
partially filled in recent years by intellectual euphemisms like "interest groups" and "elites." These words are valuable analytical
instruments, but they are even more valuable when developed
within the broader framework of social classes of which they are
subgroups.

One of the great advantages of the Soviet analytical system is
that it has been allowed to establish a virtual monopoly on class
analysis. Yet, classes, class conflict, and class analysis were not in-
vented, discovered, or contrived by Lenin or Marx. In our own
constitutional and political history, references to classes—ruling
and otherwise—to class conflict, and so on, are profuse and varied
in the writings of Alexander Hamilton, John Adams, James Madi-
son, John C. Calhoun, and others. What happened is that
Marxists effectively united a valid and reputable system of social
analysis with a disreputable and feared prognosis, and as a result
of guilt by association, the respectability of class analysis was ideologically tarnished.

Yet, it should be obvious that a class analysis can be used to
stabilize and preserve the *status quo* just as it is used to disrupt
and upset it, a point that was recognized but rejected by both Marx
and Lenin. Instead, the Marxist view that a class analysis inevitably
supported a revolutionary upheaval was accepted in the West.
What has happened, in effect, is that we have become the unwitting victims of a disease often ascribed to the Soviet leaders,

whereby we automatically deny the existence of the realities that revolt us, accepting myths as reality simply because it would be most congenial if they were true. However, if the West is effectively to rebut the Soviet challenge, it can no longer enjoy the luxury of denying what exists in many underdeveloped countries: a fierce class conflict and the existence of systems like those of Iran, Saudi Arabia, Yemen, and some Latin American countries, which have living counterparts of the Marxist caricature of the "ruling class."

The social structure of the underdeveloped countries and the role of the revolutionary bourgeoisie vary from area to area. These variations, although important to the understanding of a local situation, do not undermine the essential common bonds between these social structures. Even more striking is the almost uniform character of the emergent revolutionary middle class, irrespective of its geographical location or the cultural environment from which it emerged.

The revolutionary bourgeoisie in underdeveloped countries is distinguished from its European prototype in a number of particulars that obscure its essentially middle-class character. In general, the revolutionary bourgeoisie in some Latin American countries is closest to the European prototype, while that of the African territories is farthest removed. The bourgeoisie in the Middle East adheres more closely to the European pattern than does the bourgeoisie in Southeast Asia.

The primary reason for variations of the revolutionary bourgeoisie from its European prototype is historical and chronological. The West European bourgeoisie was an original social formation; that is, it developed spontaneously within the womb of feudal society and, hence, was the original middle class and the prototype of all others. It was, in the first place, an entrepreneurial and property-holding class. The revolutionary bourgeoisie in underdeveloped countries, on the other hand, is an imitative class and is predominantly a nonentrepreneurial and non–property-owning class. It is, in effect, a secondary proliferation from the bourgeoisie, but its proliferation was not a response to the existence of a native property-owning bourgeoisie, but a response to a foreign capital-owning class.

The main component of the middle class, its revolutionary core, is the bureaucratic intelligentsia. In Western Europe, this was a secondary emanation from the property-owning bourgeoisie, but in underdeveloped countries it was the primary component of the middle class, which assumed prominence in the absence of a strong indigenous capitalist class. As a social group, the bureaucratic intelligentsia includes the various service and professional categories that developed to service the local aristocracy, the property-owning bourgeoisie, and the civil servants, teachers, lawyers, professors, engineers, doctors, professional military officers (in the middle grades), writers, artists, and other white-collar and professional vocations. The status of the bureaucratic intelligentsia was determined not by ownership of land or other property, but by the role it played in society.

In the underdeveloped countries, the bureaucratic intelligentsia serves much the same function and enjoys a comparable social status, but it grew up primarily to service foreign and alien enterprises rather than local higher classes. Consequently, it is even more alienated from its society than was the East European bureaucratic intelligentsia. Because of the closer social proximity of the revolutionary bourgeoisie in underdeveloped countries to the bureaucratic intelligentsia in Eastern Europe, its behavior and aspirations coincide more with that historical group than with the Western European bourgeoisie. It should also be mentioned that the Bolshevik Revolution was forged in the crucibles of this component of the middle class and hence Soviet leaders are probably more aware of the ambiguous and alienated character of this group and more prepared to exploit it.

Since the revolutionary elites in underdeveloped countries fail to meet all the criteria of what constitutes a "middle class" or "bourgeoisie" in the West European historical sense, their middle-class character is rejected in some quarters. Given the unique character of their emergence, the revolutionary elites in underdeveloped countries nevertheless qualify as authentic, if unstabilized and historically distorted, middle classes for the following reasons:

(1) The functions that these elites perform in society are traditional middle-class functions.

(2) The primary ideological motivation of the revolutionary elites is *nationalism* as an end in itself. Socialist norms, whether Marxist-inspired or not, are acceptable not as ends in themselves, but as more efficient means for consolidating and strengthening the emerging national state. Nationalism is both European and bourgeois in origin and conception. As an ideological norm, it is compatible with Communism. The fact that the Soviet Union has used both nationalism and transnationalist regionalism as instruments for the achievement of its own ends should not obscure the fact

that, whereas for Moscow, nationalism is a means and socialism an end, for the revolutionary elites, nationalism is the end, and socialism the means. In the economic sector, the socialism of the underdeveloped countries is, in reality, state capitalism rather than socialism.

(3) The revolutionary elite in underdeveloped countries takes its aspirations and values from the European middle classes whom it imitates and by whom it has been educated. As an imitative middle class, it seeks the social approval of European middle classes, and much of its resentment may stem from its feeling of rejection. It does not imitate the classes in the Soviet satellites, nor does it elevate the values of the proletarian class as objectives of national or social policy, as is done in the Communist world.

(4) Revolutionary elites do not reject religious norms and principles as guidelines for the organization of society, although they do reject some of the more reactionary and stultifying institutions and attitudes of religion that sprang up to preserve the sanctity of the old order. On the contrary, in the same way that its role became transformed by the bourgeoisie in Western Europe, religion may become an instrument for stabilizing and sanctifying the new social order.

The most imposing psychological barrier to Western acceptance of the revolutionary elite as a middle class is the fact that it is not a property-owning class—the traditional form of the Western bourgeoisie. Yet, it should be recognized that the peculiar conditions under which the underdeveloped countries emerged made the development of an indigenous property-owning bourgeois class largely impossible. However, wherever the possibilities presented themselves, as in Syria, India, parts of Latin America, and scattered locations elsewhere, an entrepreneurial middle class did emerge alongside the bureaucratic-intelligentsia component. Now that the class structure of the underdeveloped countries has assumed shape, it cannot be expected that they will introduce artificial measures solely to create a property-owning middle class to conform to an abstract ideological norm.

Although centered in the social structure, the bureaucratic intelligentsia is alienated from both the foreign capitalists and its own landowning aristocracy. Poorly paid, without property, and with little access to power or opportunity for upward mobility, the bureaucratic intelligentsia thrives in a suffocating atmosphere of frustration and resentment. As the native class in a society that possesses a virtual monopoly of the technical, professional, and organizational skills, it is denied political power, social status, and material rewards. Its frustrations intensify as its own estimate of its importance in society becomes aggrandized; its expectations and aspirations consequently accelerate and spiral upward in revolutionary passion. As the most articulate social concentration of resentment and frustration, it sees that the only barriers between it and the pinnacle of power and prestige are a small foreign capitalist class and an enervated and degenerate landowning class. Since members of the bureaucratic intelligentsia have the nearest access to the instruments of violence, it is not surprising that, in a number of cases—Egypt, Iraq, Sudan, South Korea— the leadership of this class has come from the middle ranks of the professional military.

Not sufficiently large to carry through and sustain a revolutionary transformation by itself, the revolutionary bourgeoisie unfurls the banner of nationalism and mobilizes the working class and the landless peasantry against the universally hated foreign capitalists and landowning classes. Where it has not yet come to power, it seeks power; where it has come to power, it seeks to solidify its control against the former ruling groups and to expand its power through modernization and industrialization. In pursuit of the first objective, it expropriates the landowners and nationalizes foreign enterprises. In pursuit of the second objective, it enhances the national power of the state through modernization and industrialization, based mainly on public ownership and centrally directed planning, and this, in turn, enhances its own power and prestige. Since the middle class controls the state, the expansion of state-owned enterprises automatically extends its power as a class. Thus, the immediate objective of the revolutionary middle class in power is to entrench itself permanently by adjusting the socioeconomic order to its advantage. It also endeavors to demonstrate to the working class and peasantry that it merits the right to rule as the most progressive and socially responsible class; that its goals, values, and aspirations are as worthy of emulation and universalization as those of the nation or society as a whole. This was perceptively recognized by the aging Stalin during one of his shrewdest and most enigmatic moments when, at the Nineteenth Party Congress, he anticipated that the middle class would fail in this endeavor and called upon the Communists to take possession of the political symbols of the bourgeoisie:

Formerly, the bourgeoisie permitted itself to be "liberal" and defended democratic freedoms, thus creating popularity for itself among the people. Now no trace remains of liberalism. There is no so-called "personal freedom." . . . The principle of equality among peoples and nations has been crushed and has been replaced by the principle of full rights for the exploiting minority and no rights at all for the exploited majority of citizens. The banner of bourgeois democratic rights has been thrown overboard. I think that this banner must be raised by you, the representatives of the Communist and democratic parties, and must be carried forward by you if you want to rally around you the majority of the people. There is no one else to raise it. . . . Formerly the bourgeoisie was considered the head of a nation. It defended the rights and independence of a nation for dollars. The banner of national independence and of national sovereignty has been thrown overboard. There is no doubt that this banner will have to be raised by you, representatives of Communist and democratic parties, and carried forward if you want to become the leading force of the nation. There is no one else to raise it.[3]

When the revolutionary middle class comes to power in underdeveloped countries it is extremely shaky because it possesses no material economic foundation to give it permanence. This results in its social instability and ideological ambivalence. This new class is capable of either establishing a new social *status quo* or, in the interests of preserving itself as a ruling group, abdicating its middle-class outlook, undergoing unilateral communization, and continuing the revolution in more radical directions. In the last instance, it automatically subverts its own character as a middle class and transforms itself into a bureaucratic ruling class, willing to serve any ideosocial system that will ensure its permanence as a collection of ruling individuals rather than a social class. This is precisely what current Soviet thinking about the future of the "national bourgeoisie" contemplates. It is a departure from the orthodox Leninist-Stalinist position on the inherent treachery of the "national bourgeoisie" still subscribed to by Mao Tse-tung.

The alliance forged between foreign economic interests and the landowning classes of the Middle East and Latin America, and the support of this alliance by the West, threaten to divert the middle-class revolutions into the arms of the Soviet Union. Soviet leaders are prepared to exploit this alliance in accordance with theoretical formulations that have been renovated and refined for more than four decades, ever since Lenin laid down the principal lines of analysis for exploiting revolutionary movements in underdeveloped countries. His dicta have since been modified, renovated, refined, and adapted to various areas under a variety of circumstances, but the important point is that the Soviet leaders, for more than forty years, have had at their disposal a systematically articulated theoretical framework for analyzing and exploiting underdevelopment.

> The characteristic feature of imperialism [Lenin observed in 1920] is that the whole world, as we see, is at present divided into a large number of oppressed nations and an insignificant number of oppressing nations possessing colossal wealth and powerful military forces. The overwhelming majority of the population of the world . . . about 70 per cent of the population of the world belongs to the oppressed nations, which are either in a state of direct colonial dependence or belong to the outlying colonial states such as Persia, Turkey, and China, or else, after being conquered by the armies of a big imperialist power, have been forced into dependence upon it by treaties. . . . We argued about whether it would be correct, in principle and in theory, to declare that the Communist International and the Communist Parties should support the bourgeois-democratic movement in backward countries. As a result . . . we unanimously decided to speak of the national revolutionary movement instead of the "bourgeois-democratic" movement. There is not the slightest doubt that every nationalist movement can only be a bourgeois-democratic movement. . . . It would be utopian to think that proletarian parties, if indeed they can arise in such countries, could pursue Communist tactics and a Communist policy in these countries without having definite relations with the peasant movement and without effectively supporting it. But it was argued that if we speak about the bourgeois-democratic movement all distinction between reformist and revolutionary movements will be obliterated; whereas in recent times this distinction has been fully and clearly revealed in the backward and colonial countries, for the imperialist bourgeoisie is trying with all its might to implant the reformist movement also among the oppressed nations. A certain rapprochement has been brought about between the bourgeoisie of the exploiting countries and those of the colonial countries, so that very often, in the majority of cases, perhaps, where the bourgeoisie of the oppressed countries does support the national movement, it simultaneously works in harmony with the nationalist bourgeoisie, *i.e.,* it joins the latter in fighting against all revolutionary movements and revolutionary classes. . . . We came to the conclusion that the only correct thing to do was to take this distinction into consideration and nearly everywhere to substitute the term "bourgeois-democratic." The meaning of this change is that we Communists should, and will, support bourgeois liberation movements in the colonial countries only when these move-

ments are really revolutionary, when the representatives of these movements do not hinder us in training and organizing the peasants and broad masses of the exploited in a revolutionary spirit, even if these countries must fight against the reformist bourgeoisie, among whom we include the heroes of the Second International. Reformist parties already exist in colonial countries, and sometimes their representatives call themselves Social-Democrats and Socialists. . . . There can be no argument about the fact that the proletariat of the advanced countries can and must assist the backward toiling masses, and that the development of the backward countries can emerge from its present stage when the victorious proletariat of the Soviet republics stretches out a helping hand to these masses.[4]

The Cuban revolution offers entirely new possibilities because it illustrates an unforeseen metamorphosis of a "bourgeois-democratic" revolution being transformed from the top into a proletarian revolution by a national bourgeoisie, not as an elite acting as the historical agents of the proletariat, but as a group carrying out an act of volition in response to external threats and attractions. Although Castro has declared himself a Marxist-Leninist, called his regime a "socialist" system, and defined his ultimate purpose as the fulfillment of Marxist-Leninist ideological and social norms, these brazen and unilateral proclamations have yet to be recognized as acceptable in Moscow, since they contradict all previously explored paths to the Communist revolution. Just as Mao Tse-tung claims to have executed a "bourgeois-democratic" revolution without a bourgeoisie, so Castro claims to have executed a proletarian revolution with the help of neither the proletariat nor the Cuban Communist Party.

In his zeal for orthodoxy and acceptance into the Communist confraternity, Castro has implicitly condemned Fidelismo as a manifestation of the "cult of personality," and claims to have shifted to "collective leadership." The leaders of the old-line Communist Party, who played no role in the revolutionary process itself, have been assigned the mission of reorganizing various Cuban revolutionary organizations into a Marxist-Leninist party. To what extent Castro still remains master of the situation and the ultimate fount for delegation of authority to orthodox Communist leaders remains unclear, but it is certain that until such time as Castro no longer possesses the power unilaterally to renounce his latter-day conversion to Marxism-Leninism, he will continue to remain an eccentric leader of an enigmatic and curious bourgeois revolution. The character of this revolution continues to baffle Soviet ideologists, who had to invent a completely new stage to accommodate it—the "national democracy," as distinguished from either "bourgeois democracy" or "people's democracy."

The curious evolution of the Cuban revolution has already provoked ideological anguish in the Sino-Soviet bloc, for if the Cuban revolution does metamorphose completely into a Marxist-Leninist society, it will represent the first successful completion of an experiment begun in the early twenties with the Kuomintang revolution in China—the take-over from above of a middle-class revolution by the Communist Party. Mao Tse-tung, stung by the Chiang Kai-shek affair, adheres to the view that the two-phase revolution in underdeveloped countries can safely be executed only if the entire dual-phase operation is conducted under the leadership of the Communist Party, and that it is utopian to expect a bourgeois class to carry out a Communist revolution. He remains convinced that the revolutionary bourgeoisie will arrest the revolutionary movement once the anti-imperialist and antifeudal phase of the revolution has been consummated, and that it will seek to anchor itself as the ruling class in a bourgeois social order. This view, which is in accordance with the orthodox Leninist-Stalinist strategy of revolution in colonial and semicolonial countries, maintains that once the bourgeois revolution has been completed, the Communist Party should prepare a proletarian upheaval against the bourgeoisie. The Soviet view seems to be that it is now possible that the revolutionary bourgeoisie in underdeveloped countries, seeing the balance of power shifting toward the Soviet orbit, may, in its own *national,* if not *class,* interests, carry the revolution forward into its second phase, thus obviating the necessity for organizing a Communist Party and a Communist revolution from scratch.

Soviet leaders clearly perceive the ambivalent character of the revolutionary middle class. These elites simultaneously pose a threat to the middle-class *status quo* and create an opportunity to help preserve it. These revolutionary middle classes have the capability and the determination to come to power. In some countries, they will come to power with the West or without the West. The direction they take and the ideological alliances they forge will depend upon how skillfully the situation is analyzed and acted upon by Soviet and Western leaders, and how effectively the social forces working for or against the ideological *status quo* are calculated and manipulated.

At this critical juncture in history, the unparalleled success of Soviet foreign policy during the past four decades challenges the Western world to identify the forces agitating the underdeveloped world, to chart their direction, and to work with them, so that the emerging world will conform to an expanded middle-class ideo-social system rather than to a Communist universalism. Western policy must align itself with the popular aspirations of the middle-class nationalist forces in the underdeveloped countries, not out of sheer sentimentality, but out of absolute necessity. Either the Western world as a civilization—not as a hegemonic empire or series of empires—must universalize itself, its values, and its institutions, or it will inevitably shrink, shrivel up, and pass into the ashbins of history as another great civilization unable to accommodate itself to the demands and expectations of its aroused, disaffected, and discontented populations. Certainly there is no compulsion for the Western world to sow the seeds of its own destruction, as if in response to Communist expectations, by supporting decrepit and doomed feudal ruling classes all over the world.

Since the very existence of a great civilization or ideosocial system is at stake, the pressures of powerful interest groups must be resisted, since the issues transcend the narrow interests of those attempting to preserve the *status quo*. Increasingly, the national interests of the states of the Western community are colliding with the specific interests that powerful international corporations, consortiums, and cartels have in underdeveloped countries. These groups sometimes convey the impression that they "own" Western civilization and that, unless their position is preserved intact, Western civilization will be undermined. Until the necessary distinctions can be made, and until these groups recognize the necessity of diffusing part of their power and wealth to retain the remainder, the United States and the West will continue to back reactionary feudal regimes—which invariably turn out to be exceptionally congenial to those who have lucrative investments and enterprises in their countries—against revolutionary middle classes under the increasingly untenable and transparent device of supporting "anti-Communists." This point is supported in the following excerpt from an article by Peter F. Drucker in *Harper's:*

> The traditional tools of "foreign aid"—money and trained men—will never do the job until *Latin Americans* face up to the tough things which *they* alone can do: collect taxes from the rich and clean out the sinecure jobs in swollen government services; push through land reform and cheap mass housing; stop subsidizing the wrong

crops; get rid of the pettifogging regulations . . . and say "no" to the blackmail of the generals who habitually threaten to overthrow a regime unless they get a few more unneeded jet planes, tanks, or destroyers. [Italics added.]

One must inevitably ask *which* Latin Americans must face up to the tough problems enumerated? Who must "collect taxes from the rich . . . push through land reform . . . say 'no' to the . . . generals"? Obviously, the advice cannot be directed to those Latin Americans who have neither power nor property, unless they are being asked to conduct a revolution. It is this form of stereotyped and ritualized impersonal exhortation that serves to hide and distort social realities. Unless one deals in terms of social classes and elites, it is a mystery why taxes are not collected from the rich, why land reform is not being pushed through, why the wrong crops are being subsidized, why no one will say "no" to the generals; but once it is recognized that "they" refers to a concrete ruling class being asked to execute measures against its own interests, it becomes quite clear why these obviously reasonable objectives (in American context) are not being carried out.

In dealing with underdeveloped countries, it must be recognized that "the people" are subdivided into concrete social groups, classes, and elites, each with its own interests and aspirations. There are people with power and property and those without; people who are satisfied with the *status quo* and those who are not; people who have "freedom" and enjoy "justice," and those who labor under "tyranny" and "injustice." Impersonal exhortations to "the people," as if social classes did not exist or flourish, are disingenuous self-deceptions that obscure the real situation and result in incorrect analyses. If the "people" refuse to respond to the voice of reason, the attitude of most Americans is to shrug their shoulders and say that if "they" refuse to do anything to help themselves, nothing can be done for them. To say that social problems are insoluble, however, means making the Communists the only agents that can change an intolerable *status quo*. The Communists, too, appeal to the "people," not in the abstract but to certain social classes. They do not exhort them to reform their governments, which they are not in a position to do, but call upon them to revolt, which they can do. If ruling classes in underdeveloped countries refuse to carry out reforms from above, the social momentum does not simply grind to a halt. It assumes a new dimension—the dimension of a revolutionary upheaval from below.

An effective policy for defending and extending the Western

status quo must, therefore, include strategies that can be executed where ruling classes prove obstinate. Otherwise, the West will be confronted with the prospect of supporting ruling classes that are doomed, thus inescapably earning the animosity of the rising revolutionary middle classes determined to assume power. The development of a concerted strategy for defending and extending the middle-class *status quo* necessitates a realistic appraisal of class relationships and forces in each country, as well as an appreciation of the aspirations, powers, and future of given classes. The United States is not interested in manufacturing revolutions where they do not exist, nor in supporting those that are manipulated and directed by Communists, but it must be interested in why revolutions are taking place, and the directions of their movements.

Assessing revolutions and their characters is a tricky business and requires considerable caution as well as boldness, as the occasion may demand. In any given underdeveloped country and, indeed, in any social system, the population can generally be divided into three great divisions according to the attitude each bears to the social order of which they are all a part: One sector of the population is committed to the *status quo* and benefits so greatly from it that it is willing to fight and die in its defense. (The issue of patriotism is irrelevant to the *status quo* in underdeveloped countries and thus cannot be manipulated as a symbol by a regime under attack.) The second group is determined to overthrow the *status quo* and is willing to risk any sacrifice to bring about its destruction. And the third group comprises those who are indifferent and unwilling to risk their lives either to preserve or overturn the *status quo*. As long as the forces of the *status quo* can mobilize more power and support than the forces of revolution, the social order remains stabilized. But social systems are not static, and in the underdeveloped world the great reservoir of humanity that falls into the indifferent category can be stimulated into revolutionary action if its level of dissatisfaction is raised or its expectations for a better life are aroused by political agitation. Once this reservoir of indifference furnishes recruits for the forces arrayed against the *status quo,* a revolutionary situation is created and its momentum rapidly accelerates.

Communist agitation and propaganda are designed to arouse such expectations among indifferent populations. The successes of Communist propaganda are due not so much to superior techniques and methods as to their ability to create expectations that excite indifferent populations to risk their lives for a better future.

These expectations need to be generated only among a relatively small number of people to tilt the internal balance of power against the *status quo* in favor of the forces of revolution. The great mass of the population can continue to languish in indifference. That is why 180,000 well-trained South Vietnamese troops are no match for 20,000 Viet Cong guerrillas, and why 8,000 ragged Pathet Lao troops can repeatedly make a Royal Laotian Army nearly three times its size turn tail and run, although this Army is trained, equipped, and directed by American military-assistance units. The Pathet Lao and the Viet Cong are imbued with a dedication to overturn the *status quo* more intense than the dedication of the armies of the Laotian and South Vietnamese governments to defend it, since the latter are drawn mainly from the indifferent segments unwilling to risk their lives for a *status quo* from which they derive little or no benefit.

In defending the *status quo,* the United States can pursue three basic strategies as a consequence of a class analysis. It can (1) continue the symbiotic relationship with existing feudal regimes and support them against external attack and internal upheaval to the bitter end, with full knowledge of the limitations of such a strategy; (2) support "revolutions from above" carried out by existing ruling classes or elements from within them; or (3) abandon feudal classes to their historical fate and support the rising middle-class nationalist movements against internal feudalism while mitigating their assaults on Western economic interests.

The first strategy has been the preferred policy of the United States. It does not support an ideological *status quo,* but rather upholds any anti-Communist social order anywhere, no matter what its ideology, political form, or economic system. This usually takes the form of safeguarding these regimes against external attack and providing assistance against internal revolutions by supplying a margin of power that the forces of the local *status quo* cannot furnish internally to quash a revolutionary threat. This means supporting existing regimes and landowning classes in their symbiotic relation with foreign economic interests and making a purely military response to a social situation. This is the strategy that failed in Iraq, and is still being executed in Iran, South Vietnam, and Laos. It is a strategy being readied for use in Latin America, particularly in the Caribbean littoral. The most conservative of all possible *status quo* policies and likely to be the most ineffective, it receives its greatest impetus from powerful economic interests in the United States who are reluctant to permit any changes in the local *status quo* lest their interests be adversely affected. In areas of substantial European settlement, similar pressures are exerted by the colonists of other Western countries. In some countries still slumbering in the Middle Ages, like Yemen and Saudi Arabia, where revolutionary ferment has not yet developed to any great extent, the existing symbiotic relation can be left virtually intact, without any immediate danger, although it must be recognized that, sooner or later, a revolutionary middle class will assume shape.

A few caveats should be issued in connection with this strategy. The first is that a disintegrating feudal regime being shored up by foreign assistance against indigenous and spontaneous revolutionary upheaval must be distinguished from a *status quo* regime being unseated by revolutionary forces supplied by outside intervention. The latter is not a true revolutionary situation and there a policy of military intervention on behalf of the existing regime can be successful. One must not, however, naïvely mistake a genuine internal upheaval, no matter how initially stimulated, with one supported externally, since the same response will not succeed in both cases. There is real danger that intervention will give an insurrection the character of war against foreign domination and imperialism, and thus broaden the social base of the revolution, rather than narrow it. Indifferent segments of the population are likely to be provoked into joining the insurrection, and the intervening forces are then sucked into a never-ending spiral of intensified revolutionary activity. Consequently, it is of the utmost importance not to indulge in frivolous fabrication and self-deception solely to justify intervention. If the intervention fails, it becomes necessary to give false reasons for its failure, and self-deception builds upon self-deception until rational and realistic analysis becomes impossible. Although the population of the intervening country may be easily and successfully fooled into believing that intervention is justified because the revolution is being supported from the outside, it is certain that neither the population of the country in revolutionary ferment nor the population of the country accused of outside intervention will be deceived.*

---

* A further danger involved in intervention is the real possibility that intervention against a purely internal revolutionary insurrection may in fact provoke foreign intervention on behalf of revolution. While this may serve to document the charge of outside intervention, it may also be a cure worse than the disease. Khrushchev, at the Twenty-second Party Congress, threatened precisely this type of counteraction.

In any event, an interventionist *status quo* policy is likely to fail as a long-range policy, since it does not contribute to the expansion of a middle-class ideosocial system, but merely preserves feudal social systems.

The strategy of "revolution from above," however, appears to be emerging as a possible American policy, although in a somewhat pragmatic, nebulous, and not completely coherent manner. Historically, the "revolution from above" is the most effective and reliable method for bringing about an alteration in the social structure resulting in a more or less peaceful, but nonetheless fundamental, transformation of the social order. This strategy requires that existing ruling classes, or the most perceptive and intelligent elements within them, initiate necessary alterations in the internal balance of forces so that the forces of the *status quo* may be enhanced by giving hitherto indifferent elements in the population a stake in the reconstructed social order. Thus, while a revolution from below seeks to arouse expectations of a better life among indifferent elements of the population, "revolution from above" provides them with a material stake in preserving the revised *status quo*. In a mathematical sense, the only changes that need be introduced are those that will continuously maintain a social balance favorable to the *status quo* and opposed to those dedicated to destroying it. When skillfully executed, a "revolution from above" can even recruit supporters of the *status quo* from the revolutionary elements by providing them with a stake in the system meaningful enough to persuade them to desert the insurrectionary forces.

A "revolution from above" should be distinguished from a *coup d'état* or a palace revolution, in which personalities and cliques from within the existing governing class displace one another in a game of musical chairs, leaving the basic economic and social substructure of power intact. True "revolutions from above" result in a redistribution of social and economic power; the existing ruling class shares and diffuses its power and rewards with the emergent classes, eventually consummating their social fusion. The most successful continuous "revolution from above" has been that of the British, where successive ruling classes have been the most effective renovating and progressive social groups in British society, always introducing the changes necessary to divert revolutionary upheaval. As a consequence, over an extended period of time, there has been a continuous co-option and fusion between ruling classes and emerging classes. Thus, today some ruling families in a British middle-class socialist society can boast of ancestors who belonged to a ruling feudal nobility.

Not all attempts at "revolution from above" have been successful. Successful "revolutions from above" are delicate operations and can be safely carried out only if several prior conditions exist or can be created. The first requirement is that at least a part of the ruling class must be sufficiently perceptive to realize that the *status quo* cannot be maintained unaltered. Second, it must be prepared psychologically to share power and rewards with the rising and challenging social class from below, and to accept the risks and consequences of this redistribution of power. Third, it must be able to appraise unerringly the social forces, internal and external, in favor of both revolution and the *status quo,* and to introduce changes at any given moment just sufficient constantly to shift the balance in favor of a changing *status quo.* Miscalculation on the side of too little change merely weakens the *status quo,* whereas changes that are excessive are likely to stimulate expectations that cannot be fulfilled rapidly enough. In either instance, a revolutionary upheaval from below is apt to be provoked.

In countries where foreign investments are substantial, these external interests must also agree to share in the distribution of whatever economic and social power they command. Sharing may include the partial nationalization of their enterprises, a reduction of profits, an increase in royalties, better working conditions and opportunities for employees, and a greater sensitivity to local needs. In some instances, the foreign investors may have to accept eventual total nationalization or be prepared to undertake new enterprises that may be nationalized after an agreed-upon profit has been made.

"Revolutions from above" are likely to be dynamic and protracted affairs, but under existing conditions in underdeveloped countries, they would result in the gradual transformation of a neofeudal social order into a middle-class social system and would thus extend and strengthen the middle-class ideosocial system. Instead of a revolution that threatens the violent displacement in power of one class by another, a "revolution from above" would bring about a gradual fusion of the old aristocracy with the rising middle class and stabilize society as a whole.

The Alliance for Progress program announced by the Kennedy Administration is an approach to "revolution from above," but its success will depend upon the willingness of the Latin-American landowning classes to introduce the necessary changes,* and upon the ability of the Administration to persuade American corporations to make necessary accommodations. Unfortunately, both the landowning classes and the American business interests are likely to prefer reliance upon military intervention to prevent revolutions or to restore an overturned *status quo*. Yet, "revolutions from above," executed through the Alliance for Progress program, would have good chances for success in countries like Argentina, Uruguay, Brazil, Venezuela, Mexico, and Costa Rica, whose ruling classes include elements who perceive the threat and are prepared to cope with it. The strategy of "revolution from above" is not likely to succeed in Middle Eastern countries, where two middle-class revolutions have already taken place, one relatively bloodless (Egypt), and the other accompanied by savagery (Iraq). Unfortunately, the same fate awaits Iran, whose feudal landowning classes are among the most venal, corrupt, and shortsighted in the world. It is not likely, once a revolution in Iran develops its momentum, that either outside military intervention or a countercoup by the CIA will save the ruling classes of that ancient country.

The third strategy in defense and extension of the middle-class *status quo* is the most radical of all, but actually it requires less positive action by the United States than either of the previous two. What it does require is an appreciative and sympathetic attitude to encourage or permit the revolutionary middle class to come to power, and aid in its stabilization. It is not required that the United States stimulate these revolutions; they are developing spontaneously in response to existing conditions. It is not necessary to intervene and give material support to such revolutions; nor need diplomatic relations be ruptured with the government in power while moral support is being expressed for the aspirations of revolutionary middle classes. But extending such moral support to

---

* The narrow feudal character of Latin-American agricultural economies is demonstrated by the extreme concentration of land ownership in some countries. Whereas in Latin America as a whole, 90 per cent of the agricultural lands belong to 10 per cent of the landowners, some concentrations are even more extreme. In Guatemala, 516 farms (0.15 per cent) include 41 per cent of the farm lands; in Ecuador, 705 farms (0.17 per cent) account for 37 per cent; in Venezuela, 6,800 farms (1.69 per cent) comprise 74 per cent of the farm acreage; in Brazil, 1.6 per cent of the landowners hold 50 per cent of the agricultural lands; in Nicaragua, 362 landlords own one-third of the farm lands; in Bolivia, before land reform, 6.4 per cent of the farms constituted 92 per cent of the farm areas.

revolutionary middle classes is particularly important in countries where the ruling classes are irrevocably opposed to change.

Although this strategy is the only effective strategy of defending and extending the middle class *status quo* that can be pursued in many underdeveloped countries, it is likely to be the most difficult psychologically. Because of the necessity of revolutionary violence to alter the social order, a victorious revolutionary bourgeoisie will almost inevitably expropriate the landowners and destroy them as a social class, although it will not necessarily harm them physically. In some cases, depending upon the individual situation in each country, there is likely to be substantial nationalization of foreign-owned enterprises (American, in many instances), but with compensation. In countries where capitalism is not in complete disrepute or where a local capitalist class exists, localization may take place instead, whereby native capitalists are aided in buying foreign enterprises. Substantial public ownership in all countries where the revolutionary middle class comes to power is a foregone conclusion. But the "socialist" or "welfare states" that will emerge will be middle-class in character, not Soviet, and will be nationalist-socialist states, not international-socialist societies. This means that neither collectivization of agriculture nor nationalization of small business will take place. Depending upon local factors, some countries will emerge as parliamentary and democratic states, which is to be preferred; others will be authoritarian in varying degrees.

As we have seen, a policy in defense of the middle-class *status quo* can be based upon either encouraging and assisting *real* revolutions from above or supporting the rise of the revolutionary middle class. Both policies are defensible morally and historically, but deciding upon which method to choose in individual cases requires experienced and audacious statecraft operating within a systematic framework of social analysis. Current Soviet policy rests upon the expectation that the United States will continue to support feudal regimes and will assume a negative attitude toward middle-class revolutionary movements and bourgeois-nationalist regimes. If this expectation proves correct, the revolutionary middle classes may have no alternative but to alter the character of their revolution and shift it in a Soviet direction, transforming themselves into a bureaucratic ruling elite on the Soviet model, rather than stabilizing a middle-class revolution that will be under attack from both East and West. In the new Draft Program of the Communist Party, Khrushchev reveals both his expectations and apprehensions

concerning the revolutionary role of the middle class in underdeveloped countries:

> The world is experiencing a period of stormy national-liberation
> revolutions. . . . Young sovereign states have arisen, or are arising,
> in onetime colonies or semicolonies. Their peoples have entered a
> new period of development. . . . But the struggle is not yet over.
> . . . Many of them, having established national states, are striving
> for economic sovereignty and durable political independence. The
> peoples of these formally independent countries that in reality de-
> pend on foreign monopolies politically and economically are arising
> to fight against imperialism and reactionary pro-imperialist regimes.
> . . . The extent to which the national bourgeoisie [roughly, the revo-
> lutionary middle class] will take part in the anti-imperialist and
> antifeudal struggle will depend in considerable measure on the solid-
> ity of the working class and peasantry. . . . The national bour-
> geoisie is dual in character. In modern conditions, the national
> bourgeoisie in those colonial, onetime colonial, and dependent coun-
> tries, where it is not connected with the imperialist circles is objec-
> tively interested in accomplishing the basic tasks of an anti-imperi-
> alist and antifeudal revolution. Its progressive role and its ability to
> participate in the solution of pressing national problems are, there-
> fore, not yet spent. But as the contradictions between the working
> people and the propertied classes grow and the class struggle inside
> the country becomes more aggravated, the national bourgeoisie
> shows an increasing inclination to compromise with imperialism and
> domestic reaction.[5]

In areas where the revolutionary middle class meets resistance
to its objectives from the West, it can utilize the implicit protection of Soviet power to transform itself into a bureaucratic ruling
class ready to execute a Communist-type revolution from above
—as in Cuba—which, in the Draft Program, is called National
Democracy:

> In view of the present balance of world forces and the actual feasi-
> bility of powerful support on the part of the world Socialist system,
> the peoples of the former colonies can decide to take . . . the non-
> capitalist road of development. . . . This road will require conces-
> sions from the bourgeoisie, but those will be concessions on behalf
> of the nation. . . . Establishing and developing national democracies
> opens vast prospects for the peoples of the underdeveloped countries.
> The political basis of national democracy is a bloc of all the pro-
> gressive, patriotic forces fighting to win complete national independ-
> ence and broad democracy, and to consummate the anti-imperialist,
> antifeudal, democratic revolution.[6]

Whether the middle-class revolutions in the underdeveloped countries will establish "national democracies" as temporary way stations on the road to Communism, or whether they will establish authentic middle-class regimes that will "compromise with imperialism and domestic reaction," to use the quaint phraseology of the Draft Program, will depend in large measure upon the reception they receive from the United States. And American reaction will, in turn, largely depend upon how we perceive the situation and identify the interests of the West with the aspirations of these revolutionary middle-class movements.

The Cuban episode demonstrates one possibility, but it should be recalled that only a few years ago both Nasser and Kassem had been given up as crypto-Communists. Similar misconceptions have been expressed about the regimes in Indonesia, Guinea, and Ghana. There is no question that repeating the prophecy that certain regimes are "going Communist" may indeed result in its fulfillment.

X

THE RELATION OF STRENGTH TO WEAKNESS IN THE WORLD COMMUNITY

by REINHOLD NIEBUHR

THE impingement of strong nations upon weak ones has usually resulted in a pattern of political and economic domination. That pattern is a recurring one, whether the strong nation be Communist or capitalist. Communist dogma, however, attributes domination and exploitation, imperialism and colonialism, to the primary evil of capitalism. Obviously, the complex realities of history refute the simple diagnosis of imperialism and its implicit cure. Yet, though we may optimistically insist that many Communist dogmas may be eroded or modified in contact with reality, there is no sign today that the Communist dogma of imperialism will erode.

The historic facts are more complex than the simple interpretation of them in the Communist diagnosis and scheme of political salvation. Nevertheless, from the sixteenth to the twentieth centuries, the technical superiority of European nations led to the historic phenomenon of Western imperialism, giving the Communist dogma a seeming plausibility, if not in Europe, then among the victims of the extension of European imperial power.

The dogma obscures many relevant facts by concentrating on the economic or capitalistic cause of imperialism. The first imperial nations of Europe were Spain and Portugal. These two nations still have not attained even a minimal degree of industrial development. They were prompted to their imperial ventures by the impulses of the explorer, the desire for gold, and the missionary zeal to spread the Catholic faith.

The motives involved in the relation of strong nations to weak ones are as complex and varied as all human motives, particularly

196

those of collective man. We may take it for granted that they are never purely disinterested. The economic motive—the desire for gain and the hunger for raw materials and markets—was certainly a strong motive of imperialism in the nineteenth century. It was, however, never the sole incentive, and economic exploitation was never the sole consequence. The political motive—the lust for prestige and aggrandizement of power—was probably always dominant in imperial ventures, far more so, at least, than can be appreciated within the framework of the Marxist dogma. Furthermore, the missionary motive—the desire to bestow upon the weaker partner the religious, cultural, or political values most treasured by the imperial power—is certainly never absent, though it is never as pure and disinterested as the imperial powers pretend. The desire to extend our values is bound to be a mixture of the wish to display our power and the zeal to confer some political aptitude, technical skill, or cultural value upon the weaker partner.

Ironically, in the contest beween Russia and America for the allegiance of the nontechnical nations of Asia and Africa, both of these imperial contestants of our day are, in theory, anti-imperialist. Russia makes the claim because only capitalism, according to its dogma, is the fount of imperialism. Communism, therefore, by definition is not imperialistic—a simple way of proving virtue. The other imperial nation, America, considers itself anti-imperialist, too, because it is the one Western democracy in which there are remnants of the pristine liberal-democratic belief that the political institution of monarchy is the fount of imperialism, not the economic institution of property, as the Marxists claim. The possession of great economic, military, and political power involves both nations in a refutation of their original anti-imperialist theories. Both display two of the three discernible motives in the relation of strong nations to weak ones: Both seek strategic advantages, power and prestige; and both desire to extend their own system of government and values.

It is easy to see, however, why in the present condition of world affairs, the Marxist dogma is more plausible to the weaker nations of Asia and Africa than the democratic theory. Even though the democratic dogma emphasizes the right of self-determination of all nations, it seems largely irrelevant to the emergent nations. The experiences of these nontechnical nations appear to validate the Communist dogma of imperialism. Many, if not most, of the great Western powers, with their earlier technical and political competence, were involved in imperial ventures in Asia and Africa.

Though there were ancillary benefits of tutelage involved in Western domination, these are largely overlooked today. Instead, past and present experiences with such domination create resentments against real injustices for which Marxist dogma offers a simple and plausible explanation. America's own profession of comparative innocence of the imperialist guilt seems pathetically unconvincing to these new nations once they accept the notion that all capitalistic nations, including the United States, are by definition imperialistic.

An important declaration was issued at the end of the meeting of the eighty-one Communist parties, held in Moscow in November and December of 1960, to coordinate Russian and Chinese versions of Marxism-Leninism. The declaration states:

> The U.S. imperialists have set up a huge war machinery and refuse to allow any reduction. The imperialists frustrate all constructive disarmament proposals by the Soviet Union and other peaceful countries. The arms race is going on. Stockpiles of nuclear weapons are becoming dangerously large. . . . The U.S. ruling circles have wrecked the Paris meeting of the heads of government by their policy of provocation and aggression. . . . The aggressive nature of imperialism has not changed.[1]

The entire statement is an excellent example of the dogmatic and polemical approach to complex problems. The tragic dilemmas of a nuclear age are interpreted in the context of a gigantic struggle between the forces of peace and the "imperialists" or "warmongers" who are allegedly so intent on enslaving their fellow men that they will risk destroying mankind. Continued coexistence is justified, not because it will lead to accommodation between the two contestants, but because there is no doubt that Communism will ultimately triumph by peaceful means. A black-and-white picture of the tragic age of nuclear terror is not, of course, a monopoly of Communist dogmatism. It is accepted by many people in the West who have their own simple interpretations of the situation. But at least the non-Communist world as a whole allows a sufficient number of sometimes contradictory interpretations to be presented simultaneously to blur any dogmatic neatness.

The Communist declaration of 1960 was obviously directed toward the nations of Africa and Asia. It identifies Communism with national liberation and promises that "as the socialist movement grows stronger, the international situation grows more and more favorable to the peoples fighting for independence, social progress, and democracy." It speaks of the "appalling poverty" of the masses in the Western world and declares that "the domination of the monopolies is causing increasing harm to the broad peasant masses." These and other references to social conditions in the West are in such glaring contradiction to the social realities that even the Communist authors of the document could hardly have expected them to be believed. The vast majority of the men of the soil in Western areas, whether American or Canadian farmers or highly efficient Danish dairymen, do not fit this conception. There has obviously been a shift in the original Marxist dogma from a preoccupation with the messianic role of the industrial worker to the Asian conception of a similar role for the suffering peasant. The United States may have been labeled as the chief villain out of consideration for Chinese views, which did not prevail in the matter of peaceful coexistence. Nevertheless, the picture of the arch villain was derived from the original scheme of Marxist-Leninist dogma, in which Russia, in contrast to the capitalist powers, is pictured as the heavenly host in the final Armageddon.

The peculiarities of the Communist imperialist ventures, both Russian and Chinese, have left the way open for the Communist appeal to Afro-Asian anti-imperialists. Though China has dealt brutally with Tibet, and even with India, in recent years, and though the Soviet Union has subjugated a score of nations in Eastern Europe, Communist hands have remained unstained in the eyes of the Afro-Asians. This is true because the establishment of the rule of Moscow or Peking over these peoples nowhere required that they be subjected to the rule of a foreign—Russian or Chinese—colonial administration. Indigenous Communists were there to do the job. Thus it happens that Communist imperialist policies in Eastern Europe, though far more ruthless than the Western policies condemned in the Moscow declaration of 1960, escape the anti-imperialist censure. It is overlooked that the Baltic states, freed from Czarist rule at the close of World War I in the name of the Wilsonian principle of self-determination, were later robbed of their independence by the Soviets. Poland, similarly freed in 1919, is left today with a minimum of freedom and is at the mercy of Moscow. The suppression of the Hungarian rebellion of 1956, which had been the work of young Communist-nationalists, is fresh in our memory, yet the Communists in Hungary and in the other satellite countries, including the formerly democratic and highly industrialized Czechoslovakia, parade as the liberators from past agrarian-feudal rule and from social injustice. In all these countries, residual national sentiment is branded as a remnant of bourgeois-national chauvinism that will give way to the true Marxist universalism.

In short, the Leninist doctrine of imperialism clearly distorts the facts of history. Nowhere have the strong imposed their will more brutally upon the weak than in Eastern Europe. Ironically, even here the Communists claim to be leaders of the weak in the class struggle between nations. It was Lenin who transferred the concept of the class struggle from the domestic to the international scene. In his book *Imperialism, the Highest Stage of Capitalism,* written prior to the Russian Revolution, Lenin expounded this extension of the original Marxist dogma, which was a scheme of salvation for classes within nations.

Lenin was inspired, it is worth noting, to picture capitalism as the chief source of imperialism by the liberal democrat J. A. Hobson. In his anti-imperialist book *Imperialism,* published in 1902, Hobson declared: "The new imperialism differs from the old first in substituting for a single empire the theory and practice of competing empires, each motivated by similar motives of political aggrandizement and economic gain; and secondly by the dominance of investing or financial interests over the mercantile ones."

Hobson's treatise was substantially an accurate description of nineteenth-century imperialism. But Lenin amended and distorted Hobson's thesis by leaving out "political aggrandizement" as one of the chief motives for empire-building. Thus he brought the theory in line with the Marxist dogma, in which economic motivation is paramount. Lenin could then sum up the nature of imperialism more succinctly than Hobson by saying: "If it were necessary to give the briefest possible description of imperialism, I should have to say that imperialism is the monopoly stage of capitalism." This Leninist dogma has become fixed in the imagination of Asians and Africans as the key to the mystery of social and international injustice. It has, in fact, attained something of the status of an axiom on those continents. The Secretary-General of the Indonesian Ministry of Foreign Affairs, R. Abdulgani, unequivocally stated: "In our experience colonialism is the child of capitalism. In its inevitable wake colonialism brought us disunity and a degree of poverty, never known in the West. Therefore for us socialism is the essential ingredient of nationalism."[2]

Not only Communists accept this dogma as axiomatic. U Nu, the impressive Prime Minister of Burma, a social-democratic statesman of an uncommitted country, confessed: "During the entire course of our struggle for freedom, capitalist and imperialist domination have been closely associated in the minds of all of us, and it has been impossible to view the two in isolation."[3]

The rigorously anti-Communist President of South Vietnam, Ngo Dinh Diem, probably reflecting on the French colonial past, stated before the United States Congress, in 1957, that "there is a growing awareness of the colonial peoples that the origin of their poverty is the systematic withholding of technical developments."[4] Diem's statement is probably a more accurate picture of the effects of colonial domination than would appear from a strictly Marxist indictment.

The fact that Lenin's interpretation of capitalism and imperialism is widely held in Asia and Africa suggests that a dogma can gain plausibility even though it does not accord with all the facts. It is sufficient that it correspond with some of the facts that have been experienced and are particularly deeply felt.

Anti-imperialist sentiment and resentment must be regarded as one of the greatest handicaps of the "democratic world" in its contest with Communism. One really should not speak of a democratic world in this context. What distinguishes the Western from the Communist world is its empirical approach to the problems of the political order, in contrast to the dogmatic Communist approach. Resentment against Western colonial rule makes it hard for the Afro-Asian nations to accept the empirical view even after they have emancipated themselves from colonial rule. Resentment makes it difficult to undertake a sober assessment of past imperial infringement and to recognize the creative as well as negative aspects of past experience. Some of the new states that have been granted independence by Britain and France are making just this kind of assessment. They have freed themselves of much of their resentment and now maintain bonds with the former metropoles, for they wish to see some of the advantages of past relations preserved. They give recognition thereby to the fact that the strong are not wholly exploitative in their relations with the weak.

By dwelling on the economically exploitative character of colonialism, Marxist dogma obscures other aspects of imperialism. Weaker partners have borne witness by their resentments to the fact that they suffered more from the political than from the economic motives of the dominant partner. Race pride was the inevitable concomitant of the political motive, and it is the white man's racial arrogance that is most resented. Prime Minister Nehru of India, who has become a kind of elder statesman in the British

Commonwealth, does not often speak of British economic exploitation, though he obviously knows the predominant economic motivation of early British imperialism. But his autobiography testifies to the lasting impressions of racial humiliation made on a talented young Indian leader who was excluded from British clubs on Indian soil.

Unlike the British, the French displayed little or no racial arrogance in their colonial missions. Despite her tragic inability to solve the Algerian problem, France has shown success with respect to her new Community, in part because of the low intensity of French racial prejudice, which compensates for other defects in French, compared with British, colonial behavior.

Cyprus is another case in point. Cyprus gained her independence from Britain by solving the seemingly insoluble problem of tension between her Turkish and Greek populations. The solution was possible only through the wise and patient help of British statesmanship. That British patience was partly motivated by the fact that British strategic interests in Cyprus could be preserved only in a partnership relation should not be questioned. This is evidence of the endlessly complex motives of imperialism. It also points to the persistence of the relation of strength to weakness and to the necessity of adjusting this perennial relation to the new realities, which are being shaped by the equalization of power arising from the spread of technical competence and nationalism to all parts of the world.

The former Belgian Congo offers another illustration of the complex relation of power to weakness. Congolese resentment against the Belgian masters made impossible the continued partnership between the Congo and Belgium that was envisaged in the treaty of friendship drawn up before independence. Belgian copper interests did exploit and profit from the mineral wealth of the Congo. But the Congolese got a share, albeit a disproportionately modest share, of the wealth which they would not have been able to produce without the skills and the means available to the technically competent metropole. Significantly, the Belgians were not immune from the charge of economic exploitation, despite the relatively high living standards enjoyed by the Congolese. Here, too, the Marxist economic interpretation of imperialism is inadequate because it ignores the resentments produced by political factors.

Among the many Marxist dogmas that are at variance with the facts, though sufficiently plausible to impress poor and hungry peoples, two stand out particularly: One fixes the source of economic power in property alone; the other views political corruption as the result not of political power, but of the allegedly more basic economic power. Marxist dogmatism has proved strong enough to obscure even the most obvious facts. Thus the disillusioned Trotsky, recounting the sins of Stalinism in *The Revolution Betrayed* observes the growing inequality of power and privilege in the hierarchical structure of the developing Soviet state. He writes:

> From the point of view of property of the means of production, the differences between a marshal and a servant girl, the head of a trust and a day laborer, the son of a peoples' commissar and a homeless child, seem not to exist at all. Nevertheless the former occupy lordly apartments, enjoy several summer homes . . . have the best automobiles at their disposal, and have long since forgotten how to shine their own shoes. The latter live only in wooden barracks, often without partitions, and do not shine their own shoes only because they go barefoot.[5]

But this recognition of the realities of life behind the mists of dogma, this recognition of the inequalities of political power, could not be sustained by Trotsky, the consistent dogmatist. He concludes lamely, therefore, that the inequalities in power and privilege enjoyed by the Soviet bureaucracy will be subject to erosion. "The proletariat," writes Trotsky, "has not yet said the last word." It will in time oppose the bureaucracy, which will be defenseless because it "has neither stocks nor bonds." Thus Trotsky expressed his faith in the dogma of the primacy of economic power, and even in stocks and bonds, as the only guarantors of political power, even at a time when Stalin's omnipotent political power was about to destroy him. Although such confidence in a dogma may seem but a quaint reminder of the capacity of the fanatic dogmatist to blind himself to the facts, it is relevant to the understanding of the current struggle between the United States and the Soviet Union, the two imperial powers of our time.

The United States, an economic and military super power, indulged in political imperialism only briefly in the Philippines after the Spanish-American War. Such imperial power as it exercises today is the more covert type of economic power, the form of "imperialism" that seems to correspond with the Marxist dogma. All professions of innocence on the part of the United States cannot, therefore, move the hearts and minds of those who are informed by the Marxist dogma. Britain, on the other hand, is clearly an "imperialistic" nation, according to our own liberal doctrine.

Even after the most intimate wartime partnership, such a perceptive American statesman as Franklin D. Roosevelt could neither suppress his embarrassment about British imperialist motives nor appreciate the creative elements in the British tutelage of many weak nations. Our statesmen, from Roosevelt to the pre-Presidential Eisenhower, vainly sought to act as brokers between what they conceived to be a democratic but imperialist Britain and a nondemocratic but anti-imperialist Russia.

In effect, American imperial relations fail to conform with either the Communist or the liberal-democratic interpretation of imperialism. They have been neither in the nature of an exclusively economic exercise of power nor of purely political dominance. Our relations with the two small nations that came under our influence after the Spanish-American War reveal the complex interaction of economic and political power in the relation of strong to weak nations. Our anti-imperialistic scruples prevented us from annexing Cuba and prompted us to promise eventual independence to the Philippines. Yet "free" Cuba is now violently anti-American, while our relations with the Philippines are tolerably amicable.

Cuban anti-Americanism is ostensibly a reaction against economic exploitation. Our investments in Cuba have been heavy, and Castro's revolutionary government has expropriated over a billion dollars worth of American holdings. But underneath the obvious economic grievances is the resentment against a long history of uncreative dictatorial and pseudo-democratic indigenous Cuban governments that the United States has fairly consistently supported. The fact is that the "independent" Cuban people have suffered more from misgovernment by their own nationals than the Philippines suffered in their period of political apprenticeship to the United States. On the other hand, our promised emancipation of the Philippines was rather tardy and reluctant, as all such emancipations are. The delay may have been prompted by the honest conviction that the Philippines were not yet ready for self-government. Whether or not economic motives were also responsible for the delay, they certainly precipitated the final emancipation. It was in our economic interest to put the Philippines outside our tariff walls. President Woodrow Wilson, the author of the Fourteen Points and the exponent of self-determination of nations, was not particularly interested in Philippine independence. He thought of the principle of self-determination as applying to Europe with particular relevance to the multinational Austro-Hungarian Empire. Perhaps the significance of this blind spot in the mind of a liberal democrat lies in the fact that America in the past was less alive than Russia to the problem of the nascent nations of Asia and Africa. There has been a significant change in this American attitude recently.

The fact that economic penetration or partnership without political responsibility is not quite as innocent as the American theory would have it is revealed in our economic relations with the free African nation of Liberia. There an uncreative aristocracy of descendants of American ex-slaves maintain their political ascendancy, giving the Africans little of the educational or political advantages that the former British colony of Nigeria, for example, enjoyed.

The Latin American nation of Guatemala is another one that suffered from political irresponsibility in a purely economic relation. The United Fruit Company of America dominates the economic life of the little nation. The same leftist government that forced the United Fruit Company to recognize unions and raise the wages of its laborers also flirted with Communist Czechoslovakia for the purpose of purchasing military equipment. Strategic considerations thereupon prompted us to encourage rebellion against the government to save it for "democracy."

Then again, relations between Western oil companies and the oil-rich but politically primitive nations of the Near East do not conform to the Marxist image of "Western imperialism." But neither have these relations helped to promote the growth of free institutions in those nations. Here the technically competent nations join in economic partnership with nations that have oil deposits but lack the technical competence to extract and refine the oil and the transport facilities and markets for its disposal. Since the 1951 Iranian nationalist crisis, when the emotional Prime Minister, Mossadegh, temporarily halted oil production, all the oil companies there and in the Arab countries content themselves with a contractual relation with the native governments that yields the latter 50 per cent of the profits. The profits go to monarchic rulers who may or may not use them creatively for improvement of essentially pastoral economies. Though the Iranian monarchy is relatively enlightened, the new riches are not used consistently for the people's welfare.

When the Hashemite dynasty in Iraq was operating through a prime minister with dictatorial power, it made genuine efforts to use the oil royalties for public improvements, irrigation projects, and education. In 1958, the Hashemites were nevertheless overthrown and the king and the prime minister assassinated. The subsequent regime, under President Kassim, has enjoyed a fair degree of stability, though the complex relations and conflicts between Communism and Iraqi nationalism throw doubts on its prolonged duration.

Perhaps the most glaring impingement of modern wealth on a primitive culture has occurred further south on the Arabian peninsula, where the oil resources of Saudi Arabia are exploited by the Arabian-American Oil Company, and those of Kuwait by British and American companies. The impact of the partnership in oil revenues on a primitive economic and political society is particularly instructive in the case of Saudi Arabia. The present Saudi dynasty, rising to power after a long struggle between the Rashid and Saudi families, emerged as the undisputed rulers of much of the Arabian peninsula. The oil income, presently amounting to about a quarter of a billion dollars annually, is spent profligately by the royal family and its innumerable princes. The miserable Bedouins of the peninsula have received a mere trickle of the benefits in the form of schools and health services. The oil companies do not, and probably should not, interfere in Saudi Arabian politics; this compels them to remain politically irresponsible. Meanwhile, a class of indigenous technicians and bureaucrats is developing that must ultimately challenge the existing primitive political organization. The oil companies' policies of economic partnership and political lack of responsibility do not conform to the Marxist indictment of "imperialistic exploitation." But one has the uneasy feeling that their policies are hardly a match for the Communist competitor in the Middle East, particularly since Leninist Communism has learned shrewdly to combine, and alternately to emphasize, the nationalistic and the economic-revolutionary parts of its program.

The developments in the Suez Canal crisis of 1956 left the "free world" with few political laurels and only aggravated tensions. The abortive military attempt of Britain and France to force Nasser to recognize the rights of Western canal owners confirmed and intensified existing Afro-Asian resentments against Western imperialists. On the other hand, United States policy in the crisis alternated between neutrality and joint action with Russia in demanding that our allies withdraw. Our actions reinforced the suspicion of our European allies that our policies were governed more by abstract anticolonialism than by sympathetic understanding of the dependence of the whole European economy upon the Suez lifeline.

At the same time, the Soviets, who had precipitated the crisis by their arms deal with Nasser, established a virtual alliance with Egypt, a nation in which domestic Communist activity had been rigorously suppressed. Neither our pacifist idealism nor the European military realism was a match for the Russian flexibility in dealing with a nation smarting with resentment after centuries of foreign domination.

Clearly our ideological advantages are not so great in the struggle for the sympathy of the technically underdeveloped nations of Asia and Africa as we are often inclined to assume. We base our assumptions on the contradiction between Communist dogmas and the complex facts of social existence at the national, as well as the international, levels. Communist dogmas are obviously too simple and polemical to fit all the facts. But they do seem to fit not only some of the moods which have developed over centuries of subjugation, but also the realities of the dislocations in pastoral and agrarian economies that have resulted from their encounters with the West.

Only a craven defeatist could suggest that the West should capitulate before the Communist dogma and sacrifice all the treasures, cultural and spiritual, that have been bestowed upon it through the ages. But the ideological handicaps facing it must be recognized and ought to prompt great circumspection in the elaboration of Western policies toward the new and weak nations of Asia and Africa. The West cannot hope to succeed in its competition with the Soviets unless it overcomes its parochial confidence that the democratic way of organizing national communities and communities of nations is necessarily going to prove acceptable or desirable to all peoples. Its institutions may not be the only alternative to the peculiar Communist oligarchical organization of society, or to the Communist identification of cultural and religious ultimates with proximate political values.

The 1960 conference of the eighty-one Communist parties in Moscow has revealed serious conflict, particularly between the Russians and the Chinese, over the interpretation of the dogma. While the former read into Marxist-Leninist doctrine their views about "peaceful coexistence" between the two social systems, the Chinese insisted on the inevitability of war as long as capitalist imperialism continues. However, all the parties agreed, as a matter of dogma, that Communism will inevitably win. Speaking in terms of the Russian interpretation of this dogma, *Pravda* writes:

> Events in the last three years in the world arena have confirmed the correctness of the analysis of the world situation, given in the declaration and peace manifesto and the correctness of the Marxist-Leninist conclusions concerning the prospects of world development. This period has seen the further powerful growth of the world system of socialism; and the disintegration of the colonial system has gone at an accelerated pace under the pressure of the national liberation movements. . . . The great victories of Communism, the indisputable superiority of the countries in the rate of production, the development in a number of branches of science and technology, in the fields of education, culture, and art, the growth of sympathy for socialism in all countries, have once again been fully demonstrated to the entire world. . . . The question that preoccupies mankind today is the question of the preservation and consolidation of peace and the prevention of a new war. . . . The forces of peace have now grown to such an extent that there is a practical possibility of preventing war.

This *Pravda* editorial, while stressing certainty of ultimate victory, which is the staple of the Communist creed, nevertheless reveals an interesting adjustment of the dogma to the situation of the 1960's. The original core of the Marxist dogma has been abandoned; this was the anticipation of a class struggle in the highly developed industrial societies, culminating in revolution and a classless society. The emphasis has shifted to the problems arising from the awakening of the new nations of Asia and Africa —problems to which Communism is supposed to present the simple answer. Its victory is said to guarantee the emancipation of all dependent nations from domination by others, as it assures the emancipation of all suppressed classes as well as the prevention of war.

The Communist promise of technical competence and industrial development for the underdeveloped countries is most significant because it replaces the notion of the triumph of the proletariat over the bourgeoisie, which was the original promise of the apocalypse. The salvation of the proletariat is not denied, but is overshadowed and obscured by the new promise that Communism assures technical progress. Here the facts of recent history, which the authors of the Communist Manifesto of 1848 could not possibly have anticipated, have led to another change of the dogma. Recent Russian and Chinese history has revealed that a Communist regime, enjoying a monopoly of power over its people, can force the poor—in both cases the peasants—to pay for the industrial equipment required to produce abundance for their children's children. Ironically, the Communist method of capital accumulation is even more cruel, and perhaps more efficacious, than the method of early capitalism.

The success of the Soviet Union in acquiring technical competence, even technical superiority in some lines of space technology, has come as a shock to the Western world and shaken its complacent assurance that a system of economic and cultural freedom, such as its own, is a prerequisite of technical and industrial progress and a sign of the superiority of the West. The West might have been warned by the phenomenal industrial rise of Japan between 1870 and the close of the century, which occurred under economic and cultural traditions quite different from those in Western nations. It showed that there was no necessary correlation between industrial development and classical Western capitalism, a correlation more polemical than empirical. The phenomenon of universalization of technical competence both under capitalism and Communism deserves intense analysis, as does the apparent tendency in all present cultures, whether technically advanced or not, to regard technical competence as the *summum bonum* of human aspiration.

The challenge of Communism to the West transcends the competition for the allegiance of countries seeking technical advancement and competence. The West is engaged in a contest with a political system whose dogma has a disturbing plausibility to peoples who, as members of a world community, are for the first time drawn into the vortex of global political events. The seeming relevance of the Communist dogma to the particular experience of the nontechnical cultures is only part of a larger problem. What is taking place is a contest between a system with a dogmatically unified political purpose, and a system operating under conditions of freedom and therefore inevitably presenting an image of confusion and cross-purposes. The advantages of the unified position, over the diversity and contradictions of purpose characteristic of a nondogmatic world, may appear overpowering. But we must recognize that the political disadvantages from which we suffer are the inevitable concomitant of the very values that, at our best, we cherish and wish to preserve. If truth about human affairs, about ourselves and our foes, is accessible to man only as it shines through the competing and often contradictory interpretations of the same situation, then our system of freedom, with all the cross-purposes it generates, may confidently take on the task of dispelling the utopian illusions with which the Communists entice the new and impoverished nations, and unmasking the lies of the Marxist dogma and political religion. The West will be the more successful in fulfilling this task the more it is critical of its own illusions and the more it remains aware both of the polemical, nonempirical elements in its own position and of the elements of truth in the position of its Communist opponent.

XI

TRIPARTISM: DILEMMAS AND STRATEGIES

by GEORGE LISKA

THE differences between policies of neutralism and nonalignment are significant, though shadowy and fluid. They affect the influence that the uncommitted countries seek and actually bring to bear on the international system; and they condition the strategic response of the Cold War contestants.

The contemporary international system remains bipolar in the ultimate military sense. But it is becoming increasingly tripartite from the standpoint of policy and political influence, in part as a result of the East-West nuclear stalemate. In a tripartite situation, any two parties principally involved in a dispute are deeply concerned over the effects of their respective policies on any interested third party. The third party is also interested, as it stands to benefit or suffer from the dispute. If it stands to suffer from a conflict between major antagonists, the third party may try to play the role of mediator-moderator. If, on the other hand, it can benefit from a split between previously friendly or allied powers, the third party will assume the role of divisor. It is in the interest of the principal contestants to avoid policies that would seriously alienate a would-be mediator-moderator or encourage a would-be divisor.

The nonaligned countries, whose number is growing, have composed the most frequently noted "third party" in the contemporary system of policy. Their chief concern centers on the relationship between the industrial nations of the "North" and the underdeveloped, ex-colonial countries of the "South." The problem of economic development and political independence is paramount in this "North-South" relationship, which in some in-

212 NEUTRALISM AND NONALIGNMENT

stances has been overshadowing the hitherto dominant East-West conflict. What are the main characteristics, the motivations, and the rationalizations of nonalignment and its militant variety, neutralism?

STABILIZATION BETWEEN THE BLOCS

The self-styled "nonbloc" countries regard themselves as a third force for stabilizing international relations on a lower level of tension between the adversary blocs. Can and do these countries perform such a role in fact, or is it a fiction impatiently tolerated by the great powers for reasons of their own? I shall first examine some basic requirements of the role and then consider the performance itself.

To help stabilize the larger field, nonaligned countries themselves would first have to be reasonably stable and politically developed. This would mean for some or most militant neutralist regimes a delay in assuming an active international role. By contrast, mere nonalignment can, ideally, complement internal efforts to develop a national consensus capable of containing contests over fundamental foreign, as well as domestic, policy decisions when a country is just emerging from dependence or division along tribal, ethnic, or class lines. Only as a coherent community forms is the nation ready for gradual involvement in international politics at large and commitments to other nations.

Even before internal consensus, the country's leadership must first acquire an elementary sense of the reciprocity that truly equal states expect from each other whenever they relax the concept of self-interest and immediate need. Colonial status is the worst possible school for international politics as far as the acquisition of such a sense of reciprocity is concerned. First, the responsibility of a metropole for foreign relations and defense isolates native elites from relations with other states. Such isolation could only confirm the tendency of local elites to see their particular colonial power as the only embodiment of the hardships that actually mark relations among all states and collectives. Second, the colonial powers' monopoly of responsibility for internal order and welfare makes all advances—such as the lessening of internal insecurity, disease, and poverty—appear unrelated to the performance of the "exploited" colonial society. Third, in many cases, and virtually in all most recent cases, outside forces had more to do with the attainment of independence than did the efforts and sacrifices of indigenous elites.

Such colonial experiences have one thing in common: They distorted the political vision of the new elites, especially by severing in their imaginations the tie between performance and consequences in relations among self-dependent actors.

Neutralism's effect is neocolonial whenever it perpetuates the unreal world view under the new conditions of independence. The colonial experience is apparent when neutralist leaders neglect internal efforts, expecting aggrandizement from manipulating outside forces. And it is also apparent on the part of the more restrained nonaligned countries, when the attitude of nonresponsibility is carried over into the question of national capability for defense.

For a poor country to delay acquiring such capability is apparently justified on grounds of internal development, as well as external security. A nonaligned country derives a form of immunity from international configurations; and it may dispose of domestic substitutes for security-through-defense efforts. One method is immunity through imitation of the potentially dangerous power. This may currently mean the adoption of much, but not all, of the disciplined one-party system of the Communist-bloc countries. Another, and in a way, opposite, mode of immunity is through irrationality. This is the posture of a country that absorbs or deflects external pressures through chaos and anarchy instead of confronting them with organized strength. The attitude was allegedly characteristic of Iran in the past, and it has been that of some more recently nonaligned countries.[1] When a country with this kind of absorptive capacity aligns itself with an industrial power, the ally, no less than the adversary, tends to deprive it of its indigenous formless immunity, without necessarily supplying an equivalent in a rationalized means of security.

The trouble with substitutes is that they may be too effective. This may, at least for a time, be true of substitutes for self-made security. The decision to defer the burdens of a defense establishment—often prompted by the desire to avoid strains and imbalance in the structure of the developing nation's economy and political power—may actually retard both political and economic development. In many places, a modern national army has been, and will continue to be, a major agent in welding together a heterogeneous society, imparting elementary acquaintance with modern skills and arbitrating factional conflicts. Not every country can have an Ataturk, to be sure, but even the Mobutus can be useful. They can temporarily neutralize rival politicians who are unable to master the range of intractable practical problems, decisions, and influences. Being the self-appointed guardian of national interests, moreover, the army is likely to discourage outside interventions, which feuding politicians sometimes elicit and are almost always prepared to exploit.

Unless it is relatively immune to intervention, a country can itself hardly intervene with effect between greater powers, whether in the interest of stability or of anything else. And truly effective intervention must be based on some independent capability. In contemporary conditions, this capability need not be such as to permit an armed mediation; but the third party's influence must not derive only from the interplay of the powers that the party seeks to moderate. To the extent that it does so derive, the effect of third-party pressures is actually due to the regard of the great powers for the capabilities of each other. The leaders of the unaligned Bandung and, more recently, the Belgrade powers are right in asserting that rightful influence is not merely a function of material strength. But "moral" influence—no more than influence derived from the deadlock of contending forces—cannot be lastingly effective unless third-party pressures can equalize great-power behavior, even if they cannot equalize great-power capabilities. Much depends, therefore, on the meaning the neutralist leaders attach to their other contention, i.e., that independence need not mean equidistance from the two materially strongest powers.

Before we evaluate the neutralists' influence, we may ask in what framework they might best be able to exert any influence. To enhance their individual bargaining power and capabilities, the neutralists could combine in a separate bloc organization of their own; and to enhance their moral authority as a group, they might prefer to act mainly or exclusively through the similarly authoritative world organization of the United Nations.

To abstain from "permanent" bloc organization reflects more accurately the attitude toward international relations of countries that turn "independence" into a dogma. Moreover, the organization of a firm neutralist bloc would be undesirable on strictly pragmatic grounds. It would probably reduce the bargaining power that the members have individually. The more conservative of the two super powers, the United States, would shift onto the bloc leaders its preoccupation with preventing defections from nonalignment; and the expansionist superpower, the Soviet Union, might let up on courting individual countries for fear of gaining less from any one of them than it would lose in bloc good-will—or the good-will of the bloc's leaders. The strength and influence of a loose and heterogeneous neutralist bloc, as a whole, might also decrease relative to the alliance systems, after it has helped consolidate them. In order to avoid being isolated between one enemy bloc and an expanding neutralist bloc, the leaders of the alliance would have to reaffirm primary allegiance to their allies; and the governments of the lesser allies would have every reason for strengthening the existing ties in preference to joining, as a latecomer, a weaker grouping, subject to conflicting leadership ambitions.

Moreover, to add a neutralist bloc to the two alliance systems might well dissipate the greatest asset of the uncommitted countries. A neutralist bloc would weaken the standing of the United Nations and decrease the influence of the unaligned nations within as well as outside it.

Facts, as well as official ideology, have made the United Nations into an organization of the nonbloc countries for dealing with issues that are apparently separable from the struggle of the two opposing blocs.[2] Both East and West have countenanced the United Nations' evolution into a noncommitted as well as noncommitting organization, hoping to use it as the main forum for appealing to nonaligned countries in political warfare and mobilizing them for mediatory, supervisory, and policing functions in small-scale military clashes. The new ideology of the U.N. is, however, often discredited by the neutralist leaders themselves. They imitate the great powers whenever they transact a particular issue—such as that of the Congo in 1960–61—outside the U.N. framework, hoping to gain a particular advantage, compose their conflicting interests, or merely escape the contrary pressures of the super powers. More than a mere ideology, the very standing of the U.N. in the esteem of the great powers would be at stake if the neutralist countries went further and set up a permanent body of their own outside the global organization.

Within the U.N., the role and composition of a neutralist bloc organization would have to interfere with the existing informal groupings. These diversely defined voting blocs and shifting alignments have proved to be the ideal mode of exerting influence. If mere membership in the U.N. raises a small country's status above that imparted by independence, as alliance with a great power used to, membership in one or several influential voting groups raises status above that imparted by membership in the organization, and well above that implicit in material capability. The institutional arrangement has enabled the lesser countries to perform their part in adjusting global issues, while reducing to an approved scope and method the part of greater powers in local and intra-regional issues and disputes—a combination that, most of the time, has been an unattainable ideal for small states. But, if diplomatic influence of lesser states is contingent on great-power relationships, so is their diplomatic self-sufficiency. The contests of the two super powers have not only enhanced the standing of the "third force" within the enfeebled organization; they have also increased its cohesion. The presumably U.N.–supporting nonaligned countries are not themselves a self-sustaining group. To the extent that a separate organization would lessen the need to react against great-power involvement, the group's cohesion and, thus, influence, would wane.[3]

On balance, a neutralist bloc would probably decrease rather than increase its members' influence; but more important than framework is the thrust of actual policies and their impacts.

Given the necessary self-restraint of all concerned, mere non-alignment can reduce interbloc tensions and stabilize relations while favoring no contestant. On the regional plane, nonalignment counters the tendency for local states to divide between competing global powers. On the global plane, too, nonaligned states can be useful as insulating buffer states, mediators, and international policemen. The bigger nonaligned countries can serve as guarantors of the lesser buffer states; while a Laos might insulate East-West forces from each other, India might help guarantee Laos' immunity.

If nonalignment decompresses tensions between alliance blocs, militant neutralism injects pressures of its own into the field of forces. In principle, the effect can be none the less relaxing and roughly equal for each of the adversary sides. Third-party pressures do not ordinarily consolidate alliances, as do manageable pressures exerted by the adversary, for third-party pressures are likely to bear on and activate secondary conflicts within the alliance blocs. These may be conflicts over substance, like those dividing the colonial and noncolonial countries in NATO, or over strategy and tactics, like those arising between the Soviet Union and China in the Communist bloc. The resulting intra-alliance debate over policy has a positive incidental effect. It forces the publication of at least parts of the alliance's inner story. These revelations are especially valuable when they come from the totalitarian bloc, for its chief method of relaxing secrecy about its intentions and commitments is through doctrinal disagreements.

However, a more far-reaching relaxation is within the realm of possibilities. As the neutralists attract attention, adversaries may moderate their activities and objectives. The forces that might impel a head-on collision between antagonists are diverted into tangential movements; and reciprocal pressures mellow into enticements of third states. The adversary alliances may, ideally, come to behave somewhat as rivals in a two-party system, competing over a floating vote of independents and being drawn to the moderate center in the process—while continuing all the while to stress their differences.

If this is a theoretical possibility, what has been the actual state of things? It can be argued that even pressures equal in force and kind would be disadvantageous to the Western side, because the basic security postures are not comparable. The Soviet bloc has a firm offensive and defensive base because of its central position on the Eurasian land mass. The West's security depends on bases in overseas islands and rimlands. Neutralist pressure on both super powers to withdraw from advance positions and disarm tends to hamstring the West's strategic retaliatory capabilities. This might merely reinforce other compulsions to scale down levels of conflict to smaller conventional and guerrilla-type operations; but a West disengaging and disarming under pressure would be handicapped not least in conducting the "limited" kind of operations in threatened areas. To be anything like equalizing, therefore, the neutralists would have to press both super powers to withdraw into their respective national confines, following genuine self-determination of their wards and dependencies—a desideratum that would be unacceptable to the Soviets and might be distasteful to the United States, in some cases.

Thus, with the best of intentions, impartiality would be difficult to attain. The pressure of the neutralists has tended to be unequal; it has often been either coincident or openly cooperative with the Communists' pressure on the West. In the propaganda war, the neutralists have leaned toward adopting Communist meanings and attributions of categories like "deterrence" and "terror"; "disarmament," "arms control," and "arms race"; "aggressive" and "collective-security" alliances; "self-determination," "imperialism," and "neocolonialism." Individual countries supported by the West have not hesitated to accept Soviet military assistance, even when they were capable of neutralizing Western positions scheduled for early evacuation by previous agreement.[4] Collectively, the neutralists have conducted a campaign against Western alliances and bases that has threatened first to upset a delicate balance of strategic power and then to start a stampede toward the winning side—a last blow to the losing side that might exceed, and make unnecessary, the military effect of a first nuclear strike.

There has been no single reason or motive for the inequality of pressures—or, to put it differently, for the "double standard"— applied to East and West. Apart from elements of short-term opportunism and personal rivalry, the primary reason could be either the greater fear of Soviet power or the greater familiarity with the West, compounding resentment of both deprivation and indebtedness with an ambivalent sense of familial identity. The fear has engendered a tendency to propitiate the Communist bloc and be receptive to its appeals and pressures; the familiarity has engendered a more critical attitude toward the West and the expectation that it be receptive to neutralist appeals and pressures. The actual motives in particular instances must remain obscure; clearer is the pattern of effects that the *rapprochement* between neutralist countries and the Communist bloc has had on the three multilateral Western alliances and the Soviet bloc itself.

NATO has been exposed to pressures, chiefly from the Soviet bloc. The campaign against the Baghdad Pact, on the other hand, was conducted mainly by Middle Eastern neutralists. And SEATO has so far been saved from the combination fatal to the Baghdad Pact: intensification of neutralist opposition while Communist-bloc pressures apparently subsided or were transmitted and legitimized by local non-Communist powers. The lesser intensity of local antagonisms in Southeast Asia than in the Middle East has also been a factor; moreover, after 1958, the bloc (and Communist China in particular) stepped up pressure on both the SEATO powers and the nonaligned countries in the area. Of the two major consequences, one was favorable for the West and the other less so. The Sino-Soviet bloc failed to subvert to its purposes the pressures put on SEATO by local nonaligned and neutralist states; but the resumption of Communist expansion also served to stimulate the fears of these states and their subsequent inclination to apply restraints on the West.

The new Sino-Soviet thrust for expansion had another significant consequence. It advertised the failure of the nonaligned Southeast Asian countries to loosen the Sino-Soviet alliance to make it match and accelerate a like trend in the Asian alliances of the West. When making the attempt, the Bandung conferees did not apply outright pressure in order to detach the Asian power—

China—from the European ally—Russia; they relied on entice-ment, moral suasion, and verbal commitments.[5] The Bandung pol-icy toward China was thus reminiscent of Anglo-French policy to-ward Germany in the 1930's. The difference was that the object of neutralist appeasement was simultaneously being deterred by the Western alliance system. Ideally, the American strategy of deter-rence might have supplemented the neutralist strategy of attrac-tion; actually, American intransigence was no more effective than Asian wooing, and the former was not necessary to thwart the latter. In any event, the Bandung operation in Asia was both a less deliberate and a less successful division of labor between neutralists and a Cold War belligerent than was the onslaught on the Baghdad Pact in the Middle East.

The neutralists and the West complemented each other no better in the unintended effect that Bandung had on the Soviet Union's European allies, mainly Hungary. There the attraction of the neu-tralist model worked, but Western deterrence of Soviet counter-action did not. The events of 1956 showed the limits of neutralism as a force influencing both blocs. Domestic upheavals made some Communist leaders in the satellite countries receptive to the for-mula of nonalignment; but the Afro-Asian neutralists refrained from doing anything to enlarge the unaligned area at the expense of the Communist bloc. The Soviet Union was permitted to crush "counterrevolutionary" neutralism while retaining the ability to foster "objectively revolutionary" neutralism in the non-Commu-nist world—both as a matter of "internationalist duty."

After 1956, elements of both strength and weakness in the West-ern strategic posture have stimulated neutralist tendencies in non-Communist countries, albeit for different reasons and to varying degrees. On the other hand, Soviet technological and strategic suc-cesses have discouraged neutralist longings within the captive coun-tries and have failed to encourage counterbalancing shifts in the position of the Afro-Asian neutralists. Even Titoist defections, to date the Soviet bloc's major failure in regard to neutralism, have on the whole worked against Western interests. Receptivity has been a one-way street. Tito has had some success in making a Marxist type of socialism attractive to the neutralists and in setting up the Belgrade brand of neutralism as an alternative to the old-fashioned, self-liquidating anticolonialism of Bandung. But he has failed com-pletely in his efforts to induce the Communist bloc to accept non-alignment as a policy that could also be applied among "socialist" states.[6]

The imbalance that has so far marred the neutralist impact on the West and the East has been too definite to disappear in the perspective of a few analogies. Both sides in the Cold War have learned that no amount of skill and manipulation can reliably contain or master the neutralist wave. The Soviets' agreement to neutralize Austria boosted their new-look strategy outside Europe and, incidentally, added Austria to Switzerland as land barriers between NATO forces in Germany and Italy.[7] But the Austrian settlement also encouraged neutralist tendencies in Eastern Europe, which forced the Soviet Union into unpopular countermeasures. The West, in turn, has been ready to neutralize Austria's Far Eastern counterpart, Laos, albeit under military pressure from its adversary. The West's readiness to do so threatened to strengthen neutralist tendencies among the Asian SEATO allies and to necessitate costly remedies in the future.

The most acute frustration shared by the Cold War adversaries was in the area of "foreign aid." Both superpowers have been uncertain about the likely course and outcome of alternative ways of rendering material assistance to nonaligned and neutralist countries; and both sought reassurance in largely analogous doctrinaire assumptions and beliefs about the ultimately favorable effects of such assistance on their respective goals. But it is hard to see how material assistance to less developed countries could serve to expand both the socialist commonwealth and the area of freedom; and it was as natural for the Communist Chinese to oppose Soviet favors to neutralists as it was for the Thai to deplore a like diversion of American resources. There have been more pointed divergencies on both sides. As a "neutral" in the Sino-Indian border dispute, the Soviet Union has volunteered military supplies to India; and the Chinese have begun to question the Soviet monopoly of Communist influence in individual nonaligned areas, in remote Africa, and in the traditionally Chinese zone of influence. On the Western side, America has observed neutrality in the conflict of *its* ally Pakistan with India, as well as in a number of colonial contests involving European allies; and the French have contested American influence in formerly French-dominated Vietnam and Laos, both in "alliance" with neutralist elements in local upheavals and as part of plans for the neutralization of Laos.

It remained to be seen, however, whether the symmetrics are real. The "competition" of the Communist powers in particular is hardly distinguishable from a deliberate division of labor, notably in its effects. Thus India's indebtedness for Soviet support against

China may well have helped Communist strategy in Laos. The divisive impact of Bandung neutralism on the satellite belt has since been largely corrected with the cooperation of the anticolonial neutralists themselves. Their receptivity to bloc trade and assistance has helped diversify economic activities and outlets for the satellite countries and, consequently, has reconsolidated the bloc on a more substantial foundation than before.

SUBVERSION OR STAMPEDE

The utility of the neutralists as self-appointed moderators is impaired whenever they distribute pressures and opportunities unevenly between the two alliance systems and elicit from them responses that are still more upsetting. The responses add up to the strategies of East and West toward neutralism, which implement certain designs and are impeded by certain dilemmas. The designs bear on the main strategic issue of the Cold War: who contains or encircles whom by military, political, and economic means. An examination of the Sino-Soviet bloc's strategies must precede a more extended analysis of two main alternatives in the West's armory of responses.

The Communists' efforts to foster divisions among the members of the Western alliance as well as in the relations of Western allies with the nonaligned countries do not fit the model of two parties moderating their programs in order to win over the political center. The strategy is much more in keeping with the model of a multiparty system, with a revolutionary party seeking to disorder relations among all the other parties. The revolutionary party's objective is to impose its program of social transformation without concessions to anyone; its method is to divide and demoralize opponents by using "fellow travelers" to obscure and dissipate the straightforward character of the contest. The principal enemy of the moment is to be defeated with the help of a future enemy—or victim—who, for tactical reasons, is singled out as a current ally.

The Communist powers' chosen tactical allies have been the "bourgeois-nationalist" regimes in formerly colonial countries. The principal enemy, the West, is to overtax its resources and bring about its own division and isolation by ill-conceived responses to the provisional "alliance." Beyond this point, the Communists have seemed to hesitate. One possible direction for their strategy has been to try to subvert the less developed countries themselves, one by one, as they were individually ready. Another has been to work for a stampede *en masse* by eroding the non-Communist world as a whole and breaking up the West's "provocative" alliances; subversion in Iran, unlike subversion in Burma, would not so much alienate the nonaligned countries as bolster their conviction that their policy was the only right one.

The uncertainty over a key aspect of strategy has reflected the bloc's dilemmas in its relations with nonaligned countries. These dilemmas, now to be discussed in succession, concern the pace and the methods of Communist subversion on the one hand, and the revolutionary character of neutralism itself on the other.

The difficulty besetting the strategy of subversion in one country at a time has been its possible repercussions in other nonaligned countries. These countries' greater fear of the Sino-Soviet bloc serves the East best when the Communist bloc acts to intimidate the West or the world at large; but the dividends of fear decline into liabilities when the bloc encroaches on individual nonaligned countries themselves. Moreover, for the Communist powers to prevail at the center of authority in any one country, their real, subjectively committed allies—the local Communist parties—must be able to prevent a last-minute reversal by the neutralist elite; and the Soviet Union must be able to deter a Western intervention on behalf of the chastened nationalists.

Most regimes in the less developed countries have been making skillful use of the distinction between the Soviet or Chinese state as an international friend and the Communist Party as an internal enemy. These regimes can be expected to resist the transformation of a tactical, limited-liability alliance with the Communists into full membership in the "socialist commonwealth." Such a transformation would be paralleled by domestic changes from a "national" to a "popular" democracy and bring about the eventual liquidation of the nationalist cadre. The Castros willing to ignore the risk have been few.

The increasing number of countries that combine the techniques of Communist-style one-party organization with radical-leftist ideology and policy are no exception. The authoritarian one-party system is efficient in mobilizing the masses; and it is less wasteful of scarce elite resources than is the alternative, the combination of a centralized bureaucracy and a multiparty system that came into being after the French Revolution. In addition to its internal economy, the one-party system has advantages in the international politics of the Cold War. On the one hand, the one-party system may be the best available guarantee of internal security against a takeover, by imitating the Communist Party's techniques for organizing mass support. Such a regime may, therefore, lean farther toward the Sino-Soviet bloc than any other without running the risk of toppling. On the other hand, should the global balance of power shift against the West, the non-Communist elite of the one-party system could easily be stampeded into the Communist camp. The narrowness of the gap between the Soviet system and the local regime, which had so far immunized the indigenous authoritarian system, would then both predispose and qualify the regime to seek membership in the socialist "world system."

To promote such a stampede, the Sino-Soviet bloc cannot prematurely alienate nonaligned countries by the pace and techniques of subversion. To avoid loss of good-will (from forcible takeover) and of face (from a successful counteraction), the Communist powers have been assisting neutralist regimes without daring to transform support into subversion. Only when the West becomes too weak to serve as a rallying core for frightened neutrals would annexations be possible, but then they would no longer be necessary for fighting the main enemy. At the present, the main difficulty besetting the strategy of progressively eroding the non-Communist world has been the fitful interplay of countries and regimes at different stages of radical anti-Westernism and receptivity toward Communist-style socialism.

Neutralism itself shares with all revolutionary movements a pattern that confounds the outsider's attempt to harness such a movement for his ends.

The pattern is one of successive waves of radicalism and competitive thrusts of ambition, forcing most older and relatively satisfied revolutionaries into a more moderate, relatively conservative posture. Over the years, Nehru first was outdone by Nasser and then the two were brought into virtual unison in relation as well as in reaction to Nkrumah. To outdo the more radical newcomers to independence, and to reassert more than nominal leadership, the moderates will fitfully return to extreme postures; but this is unlikely either to last or to be convincing. As a consequence, not many nonaligned regimes adopt an identical nuance in attitudes toward global issues, any more than they adopt identical tactical stands on specific issues. The dynamic is unwittingly fostered by Communist-bloc policies. The bloc's special favors are highly unstable, for the bloc seeks the most extreme champion of radicalism and anti-Westernism at any particular time and place. The favors are also limited, for the bloc works with limited resources, and can effectively support only a few rivals for finite prizes. The bloc could not simultaneously back and favor Nasser and Kassim while they competed for leadership in the Middle East, or Nkrumah and Sékou-Touré in West Africa. Combined with the persistency of the Communist supreme command's "sympathy" for local Communist parties, the vagaries of bloc support for individual "bourgeois-nationalist" regimes cannot but advance the political education and moderation of the new elites.

The paucity of concrete results has increased the Communists' uncertainty about method; and this has made it all the more necessary for them to restate dramatically their ultimate intention—Communist triumph everywhere. Restatement was necessary to maintain unity and revolutionary ardor within the Sino-Soviet bloc; but as a result, the bloc's merely "objective" allies have become still more circumspect and more cynical about their own motives for the alliance. The moment the Soviet Union felt strong enough to exploit the "general crisis of capitalism" on a broad front, Lenin's idea of "uneven development" began turning against Communist strategies in underdeveloped countries. Communist advances have proved reversible in countries not adjacent to the Communist heartland, like Syria, Iraq, and Guatemala, as well as in territorially adjacent countries, like Iran (when the local Communist Party rode the wave of Mossadegh's nationalism). The bloc registers failure whenever nationalist elites retreat from a pro-Soviet line, or when an alternative leadership displaces an elite that went too far without being able or willing to go all the way—or is permitted to do so by the global requirements of Communist strategy. Until and unless a major phase of expansion has run its course, the Communists themselves have to make necessity a virtue; they have to demonstrate the possibility of coexistence, using the example of only half-controlled countries—Czechoslovakia until 1947, when Communist prospects in Western Europe collapsed, and, probably, Laos in the early 1960's, when that small country was being set up as a model of "neutrality" for Asia and Africa.

If militant neutralism is self-liquidating, and the Communist powers are beset by dilemmas, why should the West feel concerned about militant neutralism? One reason is the capacity of the Sino-Soviet bloc to shift strategies: Soviet nuclear terror can replace or supplement bloc wooing, producing superficially identical neutralist responses. This keeps the problem alive for the West and aggravates another reason for anxiety, one that bears on the Western response to neutralism.

CONCILIATION AND CONTAINMENT OF NEUTRALISM

Although directed at each other's weaknesses, the strategies of the Cold War protagonists have displayed comparable concepts and vacillations. As the bloc has seemed to waver between seeking to subvert countries one by one and inducing a mass stampede at a somewhat later date, so the West has wavered between a long-term, country-by-country approach and one stressing the immediate requirements of the free-world system as a whole. And if the Soviets have seemed to be at loggerheads with the Chinese, the West has had even less of a unified strategy. The British have inclined to a long-suffering attitude, born of experience with formerly colonial countries such as America; the French, painfully decolonizing under neutralist pressure, have inclined toward a sterner concept; and the United States has vacillated between courtship of the new countries and exasperation over them.

America's choice hung in the balance as its revolutionary myth and sentiment ran against two interrelated inclinations: cautious reformism for the free world and militant anti-Communism in the Cold War. The nation's related, and partly contradictory, concerns have been to win the neutralists over and to maintain the West's alliances and vital security positions. The two concerns and emphases imply different assumptions and minimum objectives, and entail different dilemmas. As these are made explicit and the differences between them sharpened for purposes of exposition, there emerge two contrasting strategies—a strategy of conciliating all "neutrals" and a discriminatory strategy of containing the anti-Western "neutralists."

A major premise of the strategy of conciliation, stated generally, is: The United States must identify itself with the anticolonial position. It can sympathize with the growing pains of statehood, having itself passed through the stages peculiar to most new nations: colonial dependence, emancipation, fitful expansionism under the colors of anti-imperialism and economic growth. America, too, drew on the imperial conflicts of longer-established powers—such as the conflict of the French with the British and subsequently of the British with the powers of the conservative "Holy Alliance"— while gaining and extending her independence, and she used the reprieve to develop domestically with capital assistance from abroad. In disputing the Soviet monopoly on anticolonialism, therefore, America can and must act like an older brother who understands and humors the flights of adolescence.

The conciliation strategy's key objective is for the individual nonaligned countries and regimes to uphold their commitment to independence. Such a commitment is taken to constitute the West's main political capital in the so-called uncommitted countries; its manifestations are of secondary importance. The strategy takes into account only one class of nonaligned countries, whatever its label, and within that undifferentiated group it stresses each country's unique characteristics and individual needs. As the West meets these needs with properly adjusted policies, the new nations' spirit of independence is expected to come into conflict with Sino-Soviet imperialism. This will bring into the open the impartiality latent among the Westernized elites. Meanwhile, the West must foster an image of itself as a selfless friend and helper. The West can afford to take the long view, because it is both sufficiently strong and cohesive.

In the second strategy, which derives from a somewhat less optimistic view, Western policy should not only conciliate but also contain the apparently irreconcilable. It should be concerned with the contemporary requirements of the non-Communist state system as a whole, rather than with analogies from the American past, with utopias in the future, and with individual nonaligned countries in the present. The spirit of independence in less developed countries is valuable; but, like the stable growth of its material base, it cannot be prized regardless of its foreign-policy manifestations. The key, or minimum, objective is, therefore, not to foster commitment to independence for its own sake, but to contain both Communism and its neutralist "allies" to ensure an elementary pluralistic order in the non-Communist world. Within such an incipient order, the developing countries must be able to progress *and* regress in their decolonization, politico-economic development, and foreign-policy attitudes at such uneven rates and in such a staggered phasing, that at no time will all or most of them be ripe for simultaneous Communist takeovers.

The number of independent countries has been growing, and the great powers' means for directly influencing their behavior has been waning at about the same rate. For both reasons, Western policies can have a wished-for impact only if they are consistent; hence the need to differentiate comparable types of behavior within the universe of nonalignment. Differently oriented elites interact and influence each other's behavior; to make their interaction orderly at any one time is as important as to promote an individual country's movement along successive stages of economic growth. The West is not infinitely secure; the global distribution of power is adversely affected by a particular type of neutralist policy, and the distribution would be more substantially altered by the disintegration of the Western core-alliance than by the adhesion of all nonaligned countries to it. Hence the vital importance of repercussions of policies toward neutralism among Western allies. There may be occasional conflicts of interests between these allies and the genuinely nonaligned countries; but there is no fundamental conflict, since most of the alliances are still essential for shielding all of the non-Communist countries' "uneven development."

When material assistance is employed under the strategy of conciliation, it is ideally apportioned according to a country's need and absorptive capacity. The strategy of containment would employ assistance and other means in ways determined by the requirements of two vital and related balances. One is the balance of apprehensions, which has favored the Soviet bloc and channeled neutralist fears into one-sided restraints on the West; another is the balance of rewards and sanctions, which has apparently favored the more militant neutralists and made the West suspect of wooing them over against genuinely nonaligned countries and outright allies.

Before evaluating the two alternative strategies, I shall descibe the two balances and outline the means of redressing them.

The balance of rewards and sanctions concerns support for stable growth and assured status of new countries and their regimes. It is unusually difficult for one government to impart status in the form of prestige and influence to the regime of another, weaker state. To give flagrantly is to detract; to impart conspicuously is to impugn. The difficulty is greatest in a fluid society, like the present international one, when status depends neither on tradition nor on accomplishments and inherent potential. Many past "diplomatic dictatorships" over the state system were the precarious expressions of some powers' momentary ability to manipulate their freedom of alignment. This freedom being now virtually foreclosed to committed states, it is incumbent upon the leader of a free alliance to contest the pretensions of "independent" neutralists; beyond that he may try to distinguish friendly regimes by well-advertised consultation and other means.

The task is easier when, instead of status, a great power dispenses material assistance toward stable internal growth. The criteria for allocating assistance among recipients are as important as the assistance itself. The criteria need not be left to inference from ambiguous statistics and coincidences in donor's and recipient's policy and conduct. To encourage favorable alignment and concurrence of policy is not the same as to penalize impartial nonalignment; and the Western donor must be neither blackmailed into conspicuous assistance to anti-Western neutralists nor coaxed into it by friendly recipients. If the friendly regime in Senegal, for instance, needs large-scale American assistance to neutralist Ghana in order to appease its own opposition (while ignoring that to Nkrumah), it is unlikely to remain in power. On the other hand, the United States was justified in continuing economic and military assistance to Morocco after it had agreed to evacuate American bases there under nationalist pressure; an attempt to use the occasion for serving a warning to other host-countries might only accelerate demands for withdrawal from facilities too patently "bought." It is less certain whether the decision actually to increase assistance to Morocco was wise in terms of its over-all impact, even though the desire to show good-will for the hard-pressed and supposedly moderate dynasty was probably valid. But, without question, it must be advertised in advance that tolerance will stop (in Morocco and elsewhere) when nonalignment veers into opportunistic alignment with the Soviet bloc in support of regional ambitions.

When such an alignment materializes, a discriminatory policy of assistance may not suffice. It may have to be reinforced with the policy of graduated commitment, bearing on the second balance, that of apprehensions, which must be enlarged before it can be redressed.*

The West must be manifestly able and willing to help defend friendly countries with minimum devastation and prior "provocation"; but it must also differentiate its commitments against Com-

---

* One extreme in the spectrum of "graduated" commitment is unconditional, automatic mutual-assistance commitment; the other extreme is denial of assistance under any conditions—and, possibly, opposition in support of a non-Communist victim. The vital middle of the spectrum, primarily relevant for the genuinely nonaligned states located politically in the center of the East-West spectrum might best be covered by a two-level commitment. The minimum commitment would be to equalize the balance of belligerent power and localize a conflict by means of "benevolently" implemented neutrality, if that is enough to safeguard the guaranteed friendly state; its maximum level would be direct intervention when the guaranteed state is confronted with a superior coalition of "two or more" powers or with a qualitatively superior armed force—nuclear or other—of any one state. The graduated commitment is additional to the feasible collective action under the general commitments of the U.N. Charter. The historical background and contemporary politico-military requirements and applications of this kind of commitment are discussed in my *Nations in Alliance* (1962).

munist expansion as well as extend them to expansion by non-Communist states. Incipient expansionism by would-be national or regional unifiers may not greatly threaten international stability in every instance; the same is not true of overreliance on an apparently unconditional Western commitment to aid against Communist encroachments, regardless of a regime's prior disregard for the security needs of the West and for its own security risks. Supplementing the graduated deterrence that the West opposes to the Communist bloc, the policy of graduated commitment would also extend to neutralists the restraints that they would apply to the "committed" nations and that allies apply to each other.

The problem of communicating the policy and making it credible is still greater than it is with regard to graduated deterrence. The deterrent policy is implicitly communicated as the capabilities that are required to implement it come into being. By contrast, the principles of graduated commitment (as well as of discriminatory assistance) have to be enunciated, at least in general terms. Short of that, having capabilities for making assistance possible and denial of assistance politically significant might merely confirm belief in an undifferentiated, universal commitment. The communication is heard by the potential major expansionist, too. This may call for some ambiguity, unless an explicit statement is part of a policy of pressure on an unfriendly non-Communist regime.

To compel choices from a position of weakness would result in permanently consolidating adversary alignments and creating new enemies, without compensating advantages. There are, however, two classes of reasons why a discriminatory policy is a credible one for the West to adopt. On the one hand there are the dilemmas of Soviet-bloc strategy; on the other, the discriminatory strategy's conformity with immediate Western requirements and its compatibility with long-term Western objectives.

The West's dilemmas are not altogether different from those of the Sino-Soviet bloc. Both sides face an identical strategic quandary: They can seek subversion or stability, in the more or less remote future, by action concentrating on individual countries or on entire groups and classes of countries; or they can adhere to a one-country or a one-system strategy. And both sides share the pitfalls inherent in dealing with a self-willed, faction-ridden revolutionary movement. Regardless of which strategy it follows, the West's peculiar dilemmas are less intractable, because its designs are less far-reaching. Its dilemmas concern the criteria and likely effects of the two alternative strategies.

The strategy of conciliation stresses needs and conditions in non-aligned countries; the discriminatory strategy of containment stresses attitudes and policies. The two sets of criteria differ fundamentally and cannot be combined without producing some confusion; for both have shortcomings. The criterion of structural needs and conditions may contravene the immediate policy needs of the Western party when internal conditions apparently require the local government to pursue an anti-Western foreign policy. The criterion of policy may play havoc with the lesser country's economic needs and merits. The criterion of policy must, moreover, be combined with consistency in Western responses, if these are to influence comparable behavior in the system as a whole; but the policies of the local actors themselves are often internally inconsistent.

The Soviets also face this dilemma, and in some cases this may help to make the problem a temporary one for the West. Thus Nasser, soon after being provoked by the Communists into repressing them internally, has moved to offset their ultrarevolutionary drive and his own failures abroad, which are in part due to Western opposition, by turning seriously to domestic reconstruction. And the complicating feature of the dilemma faded when Nasser's regional rival, the Kassim regime in Iraq, evolved toward a Nasser-like combination. The revolutionary regime's initial dependence on Communist support has given way to anti-Communism at home; and defensiveness abroad has given way to propagation of unifying regional designs (at the expense of Kuwait)—confined, again, to verbal expression because of local opposition and British counteraction. While the dilemma lasted, however, it called for a decision on priority and an acceptance of the resulting liabilities. A strategy that is concerned with the international system as a whole logically considers a regime's foreign-policy behavior over its domestic-policy behavior. It would destroy the rule-making and limit-setting impact of a consistent policy to try to combine the two criteria in an index of external-internal behavior to be encouraged or discouraged.

It is uncommonly hard to say which of the two criteria—a country's needs or its policies—has more serious drawbacks. A general principle of evaluation may follow from a hypothetical question: Are efforts by individual countries (and weak nonaligned countries in particular) capable of compensating for erosion of the non-Communist state system as a whole; and are they more, or less, capable of doing so than a resilient system of states is of adapting itself to subversion and defection of individual countries?

There is another, somewhat less hypothetical, approach to evaluation, i.e., an examination of the likely effect of the two strategies (identified with the two sets of criteria) on the Western alliance system and the neutralists themselves.

Alliance members respond in a variety of ways to outside pressures. The allies' response to pressures from the adversary is divisive when the adversary is not blocked or repelled by the response; by contrast, an alliance may try to absorb, or deflect onto the adversary, the weaker pressures coming from third parties. A more flexible response is needed to absorb and deflect an outside pressure than to block and repel it; this is a point in favor of a conciliatory strategy toward neutralism. However, the response must be coordinated as well as flexible. Allies are generally able to control each other's separate approaches to the adversary. When allies individually conciliate third parties, the resulting prejudice is likely to be against some member of the alliance rather than against the security function of the entire alliance; this will impede a unifying joint response. When the injured ally is unable to block intra-alliance initiatives favoring an outside party, he himself must absorb the combined pressure—from both allies and third parties —pending possible compensation by his allies for the loss suffered in the process.

The United States has contended with problems of this kind in its relations with the European allies over the issue of colonialism, and with non-European allies over local conflicts and jealousies. The bone of contention has been the distribution of America's political and material support. Two situations must be distinguished. One occurs when the United States alone woos the nonaligned countries; the other, when several Western allies do so concurrently and, at times, competitively.

The first situation may be the less dangerous for the Western alliance. Countries like Portugal or Thailand or Pakistan are, in the last resort, less decisively swayed by what they regard as American courtship of neutralists than by NATO's and SEATO's ability to perform their functions. The two kinds of considerations can, however, be virtually indistinguishable from each other. Thus a relatively secure Portugal expects the alliance to safeguard its stability and status, intimately dependent on Portugal's extra-European possessions; and the security, status, and, possibly, internal stability of countries like Thailand and Pakistan are largely dependent on their standing with local nonaligned countries. Only in allied countries free of direct concern with nonaligned countries—Canada and, decreasingly, Japan—is American policy toward neutralism definitely less significant in preserving or loosening ties than the alliance's security performance and economic advantage.

The danger to the alliance grows with the number of partners that can and do nurse their relations with nonaligned countries without constant regard for their allies' interests. Many of America's allies can do so from superior past experience as they recover economic strength—e.g., West Germany—or as they shed the colonial incubus—e.g., Britain and France—or as they atone for past aggressions—e.g., Japan. When competitive wooing in peripheral areas does take place, it may cause strains at the center of the alliance in the age of neutralism similar to those of interallied contests in such areas in the age of imperialism.

Almost by definition, the discriminatory strategy of containing neutralism should have the clearest advantage over the more conciliatory approach when it comes to alliance cohesion. The great risk is that avoiding division may bring about the allies' isolation no less than avoiding isolation may cause their division. The question of risks and one's attitude toward risk-taking are at the root of any decision on strategy; the uncertain gains and liabilities of any course of conduct are notoriously hard to calculate. The advantage of a deliberate risk-taking policy is that more of the risks are of one's own choosing, by contrast with the unknown risks of an apparently prudent policy.

As they impinge on the nonaligned and neutralist countries themselves, the two strategies incur different kinds of risks for the West. The conciliatory strategy's risks are mostly speculative and easy to underrate. The risks of the discriminatory strategy appear to be manifest and can easily be overrated. A reverse pattern seems to characterize the two strategies' advantages.

In the relations between the neutralist countries and the West itself, conciliation can easily lapse into appeasement, and self-identification into the condescension of adults toward adolescents. An air of condescension would bring resentment; appeasement would forfeit respect. Intangible as they are, such matters govern relations between parties with highly unequal capabilities and inhibitions. More tangibly, the conciliatory strategy enables the courted countries to retain and compound gains from both sides while leaving intact the imbalance in their fear-induced restraints on the two main parties to the Cold War.

This makes things more difficult for the West. The West seeks to demonstrate the expansionist ambitions of the Sino-Soviet bloc;

but it reduces the danger's imminence as it shows itself capable of dealing with the bloc. The neutralists can go on exploiting the East-West conflict and propitiating the bloc while claiming to have no fear of it. Moreover, if both the United States and the Soviet Union "reward" anti-Westernism, another premium is put on the most radical form of neutralism; the nonaligned and neutralist countries and groups then have no alternative course to tempt them. It is more difficult to contend with neutralism in allied Japan— and to apply strict criteria to the use of American assistance by allied Pakistan—when India is courted by both sides; and Senegal and Nigeria might not stay long on their relatively pro-Western course were Mali and Ghana to receive equal or greater attention and support from the West. Moreover, a policy of indiscriminate conciliation would counteract the competitive interplay among neutralists themselves, an interplay that tends to confine extremism to a minority position.

The long-term risk of the nondiscriminatory policy lies in the possibility of gaining no new friends and of losing old ones. The immediate risks of the discriminatory policy of containment are those of seeing one or several countries become positively hostile to the West, aligning themselves more closely with the Sino-Soviet bloc, or moving into full membership within it. The long-term risks are those of any policy that presses two opportunistic allies together in the belief that enforced intimacy, if prolonged beyond the initial *rapprochement,* will eventually reveal incompatibility. The belief that such enforced intimacy does not produce, and ultimately precludes, permanent unions squares the policy of pressure with the basic rule of a tripartite system of policy: Do nothing in relation to a third party that might benefit the chief adversary.

Incompatibilities among rival nonaligned and neutralist countries and leaders themselves are a tactical asset for the West. They helped, for example, restore Tunisia to moderate Bourguibism from a spell of extremism that sought to coerce France into promptly evacuating the Bizerte base. Of larger significance are the incompatibilities that limit the degree of possible intimacy between neutralists and the Sino-Soviet bloc. Rival expansionisms may produce even greater, or earlier, incompatibility between them than would the neutralists' will to independence. The ambitious lesser partner's concept of his independence tends to expand so as to comprise the disputed position and exclude the stronger partner-antagonist from mere influence over it. The strain between the U.A.R. and the U.S.S.R. first came into the open over the Communist bloc's activities in coveted Iraq and in the Syrian province rather than in Egypt proper.

It is, of course, always possible that as a result of the elite's pique or its Communist allies' triumph, the discriminatory strategy may backfire and actually press the neutralist country into the Sino-Soviet bloc. The risk must not be exaggerated. Generally, militant neutralism goes with a fairly resistant one-party domestic system and a remote geographic location; and neutralists can reverse themselves when they burn their fingers with the East, without completely burning their bridges to the West. For the same reasons, the West must press such regimes all the harder to make them move away from the bloc and closer to the center. A country's physical proximity to the bloc increases the immediate danger to national security; it is usually tempered by corresponding caution in the country's policy toward both East and West, although regional disputes—such as Afghanistan's with Pakistan—may still occur and tax a discriminatory strategy to the utmost.

Such as they are, the risks can be further discounted by a gain. The gain will most likely accrue when the circumstances surrounding the "loss" of a neutralist country increase desire for genuine nonalignment at large. In order to promote such circumstances, the West may have to refuse help in salvaging a sinking elite. The refusal will pay off whenever subversion in a country remote from the Sino-Soviet bloc promises to be temporary and remain isolated, while the deterrent effect on other neutralists promises to be both widespread and lasting.

There is a more serious possible liability to be considered. The policy of discrimination on grounds of present behavior might interfere with the policy of assisting the development of potentially powerful countries, in the long-range security interest of the West itself. It is possible that, in such countries, the emotional satisfactions of a conspicuous foreign policy are soon offset by the reluctance to assume specific responsibilities prematurely. But if a conflict of objectives does occur, the long-term goal of building up such a country may have to be temporarily sacrificed for the immediate need of cutting its leadership down to size. Western aloofness may produce compensating dividends when it serves to highlight Communist encroachments and miscalculations while opposition to the developing country's costly foreign policy crystallizes within.

The two strategies' possible effect on multipolarization is a long-term aspect of their impact on the international system as a whole.

Two more immediate issues arise in this connection: One bears on polarization between East and West; the other on the problem of international order in the non-Communist world.

TOWARD ORDER AMIDST CONFLICT

The geopolitical pattern of polarization can be more or less symmetrical and neat. If a number of countries geographically close to the West's heartland should adhere more closely to the Sino-Soviet bloc politically, this would make for symmetry of the pattern as long as the West retains its friends, allies, and positions geographically adjacent to the Sino-Soviet heartland. Should the West lose these positions and the Communist bloc fail to gain or retain positions in the Western orbit, the pattern would be both symmetrical and neat: two compact blocs would face each other across the adjacent nonaligned areas.

So far, the West has enjoyed a symmetry in its favor, progressively marred by setbacks in individual countries. The West's ability to uphold its wards and positions has been apparently on the decline in areas both remote from and adjacent to the Sino-Soviet bloc. At the time of the Guatemalan crisis in 1954, local Communists had still to rationalize their failure to consolidate gains. They alleged the impossibility of taking over a country placed in the "iron fist" of Western imperialism, that is, in geographical proximity to the United States. The doctrine may have been revised after the fist failed to bear down on Cuba; it was in any event invalidated by revolutions in long-range military hardware and in short-term popular expectations. The two revolutions were complementary in opening up the American sphere to Soviet influence; after a century of disparity, initiated by Napoleon III's expulsion from Mexico, something like equality of access to areas of each other's immediate concern was apparently being re-established between the United States and the unfriendly European power of the moment. The emergence of equality highlighted a persisting disparity in the two superpowers' attitudes toward forceful action against less powerful states; and the practical handicaps for the United States due to the disparity have been further increased by superficial analogies between Cuba and Hungary.

The combined impact of an inescapable equality and a largely self-imposed disparity might precipitate a reordering in the existing geopolitical pattern. Even if the Sino-Soviet bloc does not attain an asymmetry completely favorable to itself, it might enforce a symmetrical and neat repolarization. Neither of two compact blocs would then encircle the other by its outposts. Before this happened, Western positions and commitments in areas near the Soviet Union would have to be subverted, or tacitly bartered for Soviet abstinence within the Western heartland and near the United States in particular. Such a bargain may well be the provisional objective of Communist forays in areas remote from the bloc; its ethical hazards would exceed those of intervention against small states that abuse their independence.

The discriminatory strategy might affect the pattern of polarization by pressing nonaligned countries into the Sino-Soviet bloc; the conciliatory strategy might influence the pattern only indirectly, but more profoundly, by conferring on nonaligned official and public opinion a virtual veto power over Western responses to Sino-Soviet probings and pressures. Such considerations might merely rationalize moderation induced by a growing regard for rising Soviet capabilities; while deeming itself self-restrained, the West merely would be self-deceived. The effects would not stay confined to the relationship of East and West; closely related are the two strategies' implications for an elementary order in the non-Communist part of the world itself.

International order requires that the major powers exert themselves within, as well as on behalf of, the non-Communist world. In the perspective of the conciliatory strategy, the responsibility is communal even before there is a community; in the perspective of the discriminatory strategy, it must be residually imperial even when there are no more Western empires—as long as the larger ex-colonial countries do not choose to share in the task. Acts in excess of the lesser countries' rights and duties to uphold their essential internal and external independence are to be policed; these acts include threats to still weaker outside parties, and inhibitions on the security role of the greater powers. The objective is not rule by one or several powers; it is to evolve rules of mutually tolerable conduct within an embattled part of the world, and to prevent overreactions to internal problems from generating disorder abroad.

The rules may continue to inhibit direct and forcible interference in internal affairs. This is apparently at variance with the fact that domestic factors tend to determine the international behavior of the most self-assertive neutralists. However, the inconsistency decreases as the foreign policy of the great powers that try to influence the lesser ones becomes more consistent. Only consistency in demonstrating the limits of Western tolerance can substantiate those limits. Once established, the limits are of necessity taken into account by local actors. Some actors will devise substitutes for equating anticolonialism with anti-Westernism as a means for enhancing their local positions; others will be compelled to reveal fully their commitment one way or the other. Apparently uncontrollable local power fields might then become more manageable; a concurrent polarization of forces within and between non-Communist countries need not be unfavorable to the West. Many of the local actors who aim to reduce Western presence think and act within the framework of a permissive or vacillating Western strategy. They would re-examine their attitudes if they had to choose between assistance on terms satisfying vital Western interests and the transfer of Western friendship elsewhere.

Some such rationale has inspired the policy of the Fifth French Republic toward its colonial dependencies. The sanction of with-holding all French assistance was meant to encourage continued association with France in larger community or special partner-ship. The sanction was implemented against Guinea when she opted for complete independence; the sanction was threatened in order to influence Algeria's decision between severance of ties and continued association. As applied to Guinea, the policy was discredited within its own terms. The alienation of the penal-ized country was not given time to pay off in deterrent effect on other French-African countries, soon given virtually com-plete independence in a reversal of policy. Apart from being consistent, moreover, the policy must also be concerted. It is a feasible strategy for the West as a whole, rather than for any one, or any but the most powerful, Western country—notably if such a country's allies cannot also be counted upon to deny aid and forgo influence.

The West cannot concert policy for a common order—or for joint action of any kind—without in some way touching upon the identity of the conflict to be regarded as the dominant one for the global system and the non-Communist system of states for some time to come. The choice is between the East-West conflict and the South-North issue of economic develop-ment and political independence for the nonindustrial, mainly ex-colonial, countries. The conciliatory strategy implies belief that a choice between the two conflicts can be avoided as long as the West avoids stressing preventive, primarily military, ap-proaches. The discriminatory strategy implies the belief in continuing contest over priority; whenever choice is necessary, the East-West conflict and the immediate requirements of waging it must be treated as dominant.

In terms of the sweep and interplay of cultures and civilizations, the South-North issue may appear as ultimately transcending the more acute contemporary conflict in importance. The view is apparently confirmed by short-term impressions, when both East and West resort to indirect strategies and economic weapons against each other in the Southern Hemisphere; and it receives support from a statistical illusion based on the sheer number of colonial and postcolonial crises in which the powers of the North (including the industrial Soviet Union) have on occasion been reduced to secondary roles.

Yet it can be argued that changes in method do not produce changes in identity, and that ups and downs in statistical incidence do not reverse the order of priority. A conflict is "dominant" when it can transform the international system in the process of being waged and possibly won by one party. It is not easy to see what the South-North contention means in terms of particular stakes, and what a victory of the South as it is presently constituted would mean for the state system, unless it be multipolarity resulting from an enforced diffusion of Northern wealth and power. A partial diffusion and the transformation that might result are, however, being promoted only or mainly as a by-product of the East-West struggle. The stakes are indeterminate, but so are the contestants. The major industrialized powers occasionally identify themselves with the South, and more insistently resist being identified with the South's image of the North. But, so far, the South itself has neither major power of its own nor sufficient cohesion to override internal factionalism and produce an independent collective capability. And finally, commitments and loyalties won through parallel or supporting policies on the South-North issue are still less permanent and transferable to the other major issue than those won on the East-West issue.

In case of doubt, a conflict that can be defined more clearly in terms of actors and stakes, and can give rise to dependable ties, should be given primacy in resolving uncertainty over priority. This is not to say that the East-West conflict will remain dominant indefinitely. But it is not a matter of indifference whether the West or the Soviet Union would revise past policies and objectives more basically if an ascendant South moved to transform the South-North "issue" into a real conflict.

NOTES

NOTES TO CHAPTER II

On Understanding the Unaligned

1. John G. Stoessinger, *The Might of Nations* (New York: Random House, 1961), p. 25.
2. Stuart Cloete, *West with the Sun* (New York: Doubleday and Company, 1962).
3. Charles A. Beard, *A Foreign Policy for America* (New York: Alfred A. Knopf, 1940), pp. 4–5.
4. Stoessinger, *op. cit.,* pp. 406–20.
5. Ruth Benedict, *Patterns of Culture* (Boston: Houghton Mifflin Company, 1961), p. 1.
6. Louis Hartz, *The Liberal Tradition in America* (New York: Harcourt, Brace and Company, 1956, p. 309.
7. As quoted in Edward Dumbauld, *The Declaration of Independence and What It Means Today* (Norman, Okla.: University of Oklahoma Press, 1950), p. 51.
8. Hartz, *op. cit.,* p. 35.
9. *Matt.* 28:19.
10. Hartz, *op. cit.,* pp. 36–37.
11. Thomas A. Bailey, *A Diplomatic History of the American People* (New York: Appleton-Century-Crofts, 1947), p. 37.
12. As quoted in Dexter Perkins, *The United States and Latin America* (Baton Rouge, La.: Louisiana State University Press, 1961), p. 48.
13. *Ibid.,* p. 50.
14. *Ibid.,* pp. 51–86.
15. *Ibid.,* p. 57.
16. Rupert Emerson, *From Empire to Nation* (Cambridge, Mass.: Harvard University Press, 1960), p. 25.
17. *The New York Times,* November 11, 1959.

18. "Samoa's Coming of Age," *The New Republic,* February 12, 1962, p. 12.
19. Saul K. Padover, "Asia Puts Some Sharp Questions to Us," *The New York Times Magazine,* March 4, 1962, pp. 14, 88.
20. Hartz, *op. cit.,* p. 309.
21. *The Washington Post,* January 21, 1962.
22. *Ibid.,* February 11, 1962.
23. "Is it because liberty in the abstract may be classed amongst the blessings of mankind, that I am seriously to felicitate a madman, who has escaped from the protecting restraint and wholesome darkness of his cell, on his restoration to the enjoyment of light and liberty? Am I to congratulate a highwayman and murderer, who has broke prison, upon the recovery of his natural rights?" Edmund Burke, *Reflections on the Revolution in France* (London and New York: Oxford University Press, 1950), p. 8.
24. *The New York Times,* September 22, 1961.
25. Charles Burton Marshall, "Political Relations with New States," *United Asia* (Bombay), November, 1959, pp. 403, 406–7.

NOTES TO CHAPTER III
Congo Crisis: A Study of Postcolonial Politics

1. For a review of the involvement of the new states in the Congo from July, 1960, through May, 1961 see Robert C. Good, "Congo Crisis: The Role of the New States," in *Neutralism,* a set of papers published in 1961 by the Washington Center of Foreign Policy Research, pp. 9–26.
2. The Report of the United Nations Conciliation Commission for the Congo, a document prepared largely by "moderates," refers to "foreign interference by certain States." For an interesting review of the causes of the crisis, see Paragraph 112 of the Report. The full complexity of the situation is acknowledged in this summary.

NOTES TO CHAPTER IV
A Conservative View of the New States

1. Reginald Maudling, *House of Commons Debates,* October 19, 1961, col. 354.
2. Lord Salisbury, "Anglo-American Shibboleths," *Foreign Affairs,* April, 1958, p. 404.
3. F. M. Bennett, *House of Commons Debates,* October 19, 1961, col. 409.
4. John A. Biggs-Davison, *House of Commons Debates,* October 31, 1961, col. 65.
5. Sir John Slessor, *What Price Coexistence?* (New York: Frederick A. Praeger, 1961).

6. London: Allen and Unwin, 1957.
7. "The Next to the Last Act in Africa," *Foreign Affairs,* July, 1961, pp. 667–68.
8. Henry Fairlie, *Time and Tide* (London), December 8, 1961. A cogent, extended, skeptical view of the Commonwealth can be found in Hedley Bull's "What Is the Commonwealth?," *World Politics,* July, 1959.
9. "The Idea of Colonialism," *Encounter* (London), December, 1958, pp. 80, 82.
10. *Colonial Rule: Enemies and Obligations,* Conservative Political Center (on behalf of the Conservative Commonwealth Council), p. 7.
11. *The Times* (London), December 29, 1961.
12. *The Daily Telegraph* (London), July 25, 1961.
13. *Ibid.,* August 31, 1961.
14. Joseph B. Godber, *House of Commons Debates,* October 18, 1961.
15. *The Economist* (London), July 14, 1956, p. 111.
16. C. M. Woodhouse, *British Foreign Policy Since the Second World War* (London: 1961), pp. 190–91.
17. Geoffrey Goodwin, *Britain and the United Nations* (New York: Manhattan Publishing Co., 1958), p. 267.
18. *The Daily Telegraph,* December 19, 1961.
19. *House of Commons Debates,* December 14, 1961, col. 749.
20. *The Daily Telegraph,* August 31, 1961; *The Times,* December 25, 1961.
21. *The Round Table,* March, 1956, pp. 122–23.
22. R. T. Paget, *House of Commons Debates,* October 18, 1961, cols. 259–60.
23. Lord Salisbury, *op. cit.,* p. 408.
24. *Colonial Rule: Enemies and Obligations,* p. 15.
25. Lord Coleraine, *House of Lords Debates,* September 13, 1956, col. 831.
26. Lord Salisbury, *op. cit.,* p. 408.
27. *The Times,* July 21, 1961.

NOTES TO CHAPTER V

The "Third Party": The Rationale of Nonalignment

1. F. R. Moraes, *Jawaharlal Nehru: A Biography* (New York: The Macmillan Company, 1957), p. 452.
2. Lloyd A. Free, *Six Allies and a Neutral* (Chicago: The Free Press of Glencoe, Ill., 1959), pp. 11–14.
3. Prime Minister Nehru, at Bandung, as quoted in George McTurnan Kahin, *The Asian-African Conference* (Ithaca, N.Y.: Cornell University Press, 1956), pp. 64–72, 73–75. See also W. H. Wriggins, *Ceylon: Dilemmas of a New Nation* (1960), p. 467.

NOTES TO CHAPTER VI
Nehru, Nasser, and Nkrumah on Neutralism

1. Documentation for the numerous quotations in this essay will not be given here. Readers who wish to consult sources are referred to the chapter by the same title in *Neutralism,* Washington Center of Foreign Policy Research, 1961, pp. 85–110.
2. William H. Stringer, "Nehru Scans the World," *The Christian Science Monitor,* January 7, 1959.
3. See Manfred Halpern, "Egypt Discovers Africa," *Africa Report,* April, 1961.
4. See Ross N. Berkes and Mohinder S. Bedi, *The Diplomacy of India* (Stanford, Calif.: Stanford University Press, 1958), pp. 62, 74.

NOTES TO CHAPTER VII
The New States and the United Nations

1. *United Nations Document A/PV 1051,* November 10, 1961.
2. *United Nations Document A/PV 1034,* October 10, 1961.
3. *The New York Times,* October 7, 1961.
4. *United Nations Document A/PV 1015,* September 26, 1961.
5. See, for example, Hamilton Fish Armstrong, "U.N. on Trial," *Foreign Affairs,* April, 1961; H. J. Morgenthau, "Threat to— and Hope for—the U.N.," *The New York Times Magazine,* October 29, 1961; L. P. Bloomfield, "The New Diplomacy in the United Nations," in F. O. Wilcox and H. F. Haviland, Jr. (eds.), *The United States and the United Nations* (Baltimore, Md.: The Johns Hopkins Press, 1961).
6. "A Close View of the Nonaligned," *The New York Times Magazine,* October 1, 1961.
7. Speech on conciliation with America, March 22, 1775.
8. *The New York Times,* December 29, 1961.
9. Associated Press Dispatch, January 6, 1962.
10. *The New York Times,* December 13, 1956.
11. *The New York Times,* December 19, 1961.
12. *Ibid.,* December 20, 1961.
13. *Ibid.,* December 22, 1961.
14. F. O. Wilcox and H. F. Haviland, Jr. (eds.), *The United States and the United Nations* (Baltimore, Md.: The Johns Hopkins Press, 1961), p. 141.
15. *The New York Times,* December 23, 1961.
16. *Ibid.,* November 17, 1961.
17. Hamilton Fish Armstrong, "U.N. on Trial," *loc. cit.,* p. 396.

NOTES TO CHAPTER IX
Revolutionary Change and the Strategy of the *Status Quo*

1. *Pravda,* July 30, 1961.
2. *Ibid.,* October 18, 1961.
3. *Ibid.,* October 15, 1952.
4. V. I. Lenin, *Selected Works* (New York: International Publishers, 1943), X, 239–41.
5. *Pravda,* July 30, 1961.
6. *Ibid.*

NOTES TO CHAPTER X
The Relation of Strength to Weakness in the World Community.

1. *The New York Times,* December 7, 1960.
2. As quoted in Rupert Emerson, *From Empire to Nation* (Cambridge, Mass.: Harvard University Press, 1960), p. 184.
3. *Ibid,* p. 483.
4. *Ibid.,* p. 184.
5. Leon Trotsky, *The Revolution Betrayed* (New York: Doubleday Doran, 1937), pp. 238–39.

NOTES TO CHAPTER XI
Tripartism: Dilemmas and Strategies

1. L. Binder, "The Middle East as a Subordinate International System," *World Politics,* April, 1958, p. 425. The posture recalls the strategy of confounding the adversary with apparent irrationality, failure to register demands and other messages, and inability to comply with threats. T. C. Schelling, *The Strategy of Conflict* (Cambridge, Mass.: Harvard University Press, 1960).
2. See Introduction to the Annual Report of the Secretary-General, in *The New York Times,* September 13, 1960, p. 41. On bloc voting and membership see T. Hovet, Jr., *Bloc Politics in the United Nations* (Cambridge, Mass.: Harvard University Press, 1960), p. 38.
3. In keeping with this estimate, if not necessarily for the same reasons, Prime Minister Nehru opposed President Nkrumah's agitation for a neutralist bloc organization during the 1960 United Nations General Assembly session. (*The New York Times,* September 28, 1960, p. 17.) Since then, African neutralists have turned to regional organization, allegedly on the model of NATO; competing combinations have not failed to emerge. *Ibid.,* January 8, 1961, pp. 1, 3.

4. Thus Morocco received Soviet military aircraft after the United States had agreed to evacuate American bases by 1963. Guinea was reported, probably prematurely, to have gone one step further and to have granted a submarine base to the Soviet Union. (*The New York Times*, December 5, 1960, p. 13, and *ibid.*, December 8, 1960, pp. 1, 6.)
5. George McTurnan Kahin, *The Asian-African Conference* (Ithaca, N.Y.: Cornell University Press, 1956), pp. 67 f.
6. Wladyslaw W. Kulski, *Peaceful Co-existence: An Analysis of Soviet Foreign Policy* (Chicago: Henry Regnery Company, 1959), pp. 118–119, 148. For the final declaration of the Belgrade Conference of "nonbloc" nations, see *The New York Times*, September 7, 1961, p. 8; and P. Hofmann, "Bomb Jolts 'Neutrals,'" *ibid.*, September 3, 1961, p. 4 E, for comment.
7. See Kulski, *op cit.*, p. 158, for the barrier argument.

A SELECT CHRONOLOGY

1945   March: Pact of the League of Arab States signed by Egypt, Iraq, Lebanon, Saudi Arabia, Syria, Jordan, and Yemen. Libya joined League in 1953, Sudan in 1956, Tunisia and Morocco in 1958, and Kuwait in 1961.

April–June: United Nations Conference at San Francisco.

1946   July 4: Republic of the Philippines becomes independent.

1947   August 15: India and Pakistan become independent states within the British Commonwealth.

1948   January 4: Burma becomes independent and choses to leave the British Commonwealth.

February 4: Ceylon becomes independent within the British Commonwealth.

May 14: State of Israel created.

May: War between Israel and the Arab League begins. War ends July, 1949.

June 28: Cominform expels Yugoslavia.

1949   January 20: Representatives of fourteen Afro-Asian governments meet in New Delhi to discuss Dutch military action in Indonesia. They agree to act jointly on the matter in the United Nations.

April 4: North Atlantic Treaty signed.

December 27: Indonesia becomes independent.

1950   June 25: Republic of Korea invaded.

September: Afro-Asian caucusing group first meets at United Nations on *ad hoc* basis.

1951   November 28: Turkey and Greece enter NATO.

1952	January 1: Libya becomes independent.
1953	July 27: Korean armistice signed.
	November 9: Cambodia becomes independent.
1954	April: Colombo Conference attended by heads of government from Ceylon, India, Pakistan, Burma, and Indonesia. Suggestion for Afro-Asian Conference put forward by Indonesia.
	September 8: Southeast Asia Collective Defense Treaty signed by Australia, France, Great Britain, New Zealand, Pakistan, the Philippines, Thailand, and the United States.
	December 29: Laos and Vietnam become independent.
1955	March: Baghdad Pact signed by Iran, Iraq, Pakistan, Turkey, and Great Britain.
	April 18–24: Bandung Conference sponsored by the Colombo powers. Attended by delegates from Afghanistan, Burma, Cambodia, Ceylon, Communist China, Egypt, Ethiopia, Gold Coast, India, Indonesia, Iran, Iraq, Jordan, Laos, Lebanon, Liberia, Nepal, North Vietnam, Pakistan, the Philippines, Saudi Arabia, Sudan, Syria, Thailand, Turkey, Vietnam, and Yemen.
	May 14: Warsaw Pact signed by Russia, Albania, Bulgaria, Czechoslovakia, East Germany, Hungary, Poland, and Rumania.
	May 15: Austrian State Treaty establishing Austrian neutrality signed.
	May 26: Bulganin and Khrushchev meet with Tito after seven years of Soviet-Yugoslav estrangement.
	September: Following suggestion of Bandung Conference, the seventeen Afro-Asian states at the United Nations put the Afro-Asian caucus on a permanent basis.
	December 1: Khrushchev and Bulganin visit India and Burma.
	December 14: United Nations membership deadlock broken. (Between 1949 and 1955, only one new state had been admitted.) Sixteen nations—Albania, Austria, Bulgaria, Cambodia, Ceylon, Finland, Hungary, Ireland, Italy, Jordan, Laos, Libya, Nepal, Portugal, Rumania, and Spain—gain admission.
1956	January 1: Sudan becomes independent.
	March 2: Morocco becomes independent.
	October: Hungarian uprising.

October–November: Suez crisis.

October 19: Russia and Japan sign declaration ending state of war.

November 5: United Nations establishes first international police force to supervise truce in Middle East.

March 20: Tunisia becomes independent.

1957   March 6: Ghana becomes independent.

March 25: Rome treaties creating European Economic Community and EURATOM are signed.

August 31: Malaya becomes independent within the British Commonwealth.

1958   February 8: Egypt and Syria merge, forming United Arab Republic.

April 15–22: First Conference of Independent African States held at Accra.

September: African caucusing group set up at United Nations following direction of Conference of Independent African States in April.

October 2: Guinea becomes independent.

December 8–13: First All-Africa Peoples' Conference held in Accra.

1959   August 21: Central Treaty Organization of the Middle East formed by Great Britain, Iran, Pakistan, and Turkey. Replaces Baghdad Pact, which became inoperative following Iraqi coup of July, 1958.

1960   January 1: Cameroun becomes independent.

April 27: Togo becomes independent.

June–December: The following African countries become independent: Central African Republic, Chad, Congo Republic (Brazzaville), Gabon, Malagasy Republic, and Senegal (all within the French Community); Dahomey, Ivory Coast, Mali, Mauritania, Niger, and Upper Volta (choosing to remain outside the French Community); Congo (Leopoldville); Somalia; and Nigeria (within the British Commonwealth).

July 6: Mutiny of Congolese Army.

July 11: Katanga secedes from the Congo.

July 15: First United Nations troops arrive in the Congo.

August 6: Cyprus becomes independent.

September 5: Kasavubu deposes Premier Lumumba.

October 2: Khrushchev makes his troika proposal at United Nations.

December 15–19: Twelve newly independent African countries, all former French colonies—Cameroun, Central African Republic, Chad, Congo Republic (Brazzaville), Dahomey, Gabon, Ivory Coast, Malagasy Republic, Mauritania, Niger, Senegal, and Upper Volta—meet at Brazzaville to form a loose community of states closely tied to France. At a subsequent meeting, this group became known as the Organisation Africaine et Malgache de Cooperation Economique (OAMCE).

December 14: U.N. General Assembly approves Afro-Asian resolution proclaiming "the necessity of bringing to a speedy and unconditional end colonialism in all its forms and manifestations."

1961   January 4–7: Heads of state of the U.A.R., Ghana, Guinea, Mali, Morocco, and Algerian Provisional Government, and representatives from Libya and Ceylon, meet at Casablanca to discuss the Congo situation and to form a loose grouping. The U.A.R., Ghana, Guinea, Mali, Morocco, and Algeria are subsequently referred to as the "Casablanca Group."

March 15: Angolan revolt begins.

March 15: South Africa announces its withdrawal from the British Commonwealth.

April 27: Sierra Leone becomes independent.

May 8–12: Conference of Independent African States held at Monrovia. Attended by Ethiopia, Liberia, Libya, Nigeria, Sierra Leone, Somalia, Togo, Tunisia, and the members of the OAMCE. This group of states is subsequently referred to as the "Monrovia Group."

June 5–12: Preparatory meeting for Belgrade Conference held in Cairo.

June 19: Kuwait becomes independent.

August 1: Adoula becomes Premier of the Congo and gradually wins recognition from those states that had recognized the Stanleyville regime.

August 5–16: Charter of the Alliance for Progress approved in Punta del Este.

August 10: Great Britain applies for membership in European Economic Community.

September 1: Belgrade Conference on nonaligned states, attended by representatives from Afghanistan, Algerian

Provisional Government, Burma, Cambodia, Ceylon, Cuba, Cyprus, Ethiopia, Ghana, Guinea, India, Indonesia, Iraq, Lebanon, Mali, Morocco, Nepal, Saudi Arabia, Somalia, Sudan, Tunisia, the U.A.R., Yemen, and Yugoslavia; Bolivia, Brazil, and Ecuador sent observers.

September 18: Dag Hammerskjold killed in plane crash.

September 28: Syria leaves U.A.R.

November 3: U Thant named Acting Secretary-General of United Nations.

December: India occupies Goa.

December 4: Tanganyika becomes independent within the British Commonwealth.

1962 January: Meeting in Lagos of African heads of state of all Monrovia powers except Libya and Tunisia, plus the Congo (Leopoldville) and Tanganyika.

January 1: Western Samoa becomes independent.

July 1: Rwanda and Burundi become independent.

July 3: Algeria becomes independent.

THE CONTRIBUTORS

VERNON V. ASPATURIAN. Professor of Political Science, Pennsylvania State University. Author of *The Union Republics in Soviet Diplomacy* and co-author of *Foreign Policy in World Politics*.

ROBERT C. GOOD. Director, Office of Research and Analysis for Africa, Department of State. Formerly Assistant Professor of International Relations and member of the staff of the Social Science Foundation, University of Denver.

ERNEST W. LEFEVER. Foreign-policy analyst associated with the Institute for Defense Analyses, Washington, D.C. Author of *Ethics and United States Foreign Policy* and editor of *Arms and Arms Control*.

GEORGE LISKA. Author of *The International Equilibrium* and *The New Statecraft*.

CHARLES BURTON MARSHALL. Formerly consultant, Committee on Foreign Affairs, United States House of Representatives; member of Policy Planning Staff, Department of State; and Political Adviser to the Prime Minister of Pakistan. Author of *Limits of Foreign Policy*.

LAURENCE W. MARTIN. Associate Professor of European Diplomacy, School of Advanced International Studies, The Johns Hopkins University. Author of *Peace Without Victory* and co-author, with Arnold Wolfers, of *The Anglo-American Tradition in Foreign Affairs*.

REINHOLD NIEBUHR. Professor Emeritus of Applied Christianity at Union Theological Seminary, New York City. His many books include *Moral Man and Immoral Society; The Children of Light and the Children of Darkness; The Self and the Dramas of History;* and *The Irony of American History*.

FRANCIS O. WILCOX. Dean of the School of Advanced International Studies, The Johns Hopkins University. Assistant Secretary of State for International Organization Affairs, 1955–61. His most recent book is *The United States and the United Nations,* which he edited with Dr. H. Field Haviland Jr.

ARNOLD WOLFERS. Director of the Washington Center of Foreign Policy Research. Sterling Professor Emeritus of International Relations, Yale University. Author of *Britain and France Between Two Wars; Discord and Collaboration: Essays on International Politics;* and co-author of *The Anglo-American Tradition in Foreign Affairs*.